Intermediate Plus Students' Book

with DVD-ROM

CONTENTS

	LESSON	GRAMMAR/FUNCTION	VOCABULARY	PRONUNCIATION	READING
UNIT 1 LIFESTYLES page 7					
1.1	**Coffee drinker?** page 8	passive; causative *have*	lifestyle; multi-word verbs	sentence stress: causative *have*	read an article about coffee
1.2	**Life is busy** page 11	present tenses: simple vs continuous, stative verbs	verb + preposition	connected speech: linking	
1.3	**What would you take?** page 14	describing everyday objects	everyday objects	stress patterns: responses	read a blog post called *What would you save in a fire?*
1.4	**Fair Isle** page 16				
UNIT 2 MAKERS page 19					
2.1	**Genius inventions** page 20	question forms; indirect questions	adjectives to describe inventions	intonation: statement questions	
2.2	**Builders** page 23	present perfect simple and continuous	buildings; word-building: prefixes and suffixes	silent letters	read an article about an amazing builder
2.3	**Sounds like a plan!** page 26	judging and evaluating ideas	projects	intonation: sounding enthusiastic	read about making a film
2.4	**Creativity** page 28				
UNIT 3 CHALLENGES page 31					
3.1	**Surfing dreams** page 32	narrative tenses	adverbs	word stress	read an article about *The Soul Surfer*
3.2	**Personal challenges** page 35	modals of obligation: present/past	life challenges; idioms: relationships	*have*: auxiliary vs main verb	
3.3	**Conflict resolution** page 38	resolving conflict	everyday issues	intonation: sounding tactful	read about conflict resolution
3.4	**Overpopulation** page 40				
UNIT 4 SCIENCE page 43					
4.1	**Everyone's a scientist** page 44	zero, first and second conditionals	science	*would* vs *will*	
4.2	**Smart tech, lazy brain?** page 47	passive reporting structures	reporting verbs; commonly confused words	stressed words/syllables	read an article about technology
4.3	**Delete me!** page 50	hedging	internet words/phrases	hesitation devices	read an article: *Delete me!*
4.4	**Science lover?** page 52				

DVD-ROM: BBC DVD CLIPS AND SCRIPTS · BBC INTERVIEWS AND SCRIPTS · CLASS AUDIO AND SCRIPTS

LISTENING/DVD	SPEAKING	WRITING
	talk about your lifestyle	
listen to a BBC radio programme about busy-ness	do a quiz	write an article
listen to a conversation about special objects	describe everyday objects	
BBC **Fair Isle:** watch a BBC documentary about Britain's most remote inhabited island	explain the lifestyle you prefer	write a pros and cons essay
listen to a radio programme	describe some genius inventions	
	discuss an article	write a product description
listen to conversations about making a film	discuss a project	
watch people talking about creativity	discuss creativity	write an article
	tell a story	write a short biography
listen to conversations about personal challenges	discuss life challenges	
listen to people discussing everyday problems	resolve a problem	
BBC **Supersized Earth:** watch a BBC documentary about the cities of the future	discuss megacities	write an essay
listen to a radio programme about citizen science	talk about real vs hypothetical situations	write a proposal
	talk about technology	
listen to people discussing the internet	discuss your use of social media	
watch people talking about science	talk about famous scientists	write a short biography

CONTENTS

	LESSON	GRAMMAR/FUNCTION	VOCABULARY	PRONUNCIATION	READING
UNIT 5 EXPLORE page 55					
5.1	Journeys page 56	quantifiers	nature	connected speech: *of*	read a book review
5.2	My utopia page 59	*-ing* form and infinitive	types of people; formal vs informal register	connected speech: elision	
5.3	My perfect country page 62	expressing your opinion	society	word stress	read about a radio programme
5.4	Caribbean page 64				
UNIT 6 GOODNESS page 67					
6.1	Good or bad? page 68	modals of deduction	extreme adjectives; two-part phrases	intonation: emphasis	read an article about good vs bad
6.2	Kind deeds	third and mixed conditionals	money	connected speech: elision	
6.3	The good life page 74	asking for and expressing agreement/disagreement	happiness	intonation: showing agreement/ disagreement	read about the happiest people on the planet
6.4	A helping hand page 76				
UNIT 7 ARTS page 79					
7.1	Outsider art page 80	making comparisons; *so/ such*	visual arts; multi-word verbs 2	connected speech: *schwa* in comparatives	read about outsider art
7.2	The power of music page 83	*be/get used to* vs *used to*	music	the letter *A*	
7.3	Life hacks page 86	responding to suggestions	everyday objects	intonation: sounding positive or negative	read about life hacks
7.4	Graffiti page 88				
UNIT 8 KNOWLEDGE page 91					
8.1	Lessons from the past page 92	relative clauses	lexical chunks with *make, do* and *take*	stress on lexical chunks	read about knowledge and power
8.2	Big data page 95	future forms	critical thinking; numbers and statistics	numbers	read some facts about big data
8.3	Idioms and origins page 98	guessing and estimating	idioms	intonation in short responses	
8.4	Finding out page 100				

IRREGULAR VERBS page 103 LANGUAGE BANK page 104 VOCABULARY BANK page 120

LISTENING/DVD	SPEAKING	WRITING
	describe a travel destination	write a book review
listen to people discussing their dream island	discuss your idea of utopia	
listen to a conversation about policies	discuss different policies	
BBC **Caribbean with Simon Reeve:** watch a BBC programme about Haiti	talk about stereotypes	write a story
	discuss good and bad behaviour	
listen to a news story	discuss a news story	write a thank you message
listen to a conversation about the rules for a happy life	decide on the rules for a happy life	
watch people talking about helping others	a group discussion	write a short essay
	discuss art and creativity	
listen to someone talking about their musical tastes	talk about music	write an essay
listen to a conversation about life hacks	tell someone about a skill	
BBC **Graffiti artists of Taiwan:** watch a BBC news report about Taiwanese street artists	talk about a cultural experience	write a review
	tell an anecdote	write an anecdote
listen to a radio programme about big data	discuss big data and future predictions	
listen to people discussing the origins of some idioms	discuss some idioms	
watch people talking about information and knowledge	a group discussion about information and knowledge	write a response to a proposal

COMMUNICATION BANK page 128 AUDIO SCRIPTS page 134

GRAMMAR

1 A Read the paragraph. Then work in pairs and discuss. Do you have anything in common with Sandra?

My name is Sandra Costas. I'm originally from Asturias, which is in the north of Spain, but I've been living in Seattle, USA, for two years as an exchange student. I'd never travelled out of my country before this. I love music and I was told that Seattle is a great music city. I've been to lots of great concerts. I like everything here except the weather. If I'd had a choice, I would have chosen a less rainy place. My flatmate warned me it was the wettest city in the country!

B Read the paragraph in Exercise 1A again and underline examples of the grammar points in the box.

the third conditional   the superlative   the passive   reported speech   the present perfect continuous   the present perfect simple   the past perfect   a non-defining relative clause

COMMON ERRORS

2 Find and correct the mistakes in the sentences.

1 What means this?
2 If I'll have time, I'll come to the party.
3 I like drink coffee in the morning.
4 He stopped to play football because he was too old.
5 Where I can buy a laptop?
6 Yesterday I've visited the museum.
7 I suggested her to arrive early.
8 Where are your luggages?
9 I listen music every day.
10 I've known her since ten years.

VOCABULARY

3 A Match the underlined words in the sentences with the descriptions in the box.

multi-word verb   idiom   collocation   suffix   prefix   *-ing* adjective   compound noun   verb phrase with preposition

1 Learning English is so <u>frustrating</u>!
2 I <u>get on with</u> my sister.
3 I'm <u>relying on</u> you!
4 She <u>took a photo</u>.
5 What a lov<u>able</u> dog!
6 We had a problem with the <u>language barrier</u>.
7 His behaviour was <u>ir</u>rational.
8 I'm sorry. I <u>put my foot in it</u> again.

B Work in pairs. What do the sentences in Exercise 3A mean?

PRONUNCIATION

4 A Tick the pairs of words with the same vowel sound.

1 **a)** bear **b)** fear
2 **a)** though **b)** slow
3 **a)** born **b)** warn
4 **a)** weight **b)** height
5 **a)** era **b)** nearer
6 **a)** west **b)** stressed
7 **a)** solar **b)** dollar
8 **a)** should **b)** food
9 **a)** swollen **b)** stolen
10 **a)** really **b)** rely

B L.1 **Listen and check your answers.**

COLLOCATIONS

5 A Write the words/phrases in the box in the correct word web.

a good time   by car   an effort   exercise   on a diet   a dream   research   a living

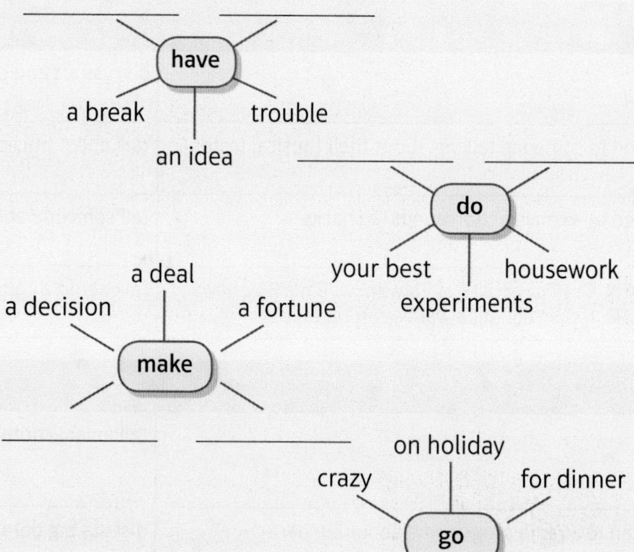

B Work in pairs. Take turns to say true sentences using some of the collocations in Exercise 5A.

REGISTER

6 Are these sentences formal (F) or informal (I)? Where might you hear/read them?

1 Gone into town. Be back at 2.
2 I'm writing to you regarding your advertisement.
3 Wow! That's fantastic news!
4 I look forward to hearing from you at your earliest convenience.
5 One of the main advantages of this program is that it is less costly than its competitors.
6 You'll never guess what!

1 lifestyles

COFFEE DRINKER? p8

LIFE IS BUSY p11

WHAT WOULD YOU TAKE? p14

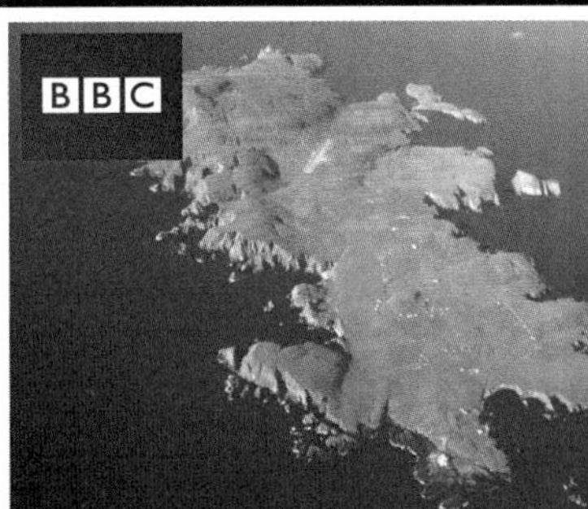

FAIR ISLE p16

SPEAKING **1.1** Talk about your lifestyle **1.2** Do a quiz **1.3** Describe everyday objects **1.4** Explain the lifestyle you prefer

LISTENING **1.2** Listen to a BBC radio programme about busy-ness **1.3** Listen to a conversation about special objects **1.4** Watch a BBC documentary about Britain's most remote inhabited island

READING **1.1** Read an article about coffee **1.3** Read a blog post called *What would you save in a fire?*

WRITING **1.2** Write an article **1.4** Write a pros and cons essay

1.1 COFFEE DRINKER?

G the passive; causative *have*
P sentence stress
V lifestyle; multi-word verbs

VOCABULARY

LIFESTYLE

1 A Read questions 1–6. What do the phrases in bold mean?

1 Are you an **early bird** or do you go to bed late and wake up late?
2 Do you **stick to a routine** every day or does your routine change?
3 Do you lead an **active lifestyle** or a **sedentary lifestyle**?
4 Do you know anyone who has an **alternative lifestyle**? What type of things do they do?
5 Do you enjoy travelling? Would you like to live a **nomadic lifestyle**?
6 What kind of work do you do? Do you **work long hours**?

B Work in pairs. Choose four questions from Exercise 1A to ask your partner.

READING

2 A Work in pairs. Discuss the questions.

1 According to *The Economist*, up to a billion people start their day with either tea or coffee. Are coffee and/ or tea an important part of your lifestyle?
2 Have you drunk any today? Will you drink any (more) today?

B Read the article about coffee. What information is new to you?

C Read the article again and answer the questions.

1 Who were Khalid and Baba Budan and what part did they play in the history of coffee?
2 What 'firsts' and 'seconds' did you learn about?
3 What are the benefits of coffee?

D Work in groups. Discuss the questions.

1 Which facts in the article did you find surprising? Why?
2 Do you think coffee is a type of medicine? Why/Why not?
3 Which is more popular in your country: coffee or tea?

THE WORLD'S FAVOURITE DRUG: ten things you didn't know about coffee

For millions of us, coffee is a big part of our lifestyle. Early birds crave it. People who work long hours need it. And those with active lifestyles drink it to give them energy. But how much do we know about it?

1 Coffee was discovered in Ethiopia in the ninth century AD. The story goes like this: a goat-herder named Khalid noticed that his goats became energetic when they ate the mysterious beans on the mountains. He took some of the beans to the village and had them turned into a drink.

2 It wasn't until coffee arrived in Mocha, Yemen, that the drink's popularity began to spread. From Mocha (the drink was named after the place), coffee beans were exported to India, Java, and eventually to Europe.

3 An alternative story says that coffee was prohibited from leaving Yemen, but a seventeenth-century traveller named Baba Budan smuggled seven coffee beans to India, where he had them planted and harvested by local people. It's said now that all of the world's coffee originates from those seven beans.

4 The word coffee comes from the Arabic qahwat al-bun (wine of the bean). It was shortened to qahwa, which became the Turkish kahve, which became coffee.

5 The world's first coffee house opened in Constantinople, now called Istanbul, in 1475.

6 There are two types of coffee: arabica and robusta. Arabica is smoother, more popular and is used in more speciality coffees. Robusta is cheaper and contains more caffeine. It also grows in tougher conditions.

7 The world's two oldest recorded cats drank coffee every day. The oldest cat ever, Creme Puff, lived to thirty-eight. Her owner, Jake Perry, fed her coffee, bacon, eggs and broccoli every day. Perry was also the owner of the previous record holder, Grandpa Rex Allen, who had the same diet and lived to thirty-four.

8 Coffee is the world's second most popular drink, after tea. 500 billion cups are drunk every year. It's also the second most commonly traded commodity, after oil. The biggest coffee drinkers are Scandinavians. On average, people from Finland, Norway and Sweden drink two cups per person per day.

9 In the seventeenth century, a French doctor suggested that his patients mix milk into their coffee. Coffee had never before been drunk with milk, and this is the origin of café au lait. In recent times, coffee has been shown to have various health benefits: it can act as an anti-depressant, help burn fat and may protect people from Alzheimer's, Parkinson's and dementia.

10 Brazil, which is responsible for a third of the world's coffee, is the leading coffee producer, followed by Vietnam, Colombia and Indonesia.

GRAMMAR

THE PASSIVE; CAUSATIVE *HAVE*

3 A Read sentences 1–4 and answer questions a)–b).

1 Coffee was discovered in Ethiopia.
2 Coffee has been shown to have health benefits.
3 Coffee had never before been drunk with milk.
4 Budan had the beans planted and harvested by local people.

a) Three of these sentences don't say who did the action because it's not the main focus. Which sentence is the exception?
b) Underline the verb forms in each sentence.

B Underline the correct alternatives to complete the rules.

RULES	**1** Use the passive to emphasise *the actions of/ what happens to* people or things. **2** The person who does the action is unimportant, obvious or *known/unknown*. **3** Form the passive with subject + *to be* + *present/ past* participle.

C Read sentences 1–4. Are statements a)–c) below true (T) or false (F)?

1 We had our coffee-maker repaired.
2 I had my hair done.
3 He had his wallet stolen.
4 She had her windows broken.

RULES	**a)** The causative *have* uses *have* + object + past participle. **b)** Use the causative *have* to say when we arrange for somebody to do something for us. **c)** We can also use it to talk about a bad experience or an action done by someone unknown or unnamed.

D Work in pairs. Find more examples of the passive and the causative *have* in the article.

▷ page 104 **LANGUAGEBANK**

4 A ▶ 1.1 **SENTENCE STRESS: causative *have***
Which word is stressed in this sentence? Listen and check.

She had her nails done.

B ▶ 1.2 Which words are stressed in sentences 1–4? Listen and check. Then listen and repeat.

1 I had my watch stolen.
2 He has his house cleaned.
3 We're having our roof fixed.
4 She's had her car broken into.

5 Complete the second sentence so that it means the same as the first, using the word in bold. Use between three and five words, including the word in bold.

1 Someone fixed our washing machine yesterday. **had**
We ____________ yesterday.
2 They gave me a prize for the best essay. **given**
I ____________ for the best essay.
3 Someone will tell them to stick to their routine. **be**
They ____________ to stick to their routine.
4 They have shown that working long hours causes stress. **been**
Working long hours ____________ to cause stress.
5 The doctor checked my hearing yesterday. **had**
I ____________ yesterday.
6 People know Mongolians for their nomadic lifestyle. **are**
Mongolians ____________ their nomadic lifestyle.
7 No one had told Lucy about the party. **been**
Lucy ____________ about the party.
8 Someone broke into their house while they were away. **had**
They ____________ into while they were away.

SPEAKING

6 Work in pairs. Choose four of these questions to ask your partner. Ask follow-up questions to find out more information.

When was the last time you:

- were given a gift?
- had something repaired?
- were taken somewhere beautiful?
- had your hair done?
- were taught how to do something?
- were photographed?
- had your opinions questioned?
- had a special meal cooked for you?

'I take after my parents in that I like working outside. We live on a farm that has been handed down from generation to generation in my family, so there are always things to do. When I was twenty, I started running the farm. Nowadays I work at least ten hours a day. I'm looking forward to retiring one day but that won't be for another few years!'

(Jake)

'I took over the family's law business ten years ago. When my mother handed over responsibility to me, I didn't realise how much work it was. I spend most of my days in the office trying to keep up with our cases. I probably sit at my desk for twelve hours a day and drink about six cups of coffee! I'm looking into employing another lawyer to ease some of the pressure.'

(Suki)

'I used to work in the city but I couldn't put up with the noise and the people. I was always dreaming about escaping. Eventually, I couldn't put it off any longer. I saved some money, left my job, and bought a camper van. I now travel all the time and make a living by doing odd jobs. I believe nothing should keep you from chasing your dreams, and I'm living my dream.'

(Meredith)

VOCABULARY PLUS

MULTI-WORD VERBS

7 A Read the texts above. Match them with the lifestyles: sedentary, active, nomadic. Which lifestyle would you prefer?

B Find ten multi-word verbs in the texts in Exercise 7A. Match them with definitions 1–10.

take
1 ________ start being responsible for a job that someone else was doing before you
2 ________ be similar to your father, mother, etc., because you have a similar character or appearance

hand
3 ________ give control or responsibility of something, e.g. a company, to someone
4 ________ give something to someone, especially to a younger person, so that they continue a tradition

put
5 ________ delay doing something until later
6 ________ accept an unpleasant situation without complaining

look
7 ________ find out about something so that you can take action
8 ________ be excited about something that is going to happen

keep
9 ________ prevent someone from doing something
10 ________ understand all the most recent facts about something

C Read sentences 1–2 about multi-word verbs and complete examples a) and b).

1 Multi-word verbs are idiomatic. You cannot usually guess the meaning from the words.
2 A multi-word verb has two or three words. The first word is a verb. The second (and third) word is a preposition.

a) verb + preposition; example: *take* ________
b) Multi-word verb with three words; example: *look* ________

▷ page 120 **VOCABULARYBANK**

SPEAKING

8 A Complete the sentences so they are true for you.

1 In my family, I take after/don't take after …
2 Something I always/never put off doing is …
3 For my work/studies, I have to/don't have to keep up with …
4 One thing that has been/hasn't been handed down in my family is …
5 Something I will/won't keep on doing for the rest of my life is …
6 I always look forward to …
7 I can't put up with …

speakout TIP

When you learn new words and phrases, always write example sentences. It's a good idea to write <u>personalised</u> sentences; this means the sentences are about you. You have a better chance of remembering the new language if you personalise it.

B Work in pairs. Discuss your sentences from Exercise 8A. Explain your answers.

WRITING

9 Write a paragraph about your lifestyle, similar to the texts in Exercise 7A. Use at least three of the multi-word verbs from Exercise 7B or other multi-word verbs you know.

VOCABULARY

VERB + PREPOSITION

1 A Work in pairs and discuss. Is your life very busy? Can you give examples?

B Read what three people say about their workload. Do any of the comments describe how you feel?

Jodi:
I **feel** completely **overwhelmed by** the amount of work I'm expected to do. I spend my life **racing around** trying to **keep up with** everything. There just aren't enough hours in the day.

Victor:
My problem is I **have no control over** my workload. My boss forces me to **take on** too much and then I **struggle with** finding time to do it all.

Alejandra:
I try not to **let** my work **pile up** too much. I prioritise my tasks and make sure that I **take time out** from work and **make time for** other things that are also important to me.

C Match the phrases in bold in the comments with definitions 1–9.

1 take responsibility for ________
2 find time to do something or be with someone even when you're busy ________
3 do something at the necessary speed ________
4 allow something to increase ________
5 how you feel when something is too much or too difficult so you are unable to do it ________
6 have trouble managing or achieving something ________
7 go fast/do lots of different tasks quickly ________
8 not have the power to direct or manage something ________
9 stop what you are doing in order to do something else for a while ________

D Complete the sentences so they are true for you. Then work in pairs and compare your ideas.

1 I sometimes feel overwhelmed by …
2 I have a tendency to take on …
3 During the week I often race around …
4 I try to make time for …
5 One thing I have no control over is …

LISTENING

2 A Read about a BBC radio programme. What problem does it focus on?

Busy-ness is NOT a competition

Oliver Burkeman

In the modern workplace, when a workmate asks you how you are, the response is almost always, 'Busy! I'm so busy!' It sounds like a complaint, but are we actually proud of the fact that we have so much to do?

Despite all the new time-saving technology we have, we seem to be busier than ever. Perhaps we are just addicted to being busy.
Oliver Burkeman has been exploring why we all feel so busy nowadays.

B 1.3 Listen to the radio programme and answer the questions.

1 How has 'the post-holiday ritual' changed in recent years? What happened before? What happens now?
2 According to the programme, why do we all proclaim to be so busy?

C Listen again. Are the statements true (T) or false (F), according to the programme? Correct the false statements.

1 We are now more likely to say we're busy than in the past.
2 Busy has become a brand. It makes us feel important and essential to the world.
3 If you're not busy, you are seen as someone who is not delivering or potentially someone that's incompetent.
4 Status comes from our reputation – the stuff that we can share on Facebook to show people what we're doing.
5 People began comparing their sixty-hour weeks, and 'busy' was equated with progress and success.

D Work in groups. Discuss the questions.

1 Do you think how busy someone is really defines their social status? Why/Why not?
2 Is busy-ness a problem nowadays? Why/Why not? If it is, how can society deal with it?

GRAMMAR

PRESENT TENSES: SIMPLE VS CONTINUOUS, STATIVE VERBS

3 A Read the sentences. Why is the simple/continuous form used in each case?

1 She's studying really hard for her exams at the moment.
2 I often work late at night just to try and keep up with everything.
3 I want people to think I'm busy.
4 I'm always racing around trying to keep up with everything.
5 We're rushing around more crazily than ever.
6 New technology saves us time, but we're still busier than before.
7 Are you taking any work with you on your holiday?

B Match sentences 1–7 in Exercise 3A with uses a)–g).

RULES

present simple
a) for habits/everyday actions
I get up at 5.00 a.m. every morning.
b) for facts/things that are always true
*Coffee **is** addictive.*
c) for states or feelings (with stative verbs, e.g. *like, love, think, want, be, know*)
*He **doesn't like** his job.*

present continuous
d) for actions happening now or around now *1*
*They**'re** both **working** too hard.*
e) to describe a situation that is in the process of changing
*The economic situation **is improving**.*
f) after words like *always, forever,* and *constantly*, to describe repeated actions (that may be annoying)
*She's always **complaining**.*
g) to describe a planned future action
*He's **starting** a new job next week.*

C Look at the stative verbs in the box and choose the correct alternative to complete the rule.

agree understand remember
depend consist realise suppose
need matter prefer forget believe

Stative verbs *are/are not* usually used in the continuous form.

▷ page 104 **LANGUAGEBANK**

4 A Find and correct one or two mistakes in the sentences. When are both the simple and continuous forms possible?

1 I'm really being busy at the moment, so I'm try to get up at 5a.m. to give me more time to get things done.
2 I try not to work in the evenings or at weekends. I'm preferring to get most of my work done during normal office hours.
3 My brother is always look at his phone while I try to have a conversation with him.
4 Sometimes I'm not realising how long I spend on the computer. I'm going on there to check some information and before I know it, two hours has disappeared.
5 I'm not really agreeing with blaming social media for making us busy. I'm thinking the problem is related to work.
6 When I go out to dinner with my husband, he's always check his phone for emails. I'm finding it really rude.

B ▶ 1.4 Listen and check your answers.

C Change three of the sentences in Exercise 4A so they are true for you. Then work in pairs and compare your ideas.

I'm not busy at the moment because my boss is away. I'm really enjoying it because I don't have to get to work so early.

5 A ▶ 1.5 CONNECTED SPEECH: linking Listen and notice how the words are linked together in fast speech.

1 final consonant + initial vowel: get‿up – I'm trying to get‿up.
2 two of the same consonants: not‿to work – I try not‿to work in the evenings.

B ▶ 1.6 Listen and write the sentences. Then mark the linking.

C Listen and check. Then listen again and repeat.

SPEAKING

6 A Work in pairs. Make questions with the prompts.

Are you too busy?

1 you / work / something important to you / at the moment?
2 on average / hours / you / sleep / night?
3 you / find / difficult / say 'no' / work / even / you / be / busy?
4 how often / you / see / friends?
5 how many emails / be / your inbox / moment?
6 you / feel / stressed / lot / time?
7 you / plan / holiday / for the near future?
8 you / have / hobby / pursue / regularly?
9 you / ever / take / day off / do nothing?
10 how often / you / come home late / from school or work?

B Add two more questions to the quiz in Exercise 6A.

C Work in groups. Ask and answer the questions in the quiz. Who do you think is too busy?

Seven reasons why being bored is good for you

As society gets busier and busier, we find that even when we're alone, we are constantly stimulated by smartphones and trying to keep up with social media. Have we forgotten the importance of being bored? We think of boredom as something negative, to be avoided, but boredom might actually be good for us. Here are some reasons why.

1 **Creativity:** Boredom leads to creativity. You get ideas from being bored. It's only when you're bored that your mind has the time and the space to develop its own creative stimulation.

2 **Problem-solving:** Our subconscious mind is usually better at solving problems than our conscious mind. This is because it is less regulated by rules and protocol. But you tend to only listen to your subconscious mind once your conscious mind has a moment to settle.

3 **Self-reflection:** Being bored encourages you to think about your current state, in a way that racing around being occupied and engaged does not. Self-reflection can be a catalyst for making changes to our jobs and lifestyle.

4 **Selflessness:** According to a study, boredom can inspire people to be altruistic, empathetic and engage in selfless tasks such as giving to charity, volunteering or donating blood.

5 **Slow down:** When we're feeling bored, it's easy to turn on your mobile phone or tablet for entertainment. Yet favouring this virtual world means we stop noticing the real world that surrounds us. Looking at the natural environment helps our minds to slow down and enjoy life.

6 **Breaking the cycle:** Research shows we get a dopamine hit each time we experience something new. In our fast-paced and constantly changing world, we have become accustomed to experiencing this hit all the time. By embracing boredom we can break this cycle and start to enjoy the simple pleasures in life again.

7 **Taking time out:** We live in a world of 24/7 connectivity. This keeps our minds constantly active. There is no downtime. Being bored allows us to take time out from the constant buzz of activity. It allows us to enter a more relaxed state and stop the roller coaster feeling that many of us struggle with. Is that really such a bad thing?

paint a picture

help others

relax

WRITING

AN ARTICLE; LEARN TO USE PERSUASIVE LANGUAGE

7 A Can you think of any reasons why being bored might be good for you?

B Read the article. Does it mention any of your ideas from Exercise 7A?

C Tick the points in the article that you agree with. Put a question mark next to any you disagree with. Then work in pairs and discuss your ideas.

D Do you think these statements about listicles are true (T) or false (F)?

1 A listicle is an article that is written as a list.
2 Listicles are a popular style for blogs and other online articles.
3 Listicles are often used in magazines.
4 Listicles tend to use very formal language.
5 Listicles are a good way to grab a reader's attention.

E Find another example for each of these persuasive devices in the article.

persuasive device	examples
using the personal pronouns *I*, *you* and *we*	We find … we are constantly stimulated by smartphones … ______
referring to research/ statistics/figures	According to a study, … ______
using declarative sentences	Boredom leads to creativity. ______
using rhetorical questions	Have we forgotten the importance of being bored? ______

8 A Work in groups. Plan your own listicle. Follow steps 1–5.

1 Decide on a suitable topic. Think of it in terms of numbers (e.g. seven ways to leave your job). Apparently, odd numbers are more popular.
2 Gather ideas about the topic. It doesn't matter if you have too many ideas – you can cut down later.
3 Choose a title.
4 Choose a style. Do you want it to be funny, informative, chatty or serious? Are you giving advice? Is it formal or informal?
5 Make some notes for each point in your listicle.

B Write your listicle (250–300 words). Add some pictures to help illustrate your ideas.

1.3 WHAT WOULD YOU TAKE?

Ⓕ describing everyday objects
Ⓟ stress patterns: responses
Ⓥ everyday objects

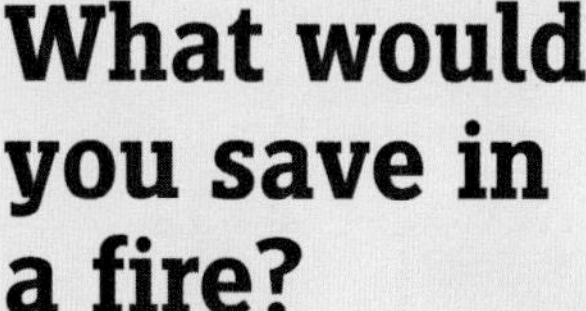

What would you save in a fire?

If your house was burning, what would you take with you? Apart from the obvious, loved ones and pets, what five possessions would you choose? Our choices reflect who we are as people – our interests, background and priorities. And they are often a conflict between what is practical, what is valuable and what is sentimental. It's a way of asking, 'What are the most important things in life?'

So what five things would you take?

1

Name: Enzo Andrade
Age: 21
Location: Recife, Brazil
Occupation: journalist

- **laptop** and **charger**
- **letters** from my parents and girlfriend
- **notebook** and **pen** – this has all my latest ideas
- my **wallet**
- my **harmonica**

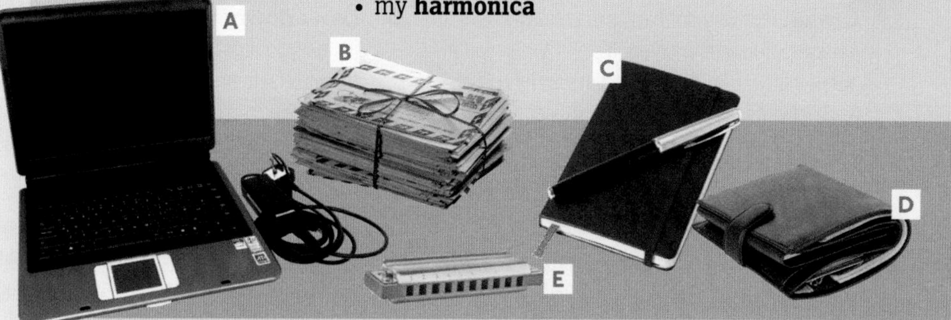

2

Name: Marie Peeters
Age: 72
Location: Antwerp, Belgium
Occupation: retired

- old **family photos**
- a **penknife** with a **bottle opener** which my father gave me
- **watch** – my late husband's
- my **camera**
- my **car key**

VOCABULARY

EVERYDAY OBJECTS

1 A Work in pairs. Read the texts. Can you find all the items from the lists in the photos?

B What do the lists tell you about the people? Are there any items you definitely would/wouldn't take from these lists?

▷ page 120 **VOCABULARYBANK**

FUNCTION

DESCRIBING EVERYDAY OBJECTS

2 A ▶ 1.7 Listen to two people discussing the question, 'What would you take with you if your house was burning?' Tick the items they mention.

coffee pot	penknife	blanket	guitar	passport
phone	watch	torch	charger	laptop
hard drive	necklace	silver ring	cooking pot	

B Listen again. Do the speakers agree or disagree about the items they discuss?

3 A Match 1–7 with a)–g) to make sentences for describing objects.

1 That's/That's definitely not
2 You can
3 It's a bit
4 You need it
5 (It's) made of
6 It's (no) good for
7 It

a) use it to get online/wear it …
b) to prove who you are.
c) telling the time.
d) essential/vital/indispensable.
e) 's really special/has sentimental value.
f) wool/metal/plastic/leather.
g) impractical/heavy/pointless.

B Listen again and check your answers.

▷ page 104 **LANGUAGEBANK**

3

Name: Patti Harrison
Age: 19
Location: Nice, France
Occupation: student

- my **phone**
- my **skateboard**
- **baseball cap**, a gift from a friend
- **silver rings** bought on my travels
- **sunglasses**

following 563 32

4 A Complete the sentences with the words in the box.

sentimental use play indispensable no heavy can that's made need

1 A phone is ______. You ______ it to keep in touch with people.
2 The necklace my grandmother gave me is ______ of gold. It's not worth very much money but it has ______ value.
3 This suitcase is enormous. It's a bit ______ but you can ______ it to carry all your things.
4 This coffee pot has a hole in it. It's ______ good for serving coffee, but you ______ use it to put flowers in.
5 Bring your guitar. ______ essential. You can ______ music and we'll sing.

B Choose three items from the photos and write sentences about them using the phrases in Exercise 4A. Do not say what the item is. Then work in pairs and read your sentences to your partner. Can he/she guess the items?

A: It's made of leather and paper. You can use it to write in.
B: A notebook?
A: Yes.

LEARN TO
RESPOND TO SUGGESTIONS

5 A 1.8 Listen again and complete the phrases for responding to suggestions.

Agreeing
1 Yeah, absolutely. I've got that, ______.
2 Definitely. I ______.
3 I was thinking the same ______.

Disagreeing/Questioning
4 Why have you chosen ______?
5 I don't think that would be my first ______.
6 Oh I'm not ______ about that.
7 That's ______ essential though, is it?
8 Are you joking?/You're ______!

Giving your opinion
9 That's quite practical./That sounds ______.
10 I'd ______ a penknife is pretty important.

B STRESS PATTERNS: responses Listen to the phrases from Exercise 5A. Underline the stressed words/syllables.

C Listen again and repeat. Copy the stress patterns.

6 A Underline the correct alternatives to complete the conversations.

1 **A:** I would take this plastic necklace. It's a bit *impractical/essential*, but I like the colours.
B: Really? I don't *think/sure* that would be my first choice.
2 **A:** I would take this old wooden box. You *can/need* use it to put things in.
B: I'm not *know/sure* about that.
3 **A:** Chocolate! It's good *for/to* use energy.
B: I was thinking the same *choice/thing*.
4 **A:** How about the television? You need it to *watch/watching* the football.
B: Are you joking? That's definitely not *heavy/essential*.

B Work in pairs. Practise the conversations in Exercise 6A.

SPEAKING

7 A Make a list of ten things you would take with you if you had to flee your home.

B Work in pairs and compare your lists. Tell your partner about the items you have chosen. Try to agree on a new list of only ten items.

C Try to agree on a final list of ten items as a class. Describe your items to the class and make a case for including them on the final agreed list.

1.4 FAIR ISLE

DVD PREVIEW

1 A Look at the fact file about a place called Fair Isle. Work in pairs and discuss. How is this place different to where you live?

FACT FILE: FAIR ISLE

LOCATION TYPE: island

COUNTRY: Scotland

AREA: 2.97 square miles

ECONOMY: fishing, agriculture, wool clothes production

OTHER FEATURES: bird observatory

INFRASTRUCTURE: one primary school (older children go to boarding school off the island), one shop, one bar/restaurant at bird observatory, road connecting inhabited areas, one nurse (no doctor)

CLIMATE: cool summers, mild winters

THINGS TO DO: walking, birdwatching, Fair Isle Museum

B Read about the programme. What might be good/bad about the lifestyle on Fair Isle?

Fair Isle

BBC

Fair Isle is a BBC documentary that looks at life on Britain's most remote inhabited island. To live on Fair Isle, you have to apply and be selected. It's a very tough lifestyle, with lots of outdoor work, but as the inhabitants mention, the island has its beauty and living there can be rewarding. The programme follows a couple, Shaun and Rachel, who are new arrivals on the island. Will they be able to adapt their lifestyle to the challenges of Fair Isle?

DVD VIEW

2 Watch the programme. According to the people interviewed, what factors make it hard to live on Fair Isle?

3 A What do we learn about the following?

1 electricity on the island
2 'every able-bodied adult'
3 Shaun and Rachel's lives before they moved (jobs and relationship)
4 the history of Fair Isle
5 the population of the island
6 the location of Fair Isle

B Work in pairs and compare your answers.

4 A Work in pairs. What do you think the phrases in bold mean? What are the phrases used to talk about in the programme?

1 You can be **cut off** for days.
2 Every … adult **holds down several jobs**.
3 The population is **at a critical point**.
4 It **cost them their life savings**.
5 The island needs people like them to **put down roots**.
6 There are no **half-measures**. If you decide to leave, you can't just come back.
7 We've had our **ups and downs**.

B Watch again to check.

5 What type of person do you think chooses to live on Fair Isle? What personal qualities do they need?

speakout explain the lifestyle you prefer

6 A 1.9 Listen to a woman talking about two different lifestyles she's experienced. What did she like about these lifestyles?

B Listen again. Tick the key phrases you hear.

KEYPHRASES

I loved the fast pace of life.
I got burned out.
I started living the quiet life.
It's important to slow down.
It's hard to say which kind of lifestyle I prefer.
I missed the buzz of my work.
I also felt a bit isolated.
In an ideal world, you'd do both.
I much prefer city life.

7 A Work in pairs. Discuss the questions.

nightlife nature noise quiet artificial light crowds open space loneliness friends public transport cinemas and theatres good views pollution natural food

1 Which of the ideas in the box above do you associate with cities (C) and which with smaller communities (S)? Which could be both?
2 Which are important to your lifestyle?
3 What else can you add to this list?

B You are going to discuss which lifestyle you prefer: living in a big city or living in a small community. Think about your answer and make notes.

C Work in groups. Tell each other which lifestyle you prefer and why.

writeback a pros and cons essay

8 A Read the first paragraph of a 'pros and cons' essay about lifestyle. What is the purpose of this first paragraph?

City life or the quiet life?

It's an age-old question. Where do we put down roots: in a big, noisy city or a quiet, calm refuge? In 1845, the writer Henry David Thoreau embraced what would now be called an alternative lifestyle. Overwhelmed by restlessness and unable to put up with society, he went and lived alone in the woods for two years, two months and two days. He then wrote a famous book about his experiences. While he found happiness in solitude, other people need the bright lights and the company of crowds to feel alive.

So, what are the benefits of city life? …

B Think about your answers in Exercise 7. What are the pros and cons of city life compared to life in smaller communities? Complete the essay in Exercise 8A.

V LIFESTYLE

1 A Rearrange the letters in bold to complete the sentences.

1 I have an **ictvae** lifestyle. I run every day, cycle to work and go climbing every weekend. *active*
2 People say I'm an **yarel dbri** because I get up at 5a.m. every morning.
3 We work extremely **lgon hsuor** – 5a.m. to 11p.m. isn't uncommon.
4 I had a **redeyntas** lifestyle. I was sitting down all day at work and I never exercised.
5 I do exactly the same thing every day. I like to **ksitc** to a **rnioteu**.
6 We move to a different place every few weeks. We've always had a **moaidcn** lifestyle.

B Work in pairs and discuss. Which of the lifestyles in Exercise 1A might match these jobs? Why?

athlete sales representative teacher rock musician airline stewardess

G THE PASSIVE; CAUSATIVE *HAVE*

2 A Read the facts about tea. Are these sentences better in the active or passive? Change any you think are better in the passive.

1 Someone invented tea bags in America in the 1800s.
Tea bags were invented in America in the 1800s.
2 People first drank tea in China 4,000 years ago.
3 People can use tea leaves to read the future.
4 Someone first added milk to tea in the seventeenth century.
5 Tea is India's second largest industry, after tourism.
6 China produces more tea than any other country.

B Work in pairs and discuss your answers. Why are some sentences better in the passive?

3 A Complete the sentences with the correct form of the verbs in brackets. Use the causative *have*.

1 I'm going to ______ my hair ______ (cut) tomorrow.
2 I ______ the bedroom walls ______ (paint) last week.
3 I've just ______ my car ______ (wash).
4 When I broke my leg, I ______ the house ______ (clean) by professionals.
5 I've got a strange rash on my arm, so I'm going to the doctor to ______ it ______ (check).
6 I need to ______ my eyes ______ (test).

B Choose two or three sentences from Exercise 3A. Change them to questions you can ask a partner.

When was the last time you had your hair cut?

C Work in pairs. Ask and answer your questions from Exercise 3B.

G PRESENT TENSES

4 A Complete the text with the correct form of the verbs in brackets. Use present tenses.

"I'm a lorry driver, so I [1] ______ (spend) a lot of time alone, listening to music while I [2] ______ (drive) at night. I [3] ______ (work) long hours – sometimes I [4] ______ (drive) for nine or ten hours a day. At the moment I [5] ______ (work) for a music company and we [6] ______ (take) musical equipment and musicians around Europe. Life [7] ______ (be) really busy. Sometimes we [8] ______ (be) on the road for five or six weeks at a time, so I [9] ______ (not have) a very good work-life balance. Next month I [10] ______ (drive) 17,000 km around Europe. I [11] ______ (look) forward to it."

B Write sentences to describe your work-life balance. Then work in pairs and compare your sentences.

V VERB + PREPOSITION

5 A Choose the correct alternatives to complete the sentences.

1 We've been overwhelmed *from/by/to* the number of applications for the job.
2 You should make time *in/on/for* the things you enjoy doing.
3 I try to be organised so that my work doesn't pile *up/in/on*.
4 I have a long journey to work and I really struggle *for/with/on* getting up early.
5 I spend my weekends racing *in/on/around*, trying to keep *up/down/on* with all the jobs that need doing at home.

B Change two or three of the sentences in Exercise 5A so they are true for you. Then work in pairs and compare your sentences.

F DESCRIBING EVERYDAY OBJECTS

6 A Match the objects in the box with their definitions.

umbrella necklace bottle camera stamp

1 It's made of glass or plastic and you use it to keep liquids in.
2 It's usually made of metal and nylon. It's waterproof. You need it to keep you dry when it's raining.
3 It's made of metal and you use it to take photographs.
4 It's made of paper and you need it to send a letter. You can stick it on an envelope.
5 It's made of silver and you can wear it around your neck.

B Write a list of five things that are special to you. Then work in pairs. Describe each thing to your partner without saying what they are. Can your partner guess?

It's a made of silver and you can wear it. My grandmother gave it to me.

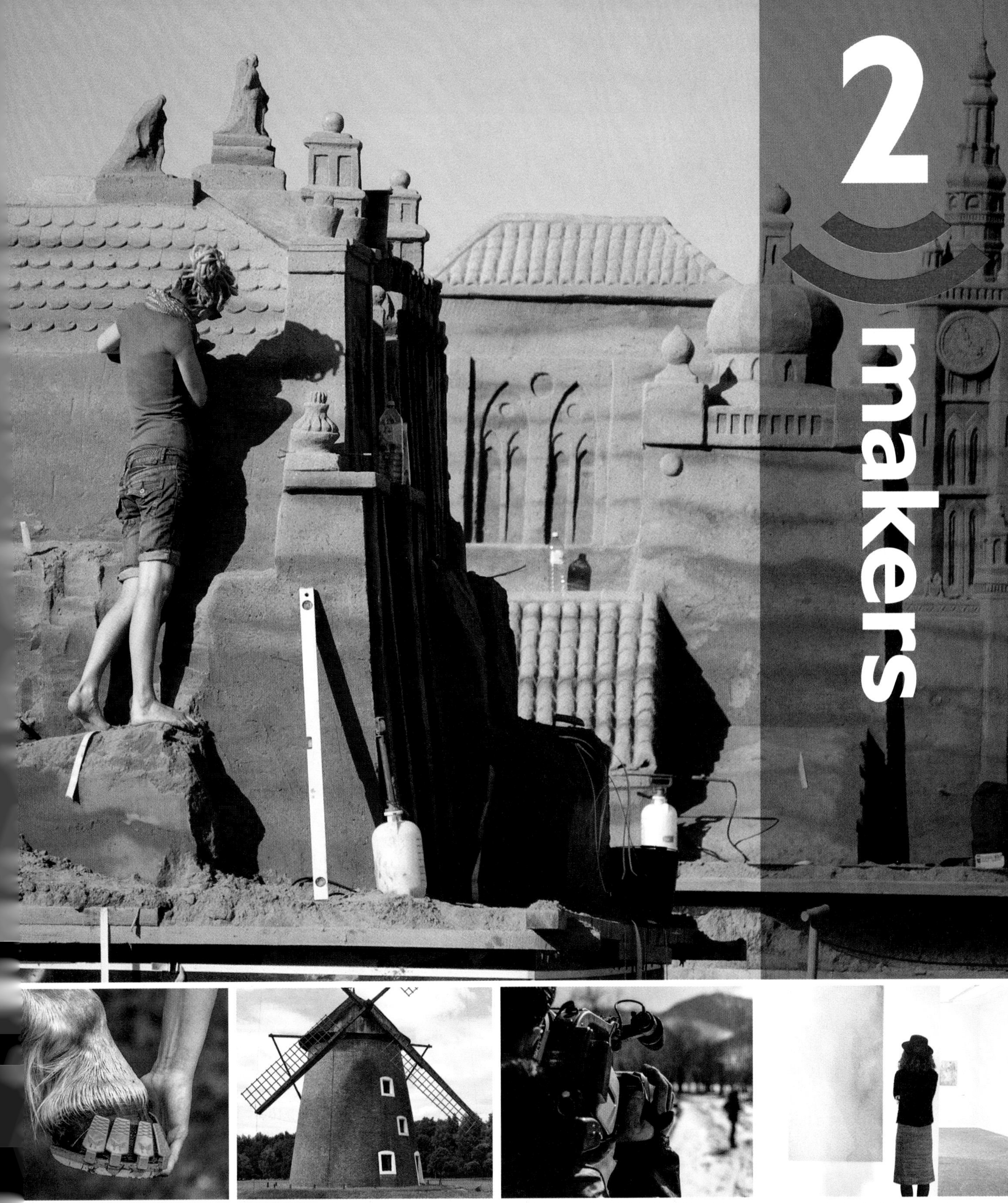

2 makers

ENIUS INVENTIONS p20 | BUILDERS p23 | SOUNDS LIKE A PLAN! p26 | CREATIVITY p28

SPEAKING **2.1** Describe some genius inventions **2.2** Discuss an article **2.4** Discuss creativity

LISTENING **2.1** Listen to a radio programme **2.3** Listen to conversations about making a film
2.4 Watch people talking about creativity

READING **2.2** Read an article about an amazing builder
2.3 Read about making a film

WRITING **2.1** Write a product description **2.4** Write an article

2.1 GENIUS INVENTIONS

G question forms; indirect questions
P intonation: statement questions
V adjectives to describe inventions

the Megasus Horserunners Horse Sneakers

Saltwater Brewery's Edible Six-pack Rings

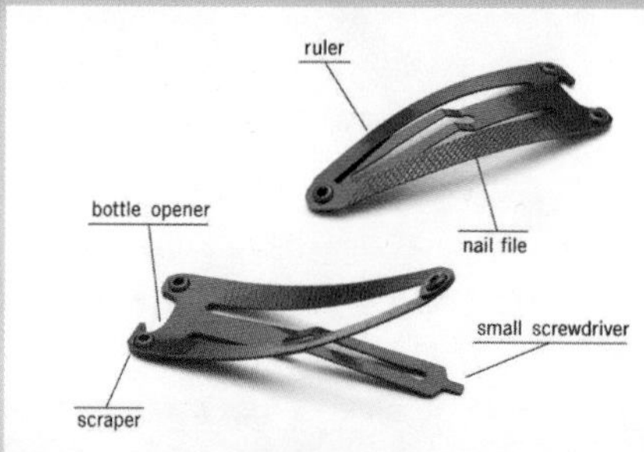

the MTA Multipurpose Hair Clip

the Edible Spoon Maker

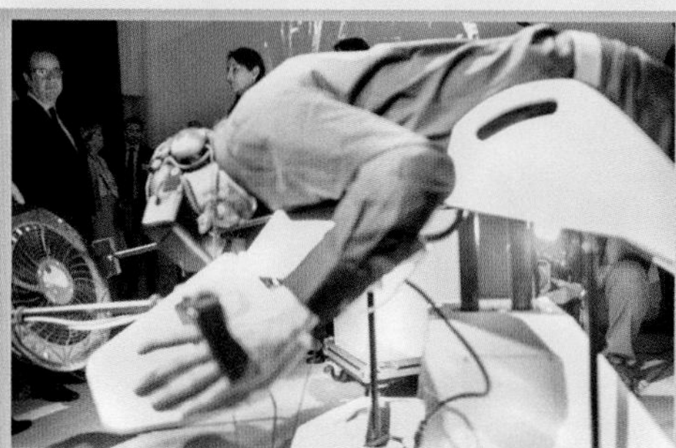

the Birdy Flight Simulator

Terra, the Grass-covered Outdoor Lawn Chair

VOCABULARY

ADJECTIVES TO DESCRIBE INVENTIONS

1 A Work in pairs. Look at the inventions in the photos and answer the questions.

1 What do you think they are for?
2 Do you think they are a good idea?
3 Who do you think would buy them?

B Match the adjectives in the box with their uses.

stunning groundbreaking flexible durable biodegradable functional portable unique edible novel flimsy clip-on

A word/Words that can be used to describe something that:

1 is new. _______, _______
2 will last a long time. _______
3 breaks easily. _______
4 has a clear use. _______
5 has lots of (different) uses. _______
6 looks very good. _______
7 can be carried around. _______
8 you can eat. _______
9 is like no other. _______
10 can be broken down (decomposed) by bacteria. _______
11 can be attached by a clip so it can be easily removed. _______

C Work in pairs. Use the words in Exercise 1B to talk about the inventions in the photos.

Aquiem Designer Boxed Water

LISTENING

2 A 2.1 Listen to a radio programme. Which of the inventions in the photos are mentioned?

B Work in pairs. Are the statements true (T) or false (F)?

1 Birdy is a flight simulator which mimics the flight of a bird flying over New York City.
2 The simulator is controlled by the body of the user.
3 The edible spoons are made of rice.
4 The spoons come in three flavours.
5 The horse trainers are the first ones to be designed specifically for horses.
6 The trainers can be easily fitted and removed.

C Listen again and check your answers.

GRAMMAR

QUESTION FORMS; INDIRECT QUESTIONS

3 A 2.2 **Listen and complete the questions from the radio programme.**

1 Can I ask what _______ about the designs?
2 _______ developed the idea?
3 Does _______ any kind of functional use?
4 Can you tell me if _______ really edible?
5 Why _______ want to eat your spoon?

B Match questions 1–5 in Exercise 3A with descriptions a)–d).

a) a direct question (with *do/does* as the auxiliary) _______
b) a direct question (with a modal auxiliary) _______
c) an indirect question _______, _______
d) a subject question _______

C Underline the correct alternatives to complete the rules.

RULES	1 We use *direct/indirect* questions to sound more polite. 2 In indirect questions, the word order is the same as in *direct questions/positive statements.* 3 When the *wh-* question word is the subject of the question, we *use/don't use* an auxiliary verb (*do, did,* etc.).

4 A Put the words in the correct order to make questions.

1 you / this / can / about / you / design / know / ask / what / I?
2 want / buy/ why / to / you / this / would?
3 idea / developed / this / who?
4 me / can / if / you / is / this / tell / biodegradable?
5 use / have / does / practical / it / a?
6 a / think / idea / you / good / is / do / this?

B Work in pairs. Student A: turn to page 128. Student B: turn to page 130.

speakout TIP

We can use statements to ask *yes/no* questions. When speaking, we understand they are questions from the context and the intonation. How do you recognise a statement question when it is written?

page 106 **LANGUAGEBANK**

5 A 2.3 **INTONATION: statement questions Listen and decide which of the statements are questions. Put a question mark after the statement questions.**

1 These are spoons. They're edible.
2 You would buy one of these.
3 He's her father. He's Iranian.
4 It's nine o'clock. We're late.
5 You've seen it before.
6 She lives here. These are her things.

B Listen again and repeat. Copy the intonation.

SPEAKING

6 A Work in groups of four. Look at the photo for your new invention idea below and imagine you need to get funding for it. How will you persuade the group to give you funding? Think about these questions to plan your pitch.

- What is it?
- Does it have a name?
- How useful is it?
- What is its function?
- What problem does it solve?
- Who would use a design like this?
- Who would buy it?
- What makes it new/unique?
- How could it change someone's experience/ the world?

B Present your ideas to your group. Ask and answer questions about the invention. Who do you think has the most brilliant invention? As a group, decide which one you would invest in.

Student A: Bubble Tank

Student B: Toasteroid

Student C: Bluetooth-enabled toothbrush

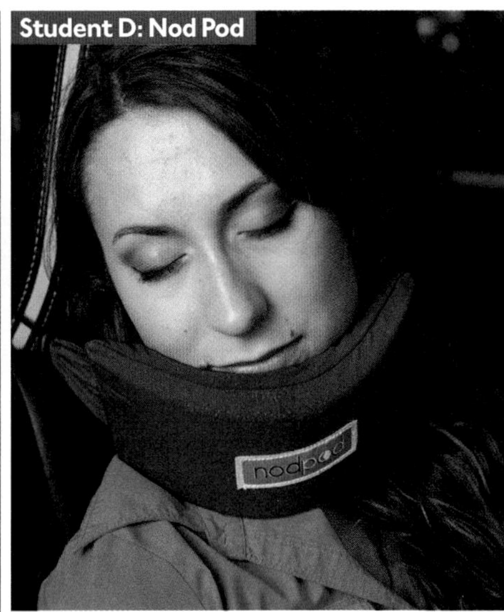
Student D: Nod Pod

WRITING

A PRODUCT DESCRIPTION; LEARN TO WRITE PERSUASIVE COPY

7 A Read the product descriptions. Would you buy either of these products? Why/Why not?

Perfect coffee water

Did you know that the coffee you drink is ninety-eight percent water? So if you want the perfect cup of coffee in the morning, you need Aquiem, the world's first designer coffee water.

Aquiem, which costs approximately $3 per litre, is a specially formulated water, which has been purified and then blended with minerals that enhance the taste and the aroma of coffee. Designed by coffee lovers, Aquiem took five years to develop, with its creators conducting extensive research to determine the precise formula for the perfect coffee water.

Aquiem is packaged in portable one-litre cartons, which are available to buy by the case, to ensure you can brew the perfect cup of coffee whenever you want it.

Clever clip

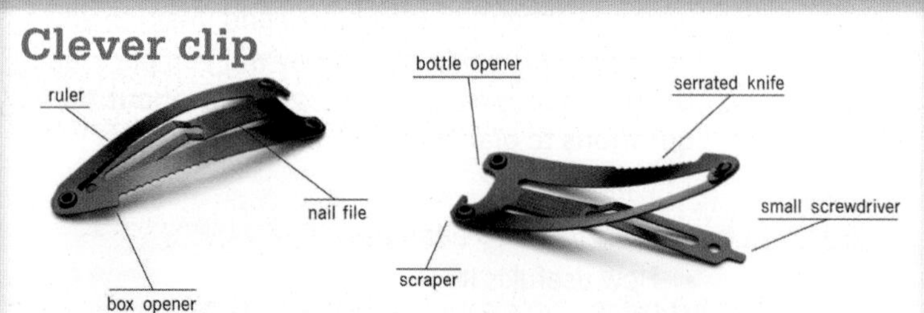

Never have a screwdriver when you need one? Then the clever clip hairclip is perfect for you. At first glance, it looks like a normal hairclip, but actually, it also functions as a tiny portable tool box. The MTA Hairclip is strengthened with steel, so it's durable, and it features a screwdriver, a bottle opener, a nail file, a trolley coin and a serrated knife, all contained within the 6x2.4-cm clip. This tool is truly multifunctional.

So next time you're out and about and suddenly need to do a bit of DIY or if you're planning a camping holiday, be sure to remember to take your MTA Hairclip. And when you're not wearing it, you can carry it on your key ring, so you never again need to be without your own personal toolkit.

B Notice the structure of the product descriptions. For each description, tick the information which is included.

	coffee water	hairclip
1 Introduce the item. (What is it?)		
2 Give details about the design of the item (colour, size, material, function).		
3 Include information about the price/ shipping/availability.		
4 Background information (e.g. who designed it, what research was involved)		
5 Closing incentive (why you should buy this item) or counter an objection (by offering an alternative use)		

8 A Read the tips for writing persuasive copy. Do you think the descriptions in Exercise 8A follow this advice?

1. Use conversational language (informal language, questions, etc.).
2. Give clear, precise details about the product.
3. Talk about the benefits of the product, not just its features (use conditionals, e.g. *If you want … , try …*).
4. Use sensory language (What does it look/taste like?) and try to appeal to your reader's emotions.
5. Use superlative language (*the best, the fastest, the first*, etc.).
6. Appeal directly to the reader (use personal pronouns).

B Match the underlined phrases in the descriptions with tips 1–6 in Exercise 8A.

C Read the descriptions again and find more examples for tips 1–6 in Exercise 8A.

D Complete the text with the phrases in the box.

truly unique	so, if you want to spend
designed by	are perfect for you
did you know that	is specially designed

Terra

1 ______ you can now grow your own armchair with grass from your garden lawn? Terra 2 ______ for gardening enthusiasts, who are looking for something a little different for their garden.

3 ______ Piergiorgio Robino and Andrea Sanna from Turin, Italy, Terra uses a clever cardboard frame, with soil placed over the top of it, where grass seeds are planted. These chairs are 4 ______ and only take two months to grow.

5 ______ a peaceful afternoon enjoying your garden sunshine, then Terra chairs 6 ______ . What could be better than having your own living furniture? Don't have a garden? No problem. You can grow your own Terra garden chair on a balcony too!

9 Choose one of the inventions on page 20 (or any invention of your choice). Write a short product description for a website (100–150 words), following the advice in Exercise 8A.

VOCABULARY

BUILDINGS

1 A Work in pairs. Look at the words in the box and answer the questions.

windmill barn greenhouse warehouse cave shed factory cathedral temple castle shelter mosque

1 Match photos A–E with words from the box.
Photo A is a cathedral.
2 Do you have any of these buildings in your town/city?
3 Have you ever visited these types of building? When/Where/Why?
4 What do the other words in the box mean?

B Write the words from Exercise 1A in the correct group.

1 religious buildings: *cathedral*, _______, _______
2 buildings used to store things: *warehouse*, _______
3 buildings for plants or animals: *barn*, _______
4 buildings for generating energy or making industrial products: *windmill*, _______
5 places where people live: *shelter*, _______
6 a large natural hole, often under the ground: _______

C Work in groups. Answer the questions using words from Exercise 1A.

Which structure:
1 is traditionally where kings and queens live?
2 uses the movement of air to create energy?
3 stores gardening tools?
4 can be a place for the homeless to sleep?
5 is made of glass?

2 A 2.4 SILENT LETTERS Listen and repeat the words in Exercise 1A. Which words have a silent *d*, a silent *t* and a silent *u*?

B 2.5 Underline the silent letters in the sentences. Then listen, check and repeat. What other words do you know that have silent letters?

1 The shed has a cupboard.
2 The cathedral has tall columns.
3 He knocked on the door of the temple.
4 The temple is on an island.
5 There's a guard in front of the castle.
6 He owns the whole factory.

▷ page121 **VOCABULARYBANK**

A

B

C

D

E

READING

3 A Work in groups of three. Student A: read *Windmill man* on page 24. Student B: turn to page 129 and read *Cave digger*. Student C: turn to page 131 and read *Shelter helper*. Then answer the questions about your text in the table.

	Windmill man	Cave digger	Shelter helper
[1]Who is he and why is he famous?			
[2]How or where did he get the idea to construct the building(s)?			
[3]Who is/are the building(s) for?			
[4]What materials does he use and where does he get them?			
[5]What has he done since creating the first building?			

B Tell the other students in your group about your text. As you listen, complete the table in Exercise 3A.

C Discuss the questions.

1 Which story do you like the best? Why?
2 What do you think of the people in the stories? What motivates them?
3 If you could build a building for your town/city, what would it be?

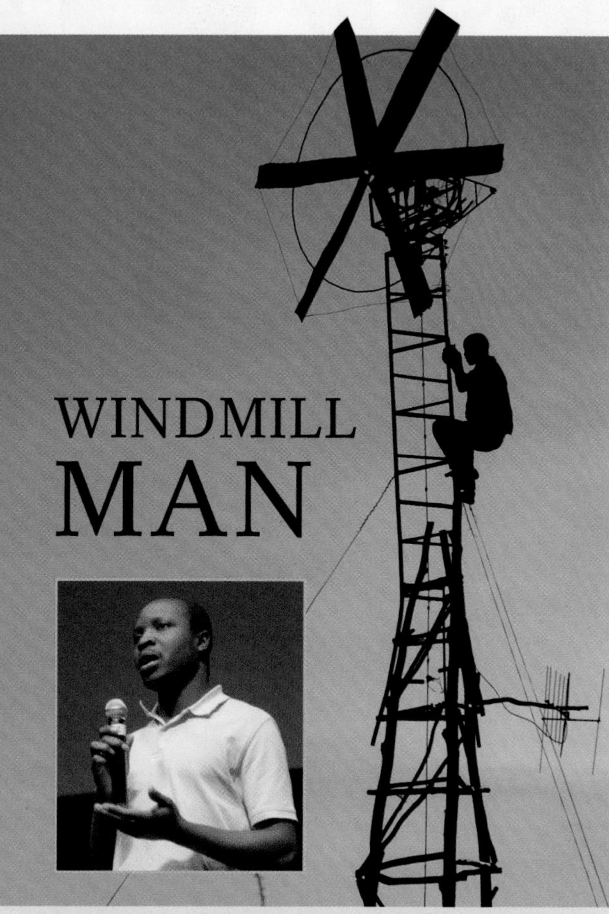

WINDMILL MAN

William Kamkwamba has become a household name in Malawi and beyond. His story shows how curiosity and persistence can defeat the greatest difficulties and turn dreams into reality.

Kamkwamba was born into a poor farming family in Malawi. In 2001 a famine struck the country. Kamkwamba's family had barely enough money to buy food and so he had to drop out of school. He was determined to continue his education, however, so he kept on visiting the school library.

One day in the library he came across a book which explained how to construct a windmill. He couldn't read English well, but he understood the diagrams and pictures. Realising that wind power could generate enough electricity to help his family, he began work on its construction. He was just fourteen years old. As he had no money, he used recycled materials: a bicycle frame, plastic pipes and scrap metal. Everyone said he was crazy.

Amazingly, despite Kamkwamba's lack of training and his youth, the windmill worked. It brought enough electricity to power four lights and two radios in his parents' house. Kamkwamba then constructed a solar-powered water pump for his village, and two other windmills. The pump helps the villagers irrigate their fields to produce food.

In the years since that first windmill, Kamkwamba has found international fame, appearing on numerous programmes. He has written a memoir called The Boy Who Harnessed the Wind, and has had his story turned into a children's book. Much of his time is spent bringing attention to the struggles of the poor in Malawi. Since 2007, Kamkwamba has been giving talks about his life and achievements. These have inspired millions and raised awareness of what needs to be done in the poor rural areas of the world.

GRAMMAR

PRESENT PERFECT SIMPLE AND CONTINUOUS

4 A Underline the verb forms in sentences 1–6.

1 Kamkwamba has become a household name.
2 Since 2007 Kamkwamba has been giving talks about his life.
3 Ra Paulette has been creating caves since 1987.
4 So far he has completed fourteen caves.
5 Since 2015 Elvis Summers has been building homes for the homeless.
6 He and friends have now constructed over forty of the wooden shelters.

B Answer the questions about the sentences in Exercise 4A.

1 Which sentences describe completed actions? Which describe ongoing, incomplete actions?
2 Which use the present perfect simple?
3 Which use the present perfect continuous?

C Complete the rules with *continuous, simple, have* or *been*.

RULES

1 We form the present perfect simple with subject + ______ + past participle.
2 We form the present perfect continuous with subject + *have* + ______ + *-ing* form.
3 We use the present perfect [3] ______ when an action is long and repeated and continues until now.
4 We use the present perfect [4] ______ when an action is shorter and complete.
5 When the main verb is a state verb, we use the present perfect [5] ______ .

▷ page 106 **LANGUAGEBANK**

5 A Complete the sentences with the present perfect simple or continuous form of the verbs in brackets. In which can we use both tenses?

1 They __________ (plan) to build a mosque for the last few years.
2 We __________ (receive) a donation of €1,000 for the homeless shelter.
3 Which of these films __________ (you/see) already?
4 She __________ (write) this book for fifteen years and she still hasn't finished!
5 We __________ (not know) her very long.
6 I __________ (try) to call you all day. Was your phone switched off?
7 She __________ (paint) the boat all morning. That's why she's tired.
8 We __________ (not include) her on the guest list because she'll be away.
9 Your clothes are covered in dust! What __________ (you/do)?
10 He __________ (work) here since he left school.

B Write two sentences about yourself in the present perfect simple and two in the present perfect continuous. Two sentences should be false. Then read your sentences to other students. Can they guess which are false?

VOCABULARY PLUS

WORD-BUILDING: PREFIXES AND SUFFIXES

6 A Read about a sculptor. What did she build when she was a child?

The midnight maker

Alyssa Levandry, sculptor

Kids are natural builders. As a toddler, I used wooden blocks to make towers that I toppled with a joyful kick. At five, I built famous empires out of Lego. Tiny plastic soldiers guarding blue castles. Houses of all colours and strange monsters with many heads. Childish things, but to me, magical.

As a seven-year-old, I built and submerged a fifty-centimetre dam in the stream by my house. It was made of sticks and leaves, mud and grass. By then, my best friend Tammy was building with me. At nine, we constructed bridges made of dry pasta and glue. They were so accurate in scale, so reliable in construction that we could stand them on my bedroom floor and run toy cars across them like the Brooklyn Bridge.

A few years later I built a musical instrument out of wood and rubber bands. I cut a hole in the wood so the sound could echo and I tied the rubber bands across the hole like guitar strings. I was a midnight maker of things – objects and structures that were the fruits of my misspent childhood.

At fourteen, my co-creator Tammy could disassemble and reassemble a radio; at fifteen, she could do the same with a computer, but I preferred natural objects. Electronics never interested me. I liked the sound and the smell of wood, the feel of mud on my hands. I did then and I still do.

7 A Read the text again. Circle the words that use the prefixes in 1. Underline the adjectives that use the suffixes in 2.

1 prefixes: *mid-*, *mis-*, *co-*, *dis-*, *re-*
2 suffixes: *-al*, *-ful*, *-ous*, *-ish*, *-able*

B Work in groups. Match the prefixes in Exercise 7A with meanings a)–e). Can you think of an example for each?

a) *mis-* : mistaken, wrong or wrongly (e.g. *mishear*, *misunderstand*)
b) ______ : again (e.g. ______)
c) ______ : in the middle of (e.g. ______)
d) ______ : positive → negative (e.g. ______)
e) ______ : together with (e.g. ______)

C Look at the suffixes in Exercise 7A again. Is this statement true (T) or false (F)?

The suffixes in Exercise 7A are usually used to turn a word into an adjective, e.g. *magic* → *magical* (relating to magic), *rely* → *reliable* (something you can rely on).

8 Add a prefix or suffix to the words in brackets to complete the sentences.

1 Don't trust him! He's completely *dishonest* (honest)!
2 I found my ________ (pilot) asleep.
3 My ________ (origin) plan was to hand over the company to my son.
4 We had to ________ (build) the temple after the storm.
5 I put off my 8a.m. meeting until ________ (morning) as I was busy.
6 The work is ________ (do) if you put in enough time and effort.
7 They ________ (judged) us. We were better than they thought!
8 The castle is protected by the ________ (mountain) landscape.
9 She looks forward to meeting her new ________ (workers).
10 I find that sticking to a routine is always ________ (help).

▷ page121 VOCABULARYBANK

SPEAKING

9 A Underline the correct alternatives to complete the sentences.

1 I sometimes make little ornaments for the house, but never anything *useful/used.*
2 People always *disunderstand/misunderstand* me and they never laugh.
3 I can cook a few dishes but I'm not very *adventural/adventurous.*
4 I'm too *disorganised/misorganised* to plan anything big, but people sometimes come to the house.
5 I'm not *musicous/musical* at all. When I sing, dogs howl in solidarity.
6 I have to *miswrite/rewrite* everything, but I do like creating fiction.

B Match sentences 1–6 in Exercise 9A with the topics in the box.

food drinks handmade objects *1* business deals music stories games for children art jokes parties conversation

C What are you good at making or organising? Choose from the things in the box in Exercise 9B and/or add your own. Tell other students.

2.3 SOUNDS LIKE A PLAN!

F judging and evaluating ideas
P intonation: sounding enthusiastic
V projects

VOCABULARY
PROJECTS

1 **Work in pairs and discuss. Have you ever made a film (e.g. a home movie, a short film for YouTube or for a project)? If so, what was difficult and what was easy? Did you enjoy it? If not, would you like to?**

2 A **Read about what you need to make a full-length film. What do the words in bold mean?**

So you want to make a movie?

First, you need **financing**. That means: start **fundraising**. Apply for **grants**. Some of these target the arts. Also, look for **sponsors**. Find people and organisations with a natural interest in your subject.

Once you have the money, you'll need to create a **budget**. How much will you spend on **venues** – the places where you'll film? How much on **personnel** – actors, directors, camera operators, etc.? And will you need to buy **equipment**?

Then you can work out the **logistics**: how many people will you need? Where will they stay and for how long? Then you'll draw up a **schedule**. What dates will you start and finish filming?

After the film is complete, you'll need to think about **promotion** and **publicity**. How will people learn about your film? It could be the greatest film ever, but you need people to know about it!

B **Answer the questions about the words in bold in Exercise 2A.**

Which word(s):

1 are related to money? (5 words) Which two of these words require things that are written down? Which one refers to people or organisations?
2 describe how you tell people about the film? (2 words)
3 is a group of people who will do the work?
4 is a set of tools for a particular purpose?
5 describes the places you'll use?
6 says when everything will happen?
7 is related to the management of resources, including buying, storing and transportation?

C **2.6 Listen and repeat the words in Exercise 2A. Underline the stressed syllables.**

FUNCTION
JUDGING AND EVALUATING IDEAS

3 A **2.7 Listen to four conversations between film students who are planning to make a short film. Match conversations 1–4 with topics a)–d).**

a) personnel **c)** schedule
b) financing **d)** venue

B **Listen again. Answer the questions.**

1 In conversation 1, what do they decide to do?
2 In conversation 2, what problems with the filming do they mention?
3 In conversation 3, what is the news?
4 In conversation 4, where do they decide to film?

4 A **Complete the sentences from the recording with the words in the box.**

that's work that might sounds think non-starter potential sound

1 I looked up this grant … What do you ________ ?
2 Yeah. I think it has ________ .
3 That ________ great.
4 I'm thinking we start filming mid-afternoon on Friday, around 3.00. How does that ________ ?
5 It's going to rain on Thursday, so that's a ________ .
6 I'm not sure that'll ________ because of the light.
7 OK. ________ a possibility.
8 That ________ work.
9 Excellent! I like the sound of ________ .

B **Which five phrases in Exercise 4A are positive? Which two are negative?**

5 A Write the phrases in the box in the correct place in the table.

That might work. I'm not convinced about that. Do you like the idea? No way. That looks/sounds great!

1 asking for an evaluation of an idea
What do you think? How does that sound? ______
2 saying an idea is possible
It has potential. That's a possibility. ______
3 saying an idea is very good
That seems like a really good idea. I like the sound of that. ______
4 saying an idea might not work
I'm not sure that'll work. I have my doubts about that. ______
5 saying an idea is completely impossible
That's a non-starter. That's out of the question. ______

B ▶ 2.8 Listen and check. Listen again and repeat.

▷ page 106 **LANGUAGEBANK**

6 Work in pairs. Role-play the conversation between two film students arranging for a speaker to come to their film school.

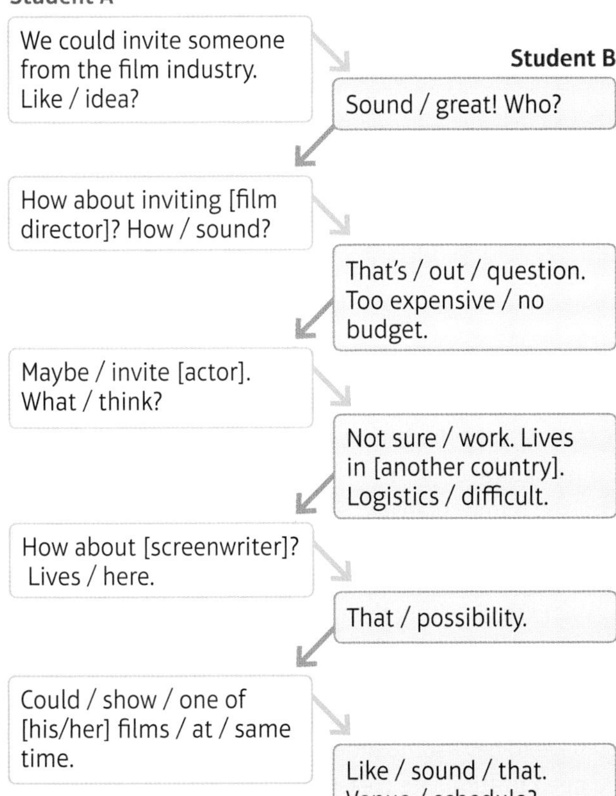

LEARN TO
GIVE PRAISE

7 A Read the words we use to say something is great and underline the stressed syllables. Which of these words do you already use?

1 Amazing!
2 Fantastic!
3 Excellent!
4 Wonderful!
5 Marvellous!
6 Brilliant!
7 Awesome!

speakout TIP

When you give praise, the intonation is as important as the words. Do Exercise 7B and focus on sounding enthusiastic.

B ▶ 2.9 **INTONATION: sounding enthusiastic** Listen and repeat. Copy the intonation.

C Work in pairs. Practise the conversations using words from Exercise 7A. Then swap roles.

1 **A:** That film is good.
B: Good? It's … !
2 **A:** It's a nice book.
B: Nice? It's … !
3 **A:** She's a good student.
B: Good? She's … !
4 **A:** We had a nice trip.
B: Nice? It was … !

SPEAKING

8 A Work in groups. Choose one of these projects to plan or create your own.

- Plan a surprise birthday party for a relative.
- Make a short film.
- Organise a concert.
- Arrange an end-of-year meal for friends or colleagues.
- Invite a speaker to your school/workplace.

B Discuss the questions.

1 What will you need to complete your project/plan?
We'll need financing, equipment and a schedule.
2 How will you finance it? Will you need a budget?
3 What logistics do you need to consider?
4 What about venues and the schedule?
5 Will you need to publicise the project/plan?

C Present your plan to the class. As you listen to other plans, think of questions to ask. Then say what you think of the project.

2.4 CREATIVITY

DVD PREVIEW

1 A Write a list of ten creative activities. Are the activities in the box creative? Why/Why not?

fixing things around the house
reading books   kayaking   cooking
going to museums/the theatre
playing the guitar   doing housework
making something new from something old   going for a walk
playing games with children

B Do you do any of the activities above or other creative activities?

DVD VIEW

2 A Watch Part 1 of the interviews. Which of the activities in the box in Exercise 1A do the speakers mention?

B Watch Part 1 again. For each speaker, make a note of what they do that is creative.

Samantha: cooking – inventing new recipes

C What do they say? Match 1–10 with a)–j) to make sentences.

1 I just love
2 She's brilliant at
3 I'd like to think I'm
4 My artwork is
5 I like to read books
6 I enjoy going to
7 I like to sort of write a few words down,
8 I suppose I appreciate
9 Basically, I have to make up stories
10 I was artistic but

a) you know, museums, libraries …
b) a little bit creative.
c) and make new things out of old things.
d) inventing new recipes with any food I can find.
e) art and things like that.
f) fixing things around the house.
g) I wasn't good at art.
h) terrible.
i) as a kind of creative act.
j) as well as, you know, write a few sort of lyrics now and again.

3 Watch Part 2 of the interviews. Which speaker likes/liked:

1 things which are already made?
2 to create things with film or photography?
3 making music?
4 to do vignettes (a type of portrait photograph)?
5 repurposing things from old to new?
6 craft activities when she was at school?

4 Watch Part 3 of the interviews. Underline the correct alternatives to complete the information.

Julian has creative friends in the industry of [1]*music/sculpture*. He used to go to school with [2]*an actor/a rapper* named Stormzy. He has a friend who is a YouTube phenomenon called Kyodai (also known as Roll Safe) who does a lot of videos for [3]*young/old* people.

Philippa has creative friends who are [4]*directors/managers* and spend a lot of time in rehearsal rooms or they [5]*play games/do sport* or make theatre. She has a lot of creative friends because she works in [6]*the music industry/theatre*.

5 Watch Part 4 of the interviews. Who says these things? Write the name of the speaker.

1 It's just natural or it is not there. ____________
2 I realised it (my creativity) got a bit rusty. ____________
3 You can inspire, not necessarily teach (creativity). ____________
4 Everyone has it within them. You've just got to find a way of bringing it out. ____________
5 You have to be able to let things flow naturally and just go with it. ____________
6 You have to have some time and patience. ____________
7 You need to stimulate creativity … so you need to practise it. ____________
8 Creativity is something that everyone has to varying degrees. ____________
9 There's no right or wrong in a creative process. ____________
10 Creativity can be inspired. ____________

Gene

speakout a discussion

6 A **Work in pairs. Use the questions in the interviews and some of the expressions in Exercise 2C to write five questions about creativity to ask another student.**

Are you any good at fixing things around the house?
Do you enjoy inventing new recipes?
Would you say you're good at art?

B **Talk to other students. Ask and answer your questions.**

7 A **Look at the quotes below from Part 4 of the interviews. Prepare to discuss the quotes using these instructions.**

1 Do you agree or disagree with the statements?
2 Think of examples from your own life and experience to support your ideas.
3 Make some notes.

'Everyone has creativity within them. You've just got to find a way of bringing it out.'

'There's no right or wrong in a creative process.'

'You need to stimulate creativity or it gets rusty. So, you need to practise it.'

B **Work in groups. Discuss the quotes in Exercise 7A. Do you agree or disagree with each other? Tell the class about your discussion.**

writeback an article

8 A **Read the text. Does the writer believe that creativity is an important skill? Why/Why not?**

The importance of creativity

Creativity is an important twenty-first-century skill. We need to be able to teach our children how to be creative in order to help them cope with the rapidly changing society that they live in. Employers of the future are looking for people who have creative ideas, who can come up with creative solutions to the problems we face. And yet, education seems to be overly concerned with teaching learners historical facts, teaching them the answers to questions rather than encouraging them to ask the questions themselves. It's incredibly important that we focus on skills like creative and critical thinking, helping people to work together cooperatively and encouraging our learners to think about the world in new and creative ways.

B **Write a short article about creativity (150–200 words). Choose one of these titles.**

1 The importance of creativity
2 Modern schooling blocks our natural creativity
3 Being creative won't make you rich but it might make you happy

2.5 LOOKBACK

G INDIRECT QUESTIONS

1 A Complete the indirect questions.

1 What are you doing later?
Can you tell me ________?

2 Where are you going at the weekend?
Can I ask you ________?

3 Who is your favourite musician/artist/designer?
Can you tell me ________?

4 Where are you going for your next holiday?
Do you have any idea ______?

5 What are your plans for the next year or two?
Do you know ________ ?

6 Where did you go to school?
Can you tell me ________?

7 Do you enjoy learning languages?
Can I ask you if ________?

B Work in pairs. Ask and answer the indirect questions in Exercise 1A.

V ADJECTIVES TO DESCRIBE INVENTIONS

2 Underline the correct alternatives to complete the sentences.

1 Where did you get that beautiful dress? It's absolutely *groundbreaking/stunning*!

2 The thing I like best about the design is that it will last a long time. It's very *durable/flimsy*.

3 I don't think anyone has ever had an idea like this before. It's *biodegradable/groundbreaking*.

4 I only bought this last month but it's broken already. The design is really *portable/flimsy*.

5 I've never seen anything like it before – it's completely *unique/clip-on*.

6 These earphones are great. They are *clip-on/novel*, so they attach to your jacket and don't fall out of your pocket.

7 These bags are 100 percent *groundbreaking/biodegradable*, so they won't harm the environment.

8 The decorations on the cake are made of sugar, so they're *functional/edible* too.

V BUILDINGS

3 A Find twelve kinds of building in the word snake.

B Work in pairs. Choose one of the words in Exercise 3A. Describe it for your partner to guess.

G PRESENT PERFECT SIMPLE AND CONTINUOUS

4 A Rana runs a small hotel. Read her to-do list and complete her sentences below. Use the present perfect simple or continuous form of the verbs in brackets.

paint walls
order bed ✓
prepare Room 1 for special guest ✓
take dog for walk ✓

1 'I ________ (work) since 5a.m.'

2 'I ________ (wait) all day for a special guest to arrive.'

3 'I ________ (clean) Room 1.'

4 'I ________ (change) the sheets in Room 1.'

5 'I ________ (listen) to the radio all afternoon.'

6 'I ________ (order) a new bed for Room 3.'

7 'I ________ (paint) the outside walls all week, but I won't finish until next week.'

8 'I ________ (take) the dog for a walk.'

B Write your own to-do list for the week. Then work in pairs and tell your partner some of the things you have done/have been doing.

F JUDGING AND EVALUATING IDEAS

5 A Complete the conversation with the words in the box.

work	possibility	wonderful
way	think	sound
doubts	sure	

A: I have an idea. Let's organise an International Food Day. What do you [1]________?

B: I like the [2]________ of that. How would it work?

A: One lunchtime, everyone brings a dish from a different country and we taste all the dishes.

B: I'm not [3]________ that'll work.

A: Why not?

B: Because most of us can't cook food from other places.

A: We could buy the food. There are lots of foreign restaurants here.

B: That might [4]________, but I have my [5]________.

A: Why?

B: Well, it would be better if we cooked the food ourselves.

A: OK, we can just ask everyone what they can cook.

B: That's a [6]________.

A: For example, I can cook an Indian curry. You can cook Turkish food, right?

B: No [7]________! I like *eating* Turkish food; I can't cook it.

A: Well, you can bring some pasta then. That's Italian. Anyway, do you like the idea?

B: It sounds [8]________!

B Work in pairs. Practise the conversation in Exercise 5A.

3 challenges

SURFING DREAMS p32

PERSONAL CHALLENGES p35

CONFLICT RESOLUTION p38

OVERPOPULATION p40

SPEAKING **3.1** Tell a story **3.2** Discuss life challenges **3.3** Resolve a problem **3.4** Discuss megacities

LISTENING **3.2** Listen to conversations about personal challenges
3.3 Listen to people discussing everyday problems
3.4 Watch a BBC documentary about the cities of the future

READING **3.1** Read an article about the Soul Surfer **3.3** Read about conflict resolution

WRITING **3.1** Write a short biography **3.4** Write an essay

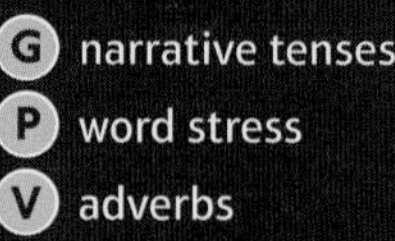

G narrative tenses
P word stress
V adverbs

SOUL SURFER

Bethany Hamilton is undoubtedly one of the best surfers in the world. She has won **numerous** awards. What makes her achievements even more incredible is that Bethany surfs with just one arm as her left arm was bitten off in a shark attack.

Born in Hawaii, Bethany grew up in a family who loved to surf. She typically spent much of her childhood on the beach and by the age of seven she was already cheerfully confident on a surfboard. She entered her first competition when she was eight and in the following years she competed in many events. At the age of thirteen, after coming second in the national championships, she was a **rising star**.

The future was looking bright. Then **tragedy struck**. On 31 October 2003, at the age of thirteen, Bethany was surfing with her best friend when she was attacked by a fifteen-foot tiger shark. The shark took Bethany's left arm and she nearly **lost her life**. Talking about the event, Bethany says, 'It literally **came out of the blue**. I had no warning at all; not even the slightest **hint of danger** on the horizon. The waves were small and I was just kind of rolling along with them, relaxing on my board, with my left arm **dangling** in the water. I remember thinking, "I hope the surf picks up soon!"'.

Then Bethany saw a grey flash and felt something pull on her arm. At first she didn't realise what had happened. But when she looked down she saw that the water was bright red and her left arm and a **huge chunk** of her surfboard had gone.

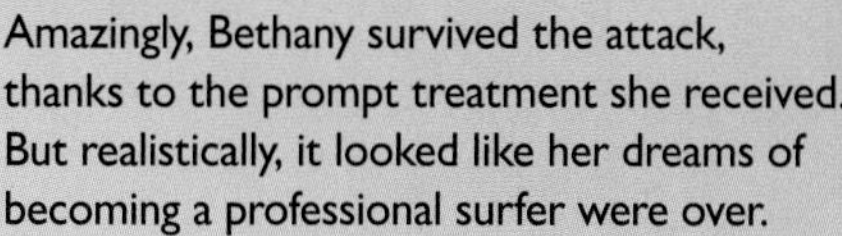

Somehow, she managed to stay calm and started to **paddle** back towards the beach, where friends desperately tried to help her and she received immediate medical treatment. Amazingly, Bethany survived the attack, thanks to the prompt treatment she received. But realistically, it looked like her dreams of becoming a professional surfer were over.

However, while many people might have given up, Bethany bravely decided she wasn't going to let her difficulties stop her from achieving her dreams. Less than a month after the accident, she was back on her surfboard and before long she was winning competitions again.

She is now **ranked** as among the top fifty female surfers in the world, despite her disability, and she has become an inspiration for many. The film *Soul Surfer* was inspired by Bethany's amazing story.

VOCABULARY PLUS

READING

1 A Look at the photos in the article and discuss the questions.

1 Have you ever been surfing? Would you like to? Why/Why not?
2 What do you think is special about the lady in the photo? What do you think happened to her surfboard?

B Read the article and check your answers.

2 A Work in pairs. Read the article again and answer the questions.

1 What is so special about Bethany's achievements?
2 When did she start to surf competitively?
3 What happened when Bethany was thirteen?
4 What were the surfing conditions like before her accident?
5 What did Bethany do when she realised the shark had bitten her?
6 How did she survive the shark attack?
7 Has Bethany managed to achieve her dreams?

B Match the words/phrases in bold in the article with definitions 1–10.

1 a very large piece
2 appeared from nowhere
3 small signal or suggestion of something bad
4 listed
5 many in number
6 someone who is becoming very successful
7 died
8 something terrible happened
9 move using your arms to push you through the water
10 hanging loosely

C Work in groups. Discuss the questions.

1 What do you think of Bethany's story? Do you think you might have behaved differently? How?
2 How do you think Bethany helps to encourage others to follow their dreams?
3 Do you have a particular dream or ambition you would like to achieve? What is it? What are the challenges?

GRAMMAR

NARRATIVE TENSES

3 A Find examples of these tenses in the article.

1 past simple: *grew up*
2 past continuous: *was looking*
3 past perfect: *had happened*

B Underline the correct alternatives to complete the rules.

RULES	1 Use the *past simple/past continuous* to talk about completed actions or the main events of a story. 2 Use the *past simple/past continuous* to give background information or to focus on the duration of a past activity. 3 Use the *past simple/past continuous* to talk about one or more actions which were in progress at the same moment in time. 4 Use the *past simple/past perfect* to talk about completed actions which happened before the main events.

C Work in pairs. What happened/What did you do yesterday? Write four sentences which exemplify the rules in Exercise 3B.

▷ page 108 **LANGUAGEBANK**

4 Complete the article with the verbs in the box.

found out struggled were waiting
had happened began decided helped
stayed had left was living

A gymnastics star

American gymnast Simone Biles, nineteen, was one of the shining stars of the Rio Olympics. But her life hasn't been easy. When Simone was five years old, she was taken into care. Her mother [1]__________ with drug and alcohol problems. Her father [2]__________ home.

Simone and her sister Adria, who was three at the time, [3]__________ in a foster home in Ohio while they [4]__________ to be adopted. When Simone's biological grandparents, Ron and Nellie, [5]__________ what [6]__________, they [7]__________ to adopt the girls themselves.

While she [8]__________ with her grandparents, Simone's talent [9]__________ to flourish. She started home-schooling so that she could spend more time training. This [10]__________ her to become one of the greatest gymnasts of our time.

VOCABULARY

ADVERBS

5 A Find eight adverbs in the article on page 32.

undoubtedly

B Complete the sentences with the adverbs in Exercise 5A.

1 He __________ wanted to compete in the Olympics.
2 They fought __________ to defend their country.
3 Dean's recent race times have been amazing. – He's __________ one of the best athletes in the group.
4 They __________ train between twenty and thirty-two hours a week.
5 She doesn't __________ stand a chance. The other competitors are much stronger.
6 It was so disgusting! The area was __________ covered in rubbish.
7 It looked like an impossible task but __________, she managed to win.
8 Ernesto was whistling __________ as he wandered through the park.

C ▶ 3.1 Listen and check your answers.

6 A **WORD STRESS: syllables** Look at the adverbs in the box. For each adverb, write the number of syllables and mark the stress pattern.

~~typically~~ bravely realistically
undoubtedly cheerfully amazingly
literally desperately

typically – 3 syllables O o o

B Listen again and check your answers.

▷ page 122 **VOCABULARYBANK**

SPEAKING

TELLING A STORY

7 A Think about a time when you or someone you know:

1 had a lucky escape.
2 achieved a long-held ambition.
3 won a competition.
4 overcame a difficult challenge.
5 went on a journey that went wrong.

B Choose one of the situations in Exercise 7A and prepare to talk about it.

1 Where were you at the time?
2 What was the background to the situation?
3 What happened? Who was involved?
4 Had anything happened before that had an impact on the situation?

C Work in groups. Tell each other your stories. Who do you think has the most interesting story?

Rafaela Lopes Silva

(born 24 April 1992) is a Brazilian judoka. She won gold medals at the 2013 World Judo Championships, as well as the 2016 Summer Olympics in the under-57 kg weight division, making her the first athlete in the history of Brazilian judo to become both world and Olympic champion.

1 ______________________________

Rafaela Silva grew up in Rio's infamously violent slum Cidade de Deus. Since opportunities were limited, the first sport she enjoyed was football, which she practised with other children in a dirt field near her home in Jacarepagua. However, when Rafaela was seven years old, her parents were concerned about fights and violence on the streets. Consequently, they signed up both Rafaela and her sister Raquel for judo classes at the Reação Institute, which had recently opened at Cidade de Deus. There, the girls trained with the former athlete Flávio Canto.

'I started judo in 2000, early in the project. My father put me in the sport as an alternative to stop [me] fighting in the street. In judo, I learnt discipline, respect for others and I began to take the sport seriously. Judo showed me the world. With the resources I get, I can support my family, help them to pay the bills.'

2 ______________________________

Silva won her first major medal by claiming silver at the 2011 World Judo Championships in Paris. In addition to this, during the 2013 World Judo Championships in Rio de Janeiro, Silva became the first Brazilian woman to ever win a gold medal for her country in a World Judo Championship. Furthermore, she repeated the feat at the 2016 Summer Olympics.

In the 2012 Summer Olympics in London, Rafaela was disqualified by the judges for an illegal move on her opponent. As a result of this, she was heavily criticised on social networks and when she returned home, she became depressed. She spent a lot of time lying down, not wanting to leave the house. 'A lot of people came to say that she needed to get over it,' says her mother. Despite the problems she had encountered, she came back to the sport later in the year, more determined than ever, and won a bronze medal at the Tokyo Grand Slam.

WRITING

A BIOGRAPHY; LEARN TO USE LINKERS

8 **Read the text about Rafaela Silva. Add two of the headings a)–c) in the correct place in the text.**

a) Personal life **b)** Early life
c) Sporting achievements

9 **A** **Look at the underlined linkers in the text. Write them in the correct place in the table.**

showing results	As a consequence, … 1 ________ So … Because of (this), … 2 ________ …
showing reasons	For this reason, … As … 3 ________
contrasting ideas	In spite of (the fact that) … 4 ________ While/Whereas … 5 ________ Although …
reinforcing/adding ideas	Besides, … 6 ________ 7 ________ 8 ________

B **Underline the correct alternatives to complete the texts.**

Pelé managed to become one of the greatest football players of all time, [1]*in spite of/besides/whereas* growing up in a poor area of São Paulo, Brazil. He often played football in the street using a grapefruit or a stuffed sock as a ball. [2]*As well as/While/Furthermore*, he was witness to crime and desperate poverty. [3]*Although/As a result/Besides*, Pelé developed an inner strength and determination to win, which he believes helped him to succeed.

When Lionel Messi was eleven, he was diagnosed with a growth hormone deficiency. [4]*Although/Because of this/Despite* a local team was interested in his skills, they could not afford the $900 a month treatment which Messi required. [5]*Whereas/Although/Consequently*, rather than be defeated by his situation, Messi focused on becoming the best player he could be. When he was thirteen, he was signed by FC Barcelona, and [6]*although/because of/in spite of* this, he was able to receive the treatment.

10 **Write a short biography (200–250 words) of an athlete you admire. Follow these instructions.**

1 Research the information you need.
2 Think about these questions: Did they have to overcome any challenges? How did they manage?
3 Use these headings: *Early life, Sporting achievements, Personal life.*
4 Try to include linkers in your writing.

PERSONAL CHALLENGES

G modals of obligation: present/past
P *have*: auxiliary vs main verb
V life challenges; relationships

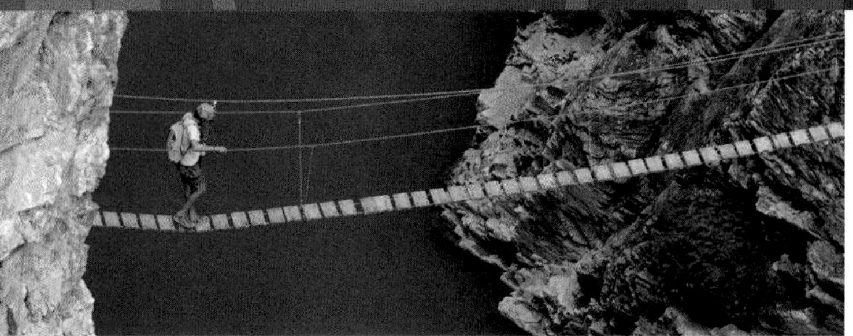

SPEAKING

1 A Look at the photos. What types of challenges do they show? Which do you think are the toughest challenges in life? Why?

B Match problems 1–9 with possible solutions a)–i).

1 My friend crashed my car. He should pay for the damage but he has no money.
2 Me and my best friend like the same boy, but he likes me more than her. She's getting jealous and it's destroying our friendship.
3 My wife wants to start a family, but we're still young and I'm not ready.
4 My fifteen-year-old daughter hates my new husband. He tries to be nice, but she doesn't respond.
5 My neighbour used to play loud music at night. I shouted at him once. Now he won't talk to me.
6 I need help moving house. I helped my brothers to move in the past but they say they're too busy.
7 My husband wants a dog. I want a cat.
8 I'm finishing school. My family thinks I should go to university. I hate studying and want to get a job.
9 My boss expects me to call him 'sir'. I don't want to.

a) Friends last a lifetime. Boyfriends usually don't. You must decide who is more important to you.
b) You should have bought him a nice pair of headphones and told him to use them at night.
c) You should go to university. You won't need to study much. If you fail, you can retake your exams.
d) He doesn't have to pay with money. Have him wash the car for a year.
e) You shouldn't get either. Animals belong in a zoo.
f) You mustn't blame it all on her. Fifteen is a difficult age. Sit down and talk about it.
g) You have to discuss this carefully. When will you be ready? Are you worried about money? Freedom? Age? Set a date and stick to it.
h) You didn't have to help them and they don't have to help you. Ask a friend instead.
i) In the past, employees had to do whatever the boss wanted. Now it's fine to be informal, but always be polite.

C Work in groups. Are a)–i) good solutions? Why/Why not? Think of different solutions to each problem. Share them with the class.

GRAMMAR

MODALS OF OBLIGATION: PRESENT/PAST

2 A Read solutions a)–i) in Exercise 1B again. Underline the modal verbs of obligation in the present (e.g. *must*). Circle the modal verbs of obligation in the past (e.g. *should have*). Which modal verbs show there is no obligation a) in the present and b) in the past?

B Complete the table.

present	past
obligation 1 ________ *to, must*	**obligation** *had to*
no obligation *don't have to*	**no obligation** 2 ________ *have to*
advice *should*	**regret, criticism** *should* 3 ________ + past participle

3 Underline the correct alternatives to complete the sentences.

1 We should *teach/have taught* our son both languages when he was still young.
2 Our teacher isn't strict. You *have/don't have* to do homework if you don't want to.
3 When I was a child, I *must/had to* do housework.
4 If you can't sleep, you *should/had to* try drinking hot chocolate before bedtime.
5 That's very kind of you! You *mustn't/didn't have to* bring me a gift!
6 You *shouldn't/don't have to* wear shorts to work. It doesn't look professional.
7 To get into university, you *should/have to* pass your exams.
8 Last year I *mustn't/had to* go to eight conferences for work.

▷ page 108 **LANGUAGEBANK**

4 A ***HAVE:* auxiliary vs main verb** Read the sentences. Is *have* the main verb or the auxiliary verb?

1 You should have come.
2 You have to come.

B ▶ 3.2 Listen to the sentences in Exercise 4A. How is *have* pronounced?

C ▶ 3.3 Listen and repeat the sentences.

LISTENING

5 A 3.4 **Listen to three conversations about personal challenges. Circle the correct topic for each conversation, a) or b).**

1 **a)** making new friends and fitting in
  b) finding a boyfriend
2 **a)** buying a house
  b) planning your future
3 **a)** getting ill
  b) getting old

B Listen again and answer the questions.

1 In conversation 1, how is the girl different to other kids her age?
2 What, for her, is 'the important thing'?
3 In conversation 2, what happened to the woman's father?
4 According to the man, how is life different after school or university?
5 In conversation 3, what does the man say about society?
6 What does the woman say about how young people on the street might view her?

VOCABULARY

LEXICAL CHUNKS: LIFE CHALLENGES

6 A Read sentences 1–12 from the recording. What do the phrases in bold mean?

1 It's not that I wanted to **fit in**.
2 I didn't want to **hang out with** the cool kids.
3 **We're just not into** partying.
4 The important thing is to **feel comfortable in your own skin**.
5 It became very hard to **make ends meet**.
6 He just **couldn't deal with it**.
7 The thing I **dread** the most is the uncertainty.
8 You have to **take a leap into the unknown**.
9 The most difficult challenges are usually **transitional moments**.
10 People just **don't take any notice of** you.
11 Do you think it's something to do with the way society is **set up**?
12 Older people have **so much to offer**.

B Match phrases 1–12 in Exercise 6a with definitions a)–l).

a) don't especially enjoy
b) times of change
c) ignore
d) have a terrible fear of something
e) had big problems with something
f) be happy with who you are
g) do something you've never tried before, even if it may be dangerous
h) spend a lot of time with particular people or in a particular place
i) organised
j) earn enough money to pay for your living costs
k) can contribute a lot, e.g. intelligence, ideas
l) be accepted by other people in a group

speakout TIP

Write down chunks of language. When you read a text, look for useful phrases – groups of words that go together. Which words in these phrases are always used in the phrase? Which can be replaced?
For example, in *the thing I dread the most*, ***dread*** can be replaced: *the thing I **hate** the most; the thing I **love** the most.*
What words could replace *comfortable* in 4 and *so much* in 12 in Exercise 6A?

SPEAKING

7 Work in groups and discuss. Do you agree with statements 1–8? Why/Why not?

1 It's not important to fit in. The important thing is to feel comfortable in your own skin.
2 If you aren't into something, e.g. partying, you should always avoid it.
3 Doing something useful for society is as important as making ends meet.
4 The thing people dread the most is uncertainty. Many people can't deal with it.
5 Taking a leap into the unknown is scary.
6 Older people become invisible to others. People don't take any notice of them.
7 Society is set up for young people.
8 Older people have a lot to offer.

VOCABULARY PLUS

IDIOMS: RELATIONSHIPS

8 **Match the idioms in bold in sentences 1–4 with definitions a)–d).**

1 There was a bad atmosphere at work, so we had a chat to **clear the air**. Everything's fine now.
2 She has **a stormy relationship** with her boyfriend. They're always arguing.
3 I really like my colleague. We **get on like a house on fire**.
4 He was just **a fair-weather friend**. When I really needed help, he disappeared.

a) have a very friendly relationship
b) a person who stops being a friend in difficult times
c) talk openly about a conflict so you can have a better relationship
d) a relationship with many disagreements and arguments

9 **A Read the stories. How many idioms connected with the body (story 1) and numbers (story 2) can you find? What do you think the idioms mean?**

1 The body and relationships

When I met Robin, we immediately saw eye to eye. During good times we had fun; during bad times he was a shoulder to cry on. After we got married, he changed. He wanted to be in control all the time and wouldn't let me live my life. I felt under the thumb. Eventually, we split up and it broke my heart.

2 Numbers and relationships

It was love at first sight. She was beautiful, intelligent and kind. She seemed like one in a million. She soon became my other half. Everything went well for three years, but then I got busy at work and stopped spending time with her. It got so bad that we broke up. After a few months, I asked her to give me a second chance. Luckily, she did!

B Match the idioms in the stories in Exercise 9A with definitions a)–h).

a) a very special, rare person
b) under someone else's control/not free
c) give someone a chance to try again after failing
d) someone who listens sympathetically to your problems
e) long-term partner, e.g. wife or husband
f) caused deep emotional pain
g) instant attraction to someone or something
h) had similar views or attitudes

C Do you have similar idioms in your language?

▷ page 122 **VOCABULARYBANK**

10 **Complete the second sentence so that it means the same as the first, using the word in bold. Use between three and five words, including the word in bold.**

1 As soon as we met, we had a great relationship. **house**
As soon as we met, we got on ________ fire.
2 There was a bad atmosphere among our personnel, so we talked about the problems. **air**
There was a bad atmosphere among our personnel, so we decided to ________.
3 She was elegant and stunning, and I fell in love immediately. **sight**
She was elegant and stunning, and it was ________.
4 I met my partner in a shelter for the homeless. **half**
I met ________ in a shelter for the homeless.
5 He fought the illness bravely but when he died, it was emotionally terrible for me. **broke**
He fought the illness bravely but when he died, it ________.
6 I was desperately sad and needed someone to listen to my problems. **shoulder**
I was desperately sad and needed ________ on.
7 We have similar views on politics. **eye**
We ________ on politics.
8 She put me in touch with this amazing man – he's a really special person! **million**
She put me in touch with this amazing man – he's ________!

11 **A Write the name of someone who:**

1 you see eye to eye with.
2 is one in a million.
3 always needs a shoulder to cry on.
4 you get on with like a house on fire.
5 you (used to) have a stormy relationship with.
6 is good at clearing the air.
7 is under the thumb.

B Work in pairs. Describe the people you named in Exercise 11A to your partner.

3.3 CONFLICT RESOLUTION

Ⓕ resolving conflict
Ⓟ intonation: sounding tactful
Ⓥ everyday issues

VOCABULARY

EVERYDAY ISSUES

1 A Work in pairs. Match situations 1–8 with responses a)–h).

1 This work is unacceptable. *f)*
2 This meat is undercooked.
3 This software is outdated.
4 This service is overpriced.
5 This information is misleading.
6 This accommodation is substandard.
7 This phone is disconnected.
8 This library book is overdue.

a) You should have returned it yesterday.
b) You have to get it reconnected.
c) You should ask for a discount.
d) You should send it back.
e) You should upgrade it.
f) You should ask them to redo it.
g) You should look for other sources.
h) You should get a new room.

B Which situations can you see in the photos?

2 A ▶ 3.5 Listen to sentences 1–8 from Exercise 1A. Mark the stressed syllables in the words with prefixes.

B Listen again and repeat.

C Work in pairs. Student A: cover sentences 1–8 in Exercise 1A. Student B: read one of the sentences but change the noun. Student A: Respond.

A: This homework is unacceptable.
B: You have to redo it.

SPEAKING

3 A Read about some everyday problems. Have you experienced any of these?

1 You are trying to work or study and someone is making lots of noise.

2 You paid for a product that you later discovered was substandard.

3 Someone borrowed something from you and returned it broken or damaged.

4 You received misleading information which caused a problem.

5 Someone did work for you but it was unacceptable.

B Work in pairs. Discuss the problems in Exercise 3A and think of solutions.

A

B

C

D

FUNCTION

RESOLVING CONFLICT

4 Read the text. What do you think are the three best pieces of advice?

How to resolve a conflict

1 **Pause and stay calm.** Don't get angry unless it's a very serious issue.

2 **Get to the bottom of the problem.** If people are behaving unacceptably, often it's because of something else happening in their lives. Sometimes people don't even realise they are causing offence.

3 **Talk to the right person.** Often, problems can only be resolved by people with power. It's useless arguing with someone who isn't in a position to help.

4 **Focus on a solution, not on the problem.** Blaming people rarely resolves the issue.

5 **Be kind.** Be a model of good behaviour rather than responding unpleasantly. The one thing you can control is your own behaviour.

6 **Be creative.** Look at the problem from different angles and be prepared to compromise.

7 **Listen with your whole body and show you understand the other person's perspective.** Resolving conflicts isn't about winning. It's about making a bad situation better for everybody.

5 A ▶ 3.6 Listen to Eric and Daniela discussing a problem. What is the problem and what is their solution?

B Which pieces of advice from Exercise 4 do the speakers follow?

6 A Complete the extracts from the recording. Use one word in each gap.

E = Eric   D = Daniela

1 **E:** Hi, how are you?
D: Fine, thanks.
E: Look, there's _________ I need to talk to you about.

2 **E:** I have an exam coming up and I'm studying, and … well, the _________ is there's a lot of noise coming from your flat at night.

3 **D:** Really? We had a party on Saturday.
E: Yeah, the thing is I _________ study because of the noise.

4 **D:** I didn't realise, to be honest.
E: It's OK. So I'm thinking perhaps you _________ lower the music?

5 **D:** I can turn the music down.
E: Yeah, or _________ you be able to wear headphones?

6 **D:** Sorry?
E: What _________ wearing headphones?

7 **E:** It's coming up next week.
D: Right. Well, you know what? We _________ just play music quietly for a week or two.

B ▶ 3.7 Listen and check your answers.

C Write the phrases in the box in the correct place in the table.

Perhaps you could … We can just … The problem is … I can't … because of … There's something I need to talk to you about. What about …? The thing is …

resolving conflict	
preparing the other person for the conversation	Can I talk to you about something? 1 _________
introducing the subject	It's about … 2 _________ 3 _________
explaining the problem	This is making it impossible to … 4 _________
suggesting a plan of action	Would you be able to …? What if we …? 5 _________ 6 _________
describing next steps	So for now, we'll (do this). 7 _________

▷ page 108 **LANGUAGEBANK**

LEARN TO
SOUND TACTFUL

> **T** **tactful** /ˈtæktfəl/ *adj* not likely to upset or embarrass other people.
>
> from *Longman Active Study Dictionary*

7 A Which sounds more tactful, a) or b)?

1 **a)** I can't study because of the noise.
b) The thing is, I can't study because of the noise.

2 **a)** You could lower the music.
b) I'm thinking perhaps you could lower the music?

3 **a)** Just keep it down.
b) I wonder if you could just keep it down.

B ▶ 3.8 **INTONATION: sounding tactful** Listen and check your answers. Then listen again and repeat. Copy the intonation.

speakout TIP

By adding some short phrases to the beginning of sentences (e.g. *Perhaps*, *Maybe*, *The thing is*), you can sound more tactful and less direct.
Find three phrases in Exercise 7A that you can use to sound tactful.

8 Find and correct the mistakes in the sentences. Two sentences are correct.

1 There's something I need to talk you about.
2 This is making it is impossible to study.
3 It's about the budget.
4 Perhaps you could speak to your manager?
5 What if we are agree to do this together?
6 Would you be able for to organise a meeting?

SPEAKING

9 A Work in pairs. Student A: turn to page 128. Student B: turn to page 130. Read and prepare your roles.

B Role-play the situations.

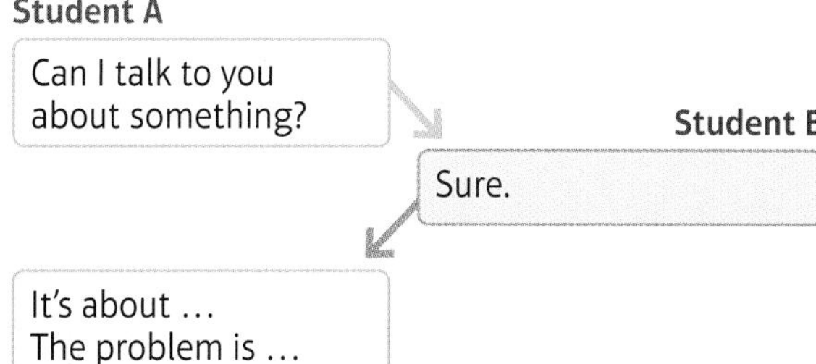

DVD PREVIEW

1 A Work in pairs or groups and discuss the questions.

1 Which are the biggest cities in your country?
2 Why are people moving to cities?
3 What problems are caused by mass urbanisation – when a large number of people move from the countryside to cities?

B Read about the programme. What might be some of the problems for residents living in the favela?

SUPERSIZED EARTH: Living in a Rio favela

BBC

More than half of the world's population now lives in cities, causing many of them to be overpopulated. We need to build more places for people to live in. *Supersized Earth* is a BBC documentary that examines how humans are redesigning the planet to build the cities of the future. This programme looks at the challenges of living in a Rio favela (slum), which includes the issue of how to get from one place to another. In Rio, a new urban cable car system has been installed to improve the residents' lives and make mobility easier. Dallas Campbell travels to Rio to investigate.

DVD VIEW

2 Watch the programme. Work in pairs and answer the questions.

1 What is Ubi Rojara building and why?
2 How has the cable car system changed the lives of people in the favela?
3 Who wins the race and why?

3 A Can you remember what the numbers in the box represent? Work in pairs and compare your ideas.

four 1.5 million 3½ minutes
$133 million eight months over 700

B Watch again to check your ideas.

4 Work in pairs. What does the presenter mean when he says the following? Can you explain the words/phrases in bold?

1 'That's double the population of Leeds, **crammed** into slums.'

2 'This **chaotic** approach to urban planning that makes districts like this so **cramped and overcrowded**.'

3 'Favelas, wherever you are in the world, they **get a lot of bad press**.'

4 'It is a **genius solution**, isn't it?'

5 'The boys' journey's **a baffling labyrinth** of narrow streets and endless steps.'

6 'The houses are so **tightly packed** together.'

5 Do you think a cable car system is a 'genius solution'? Why/Why not? What else do you think the government could do to improve life for the residents of the favelas?

speakout megacities

6 A 3.9 **Listen to someone talking about overcrowding in Hong Kong. Answer the questions.**

1 What causes overcrowding in Hong Kong?
2 What examples does the speaker give of the problem?
3 What happened to the Kowloon Walled City?
4 What does she think could be done to improve the situation?

B Listen again. Underline the correct alternatives to complete the key phrases.

KEYPHRASES

One of the biggest problems in Hong Kong **is** [1]*pollution/overcrowding*.

The issue is that real estate is very [2]*expensive/difficult to find* in Hong Kong.

... **which means that** people who need to [3]*live in/travel to* the city for work.

It's a real [4]*problem/solution* ...

One solution would be to put a limit on how much the [5]*landlords/businessmen* can charge for rent.

Or perhaps introduce a system for increasing the [6]*accommodation/wages*.

I think those two [7]*suggestions/things* **would certainly help**.

C In your opinion, what are the biggest problems of megacities (cities with more than ten million people)? Can you think of a solution to any of the problems? Make some notes.

D Work in groups and discuss your ideas. Aim to talk about three problems. For each problem, try to propose a solution. Share your ideas with the class.

writeback an essay

7 A Read the introduction to the essay. What challenges does it mention?

Megacities: problems and solutions

More people are living in cities than ever before. One tenth of the world's urban population live in megacities. These megacities act as magnets for trade, culture, knowledge and commerce. They also attract hundreds of thousands of people from poor rural families looking for work. These people often end up living in terrible conditions and working for poor pay in order to send money to their families back home. The scale and speed of urbanisation across the developing world is extraordinary, and it's bringing with it a number of challenges that have never been met before.

B Complete the essay in Exercise 7A. Think about your answers in Exercise 6D.

G NARRATIVE TENSES

1 A Complete the text with the verbs in the box.

drank was looking took was going wished had been happened disappeared was travelling arrived had travelled had planned continued was shining had already finished

Update Status | Add Photos/Video

This [1]________ a few years ago when I [2]________ around Italy with some friends. We [3]________ to visit the lakes in Northern Italy and spend a week travelling together. So my boyfriend and I were driving in our small, rusty, old Renault. Our friends [4]________ across Europe from the UK on their enormous motorbikes.

On the first morning we arranged to meet near Lake Garda at lunchtime. I remember as we set off through spectacular countryside that the sun [5]________ and I [6]________ out of the window at mountains and lakes. But the roads were very steep and the car [7]________ very slowly. It [8]________ us hours to get to the meeting point. By the time we eventually [9]________, the bikers [10]________ lunch and were ready for the next part of the journey. They [11]________ their coffees and then [12]________ into the distance again.

It [13]________ like that all week. That holiday I [14]________ I [15]________ on a motorbike too.

B Think of a memorable holiday story – it can be good or bad. Prepare to tell a partner about it. Make some notes.

C Work in pairs. Tell your partner your story.

V ADVERBS

2 A Underline the correct alternatives to complete the sentences.

1 Corfu is *desperately/undoubtedly* the most beautiful island I have ever visited.
2 *Typically/Cheerfully*, I try to run two or three times a week.
3 I was so surprised I *literally/amazingly* couldn't believe what I was seeing.
4 *Amazingly/Realistically*, I do not see how the government can survive this latest scandal.
5 We *typically/desperately* wanted to get tickets to see the band but there were none available.
6 The children played *undoubtedly/cheerfully* in the park until their mother arrived.
7 We were worried we wouldn't like the food but we were surprised by the *amazingly/literally* varied menu.
8 He *desperately/bravely* decided to speak out against the injustice.

B Choose two or three of the adverbs in Exercise 2A and write sentences which are true for you. Then work in pairs and compare your sentences.

V LEXICAL CHUNKS: LIFE CHALLENGES

3 Complete the sentences with the words in the box.

fit deal offer dread notice

1 When I lost my job, I found it hard to ________ with.
2 At school I was different to the other kids and didn't ________ in.
3 When people teased me, I tried not to take any ________.
4 Luckily, my manager realised I had a lot to ________ the company.
5 The one thing I really ________ is getting sick.

G MODALS OF OBLIGATION: PRESENT/PAST

4 Choose one of these situations. What would you say? Use modals of obligation. Then share your ideas with the class.

1 A friend is learning to drive.
2 Someone is visiting your town/city of the first time.
3 Someone asks you how to cook a special dish.
4 A friend wants to learn a sport.

F RESOLVING CONFLICT

5 A Two words are missing from each conversation. Add the missing words.

1 **A:** Can I talk to you something?
B: Yes, of course.
A: Problem is your cat keeps coming into my house.
B: Oh really? Perhaps you could call me the next time it happens.

2 **A:** There's I need to talk to you about.
B: What is it?
A: Would you able to tidy the living room?
B: Why?

3 **A:** I need to talk to you.
B: What's the problem?
A: It's about your parties. The thing, I can't sleep because of the noise.
B: What joining us and not worrying about sleep?

4 **A:** Can I ask you about something?
B: Of course.
A: It about that money you owe me. Perhaps could pay me back?
B: What money?

B Work in pairs. Practise the conversations in Exercise 5A. Continue each conversation until you resolve the problem.

4 science

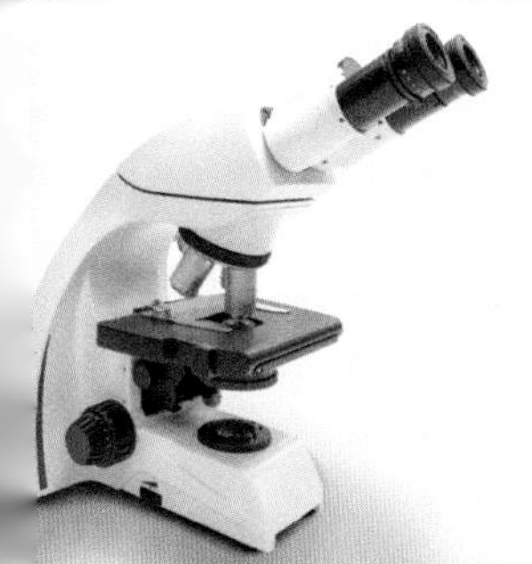

…YONE'S A SCIENTIST p44

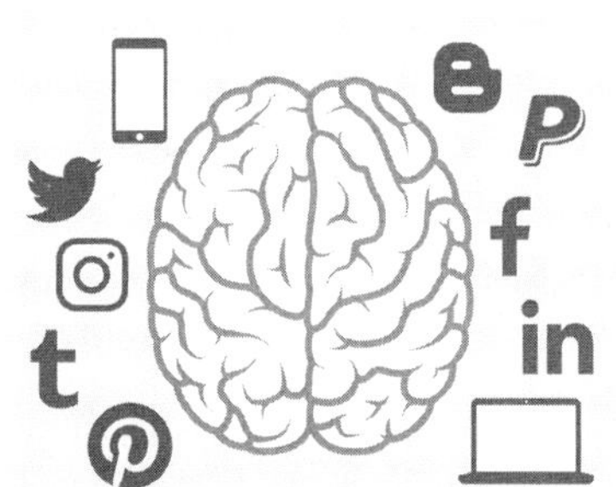

SMART TECH, LAZY BRAIN? p47

DELETE ME! p50

SCIENCE LOVER? p52

SPEAKING **4.1** Talk about real vs hypothetical situations **4.2** Talk about technology
4.3 Discuss your use of social media **4.4** Talk about famous scientists

LISTENING **4.1** Listen to a radio programme about citizen science
4.3 Listen to people discussing the internet
4.4 Watch people talking about science

READING **4.2** Read an article about technology **4.3** Read an article: *Delete me!*

WRITING **4.1** Write a proposal **4.4** Write a short biography

G zero, first and second conditionals
P *would* vs *will*
V science

VOCABULARY

SCIENCE

1 A Work in pairs. Are any of these statements true for you? Explain to your partner.

1 I love/loved science at school.
2 Science is far too complicated for me.
3 I can see how science is used in everyday life.

B What do scientists do and why is their work important?

2 A Read sentences a)–f). What do the words in bold mean? Match them with definitions 1)–10). Which words match the photos?

a) We put the **data** into a **database**.
b) We **monitor** changes in the animals' **habitat**.
c) We try to publish our research **findings**.
d) We take water **samples** from the river and **analyse** them.
e) We do **experiments** to **measure** changes in the environment.
f) We use a microscope to examine tiny **organisms**.

1 facts or information
2 find out or prove something
3 a living thing – usually very small
4 a large amount of information stored in one place in a computer system
5 a small amount of something that you take in order to examine it
6 find out the size, weight or quantity of something
7 the natural environment in which a plant or animal lives
8 information people have learned as a result of their study or work
9 examine or think about something closely in order to understand it
10 carefully watch something to see how it changes over time

B Put sentences a)–f) in Exercise 2A in a logical order (1–6).

1 We do experiments to measure the changes in the environment.
2 We monitor changes in the animal's habitat.

▷ page 123 **VOCABULARYBANK**

LISTENING

3 A Read the introduction to a radio programme. How does citizen science work?

Science Matters ON NOW 14:15–15:00

Citizen science

On *Science Matters* today, Anthony Walker looks at how we can all be scientists. For years, real scientists have been giving scientific tasks to amateurs – ordinary, unqualified people. Once they are trained, these citizens go out and use special tools to monitor and measure the natural world. Then they report their findings to a central database. This fast-growing trend in science means that everyone can be a scientist!

B  **4.1 Listen to the radio programme. What else do you learn about citizen science?**

C Listen again and answer the questions.

1 What do citizen scientists study?
2 How important are the contributions of citizen scientists?
3 Who are these scientists and what exactly do they do?
4 How is technology a part of this?
5 Can citizen science make the world a better place?

D Work in pairs. Discuss the questions.

1 Why do people want to become citizen scientists?
2 Would you or anyone you know like to become a citizen scientist? What area would you explore: weather, animals, pollution, the ocean? Why?

GRAMMAR

ZERO, FIRST AND SECOND CONDITIONALS

4 A Match sentences 1–3 from the recording with rules a)–c) below.

1 If it's in the natural world, they study it.
2 If we didn't have citizen scientists working on these research projects, we wouldn't be able to do them.
3 If you can make a model of how a disease like malaria might spread, you'll have a chance to stop it.

RULES	
	a) zero conditional (*if* + present simple + present simple): to talk about a general situation which is always true **b)** first conditional (*if* + present simple + *will/won't*/a modal verb): to talk about a specific situation in the future **c)** second conditional (*if* + past simple + *would/wouldn't*): to talk about hypothetical/ imaginary situations

B Read sentences 1–4. Then complete rules a)–d) below with *unless*, *as soon as* or *when*.

1 Unless you have the tools, you can't do the work.
2 When you have the tools, you do the work.
3 When you have the tools, you'll be able to do the work.
4 As soon as you have the tools, you can do the work.

RULES	
	a) Used with the zero conditional, *if* and _________ mean the same. **b)** With the first conditional, if something is certain to happen, we use _________. **c)** _________ + positive verb means *if not*. **d)** We can use _________ instead of *if* to show that something happens immediately.

C Rewrite the sentence using *when*, *as soon as* and *might*. How does the meaning change?

If I see you, I'll give you the money.

D Rewrite the sentences using *unless*.

1 Scientists couldn't do all the research if citizens didn't help.
Scientists couldn't do all the research unless citizens helped.
2 If we don't find an answer to global warming, we are in trouble.
3 We won't get enough data if we don't monitor the habitat.

▷ page 110 **LANGUAGEBANK**

5 Match 1–8 with a)–h) to make sentences. What type of conditional does each sentence use?

1 When we get new data, *h), zero conditional*
2 You'll have nothing to analyse
3 She won't be able to join us
4 If he didn't do these experiments,
5 You'll know it's a dinosaur fossil
6 They would help us
7 As soon as we get an idea for a new project,
8 Unless you have the right tools,

a) unless her flight arrives early.
b) it's impossible to do this research.
c) as soon as you see it.
d) we look at ways of funding it.
e) he wouldn't be able to find new organisms.
f) if they had time.
g) if you don't take samples.
h) we add it to the database.

6 A ▶ 4.2 *would* vs *will* Listen and circle the sentence you hear, a) or b).

1 **a)** Where would she go? **b)** Where will she go?
2 **a)** He'd like that very much. **b)** He'll like that very much.
3 **a)** They wouldn't ask for money. **b)** They won't ask for money.
4 **a)** What would you eat? **b)** What will you eat?
5 **a)** I'd stay longer. **b)** I'll stay longer.
6 **a)** Would you do it for me? **b)** Will you do it for me?

B Listen again and repeat.

C Work in pairs. Say some of the sentences from Exercise 6A fast. Your partner decides if you said a) or b). Then swap roles.

SPEAKING

7 A Are situations 1–6 real or hypothetical? Write conditional sentences about them. Then work in pairs and discuss your ideas.

1 I become a citizen scientist.
If I became a citizen scientist, I'd monitor changes in the environment.
2 I start a new course.
3 I have some free time tomorrow.
4 I visit a foreign country next summer.
5 I get a new job.
6 I join a new sports team.

WRITING

A PROPOSAL; LEARN TO USE POSITIVE LANGUAGE

8 A Read the proposal below. What are the goals of the proposed project?

B Which section of the proposal describes:

1 what you are asking for and why?
Executive summary
2 how the money will be spent?
3 who you are?
4 what the project will achieve?
5 how success will be judged?
6 the processes involved: who, when, how, where?

GRANT PROPOSAL
for Hollins Chubb Foundation

EXECUTIVE SUMMARY

Smartsurf is seeking a grant of 20,000 euros to develop a smart surfboard that can provide data about the oceans.

ORGANISATION INFORMATION Smartsurf was founded in 2017 to help save the oceans from environmental damage. The organisation is located in Cornwall, UK, and consists of six full-time personnel.

GOALS AND OBJECTIVES Our goal is to develop a smart surfboard that is equipped with the tools to measure the effects of climate change on the world's oceans. The project will begin in Cornwall, UK, where Smartsurf is based. However, because surfing is a worldwide sport, we believe the smart surfboard will be used globally. It will allow us to monitor changes in the oceans' temperatures around the world and to measure the damage caused by climate change. The objective is to make data collection easier and to make this data available to climate scientists. Through this, Smartsurf will make a valuable contribution to protecting the oceans.

PROJECT DESCRIPTION We are working with designers, engineers and a research team to develop a prototype of the smart surfboard. The board uses sensors that measure the immediate environment. When we complete the prototype, we will identify and train surfers to use the board. We will send our data to an already existing database, the British Oceanographic Data Centre. The data includes information about temperatures and acidity. The boards will remain the property of Smartsurf and will be loaned to surfers for a period of six months at no cost.

EVALUATION CRITERIA The smart surfboard will be measured by the amount and quality of data collected, cost-effectiveness, and user-friendliness rating by the surfing community.

BUDGET Our main cost is the prototype for the smart surfboard: 20,000 euros. This figure includes payment of research scientists, engineers, designers and a project manager. We attach a breakdown of the costs involved.

9 Underline the correct alternatives to complete the sentences.

Proposals:

1 are written in *an informal/a formal* style.
2 use *subheadings/only a major heading*.
3 must describe *who, what and why/previous grants won by the company*.
4 *use/don't use* very positive language.
5 use *'may', 'might'* and *'could'/'will'* a lot.

10 A Cover the proposal in Exercise 8. Replace the words/phrases in bold in sentences 1–6 with the more positive words/phrases in the box.

~~goal~~ develop identify objective make a valuable contribution to will allow us to

1 Our **wish** is to develop a smart surfboard. *goal*
2 It **may let us** monitor changes.
3 The **hope** is to make data collection easier.
4 Smartsurf will **help in** protecting the oceans.
5 We are working to **make** a prototype.
6 We will **look for** and train surfers to use the board.

B Look at the proposal again and check your answers.

speakout TIP

When writing a proposal:
1 don't use acronyms unless they are very famous (e.g. *BBC, USA*).
2 don't use negative language or sound uncertain (use *will*, not *could*).
3 check you followed all the instructions.

Do you think the proposal in Exercise 8 follows the advice above?

11 A Read the invitation to apply for a grant below.

B Choose one of these ideas or use your own. Plan and write your proposal for the GoodWorks Council.

- an app for monitoring local environmental damage
- a science/nature club for bored teenagers
- a new playground for children
- a centre for homeless people to sleep and eat in

GoodWorks Council:
invitation to submit proposal

GoodWorks Council invites applications for grants of up to 25,000 euros. We are looking for projects that will benefit the community. Please include the following sections: *Project summary, Organisational background, Goals and objectives, Project plan, Evaluation criteria, Budget.*

Send proposals and supporting documents to **GWCproposal@goodworks.orgs** before 10 December.

SMART TECH, LAZY BRAIN?

G passive reporting structures
V reporting verbs
P stressed words/syllables

4.2

Is tech rewiring our brains?

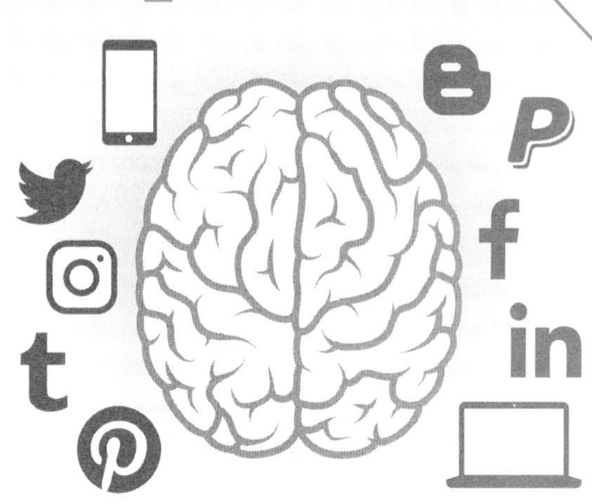

We increasingly rely on social media to talk to friends, GPS to navigate and the web for information. But reports suggest that modern technology is making us less intelligent and more antisocial. We struggle to remember our own phone number when only a few years ago we could recall dozens. Online readers have short attention spans and many of us panic when separated from our smartphone. So what's happening?

The reality is that our brains do change when we use a smartphone or computer–but they also change when we use a pen, a screwdriver or any other tool. They change when we mow the lawn, play golf or cook dinner. Our experiences continually shape the way the brain works.

So how are our brains adapting to living in today's screens-first, always-online, networked world?

Attention

Phones buzzing with text messages, Facebook notifications and news alerts continually distract us. Many experts believe that this continuous bombardment has decreased our ability to focus. A study by Microsoft found that the average human attention span had dropped from twelve seconds in the year 2000 to just eight seconds in 2015.

Memory

With phone numbers, routes and facts just a touch away, we're becoming less dependent on our memory. German neuroscientist Manfred Spitzer warns that this 'cognitive offloading' could lead to a kind of 'digital dementia', where people can no longer remember everyday information because they rely on technology to remember for them. Studies on internet and gaming addicts have shown their brain's grey matter actually shrinking. Digital offloading may also make memories less vivid. A US study showed that we are actually less likely to clearly remember things or events which we have taken photographs of.

Mood

Scientists have reported strong links between heavy internet use and depression. Health education expert Dr Aric Sigman says, 'There's a relationship between the amount of time you spend on social media and increased body dissatisfaction.' Sigman also cites a study in which girls who instant messaged their mothers released the stress hormone cortisol, rather than the feel-good hormone oxytocin associated with face-to-face interaction.

Multitasking

Our 'always-on' culture has been referred to as 'infomania' by psychologist Dr Glenn Wilson. It has been reported that working in a room full of distractions (mobiles ringing and emails arriving) reduces workers' IQ by ten points. Research also shows that multitasking while learning is likely to lead to knowledge which is not as deeply embedded in our memory.

Sleep

<u>We now spend more time on our devices than we do sleeping.</u> According to a survey, we engage in media or communication activities for eight hours and forty-one minutes daily, and sleep for eight hours and twenty-one minutes. Technology keeps us up for two reasons. First, we are stimulated by the content. Second, the LED screen uses blue light, which prevents the brain from producing the sleep hormone melatonin.

READING

1 A Work in pairs. Look at the headings in the article. How do you think technology affects these things? Read the article and check your ideas.

• attention • memory • mood • multitasking • sleep

B Work in pairs. Read the article again and answer the questions.

1 What examples does the article give of how people rely on technology?
2 What effects does it claim that this has on our brains?
3 According to the article, why has our attention span decreased?
4 How can you explain the term 'cognitive offloading'? Why might it be a problem?
5 Why might it be a bad idea for girls to text their mothers?
6 Can you give two reasons why technology makes us sleep less?

2 Work in groups. Discuss the questions.

1 Does any of the information in the article surprise you?
2 Look at the underlined sentence in the article. Who does *we* refer to?
3 Do you trust research like this? Why/Why not? Do you believe IQ drops by ten points in a room full of distractions? Doesn't it depend on the kind of work you're doing?
4 Do you see your own use of technology reflected in the research claims in the article?

VOCABULARY

REPORTING VERBS

3 A Work in pairs. Discuss the statements. One of the statements is false. Which do you think it is?

1 Reports **suggest** that modern technology is changing our brains and our personalities.
2 Experts **agree** that children who spend too much time in front of screens have short attention spans.
3 A US study **showed** that searching on the internet can increase brain function in older people (aged 55–76).
4 Scientists **report** that some teenagers spend eighteen hours a day interacting with technology.
5 Research **claims** that millennials (people who reached adulthood around the year 2000) have better memories than older people.
6 Experts **believe** that the more we constantly interact with technology, the harder it is for us to experience deep emotions.
7 A report has **confirmed** that digital screens affect the brain like cocaine.
8 Research **proves** that our brains physically change as a result of using technology.

B Check you understand the verbs in bold in Exercise 3A.

GRAMMAR

PASSIVE REPORTING STRUCTURES

4 Read the pairs of sentences. Then underline the correct alternative to complete the rule below.

1 **a)** People say that using your phone at night is bad for your sleep.
b) It is said that using your phone at night is bad for your sleep.
2 **a)** People say that social media is responsible for increased feelings of loneliness.
b) Social media is said to be responsible for increased feelings of loneliness.
3 **a)** People think that teenage overuse of technology impedes their social skills.
b) It is thought that teenage overuse of technology impedes their social skills.
4 **a)** Studies have suggested that brain activity seen in excessive internet users is similar to that of drug addicts.
b) It has been suggested that brain activity seen in excessive internet users is similar to that of drug addicts.
5 **a)** A study showed that the grey matter in the brains of internet addicts was shrinking.
b) The grey matter in the brains of internet addicts was reported to be shrinking.

RULE

Use the following passive reporting structures in *formal/ informal* writing to report opinions and beliefs:
***it* + passive reporting verb + *that* + clause**
It is said that …
It was thought that …
It has been suggested/estimated/claimed that …
subject + passive reporting verb + infinitive clause
It is thought/reported/estimated to be …
He was claimed to be …

5 A Complete the second sentence so that it means the same as the first, using the word in bold. Use between two and five words, including the word in bold. More than one answer may be possible.

1 People are using their mobile phones more than before. **thought**
Mobile phone use ________ increasing.
2 Experts have said that people aren't getting enough sleep. **claimed**
It ________ people aren't getting enough sleep.
3 People agree that too much gaming causes addiction. **reported**
Too much gaming ________ addiction.
4 Research says that thirteen percent of Americans do not use the internet. **shown**
It ________ thirteen percent of Americans do not use the internet.
5 Police think teenagers may have been responsible for the explosion. **suggested**
It ________ teenagers may have been responsible for the explosion.
6 Experts said that the overuse of the device can cause depression. **confirmed**
It ________ that overuse of the device can cause depression.
7 People think that around 500 students attended the event. **estimated**
Around 500 students ________ attended the event.
8 The parents have said they will supervise their children. **agreed**
It has ________ will supervise their children.

B ▷ 4.3 **Listen and check your answers.**

▷ page 110 **LANGUAGEBANK**

6 A STRESSED WORDS/SYLLABLES Listen again and underline the stressed words/syllables in the sentences.

Mobile *phone* use is *thought* to be incr*eas*ing.

B Listen again and notice how the unstressed words become weaker (e.g. *to be* in *thought to be:* /təbiː/). Then repeat the sentences. Copy the sentence stress.

SPEAKING

7 A Look at the mind maps and write some questions to ask a partner.

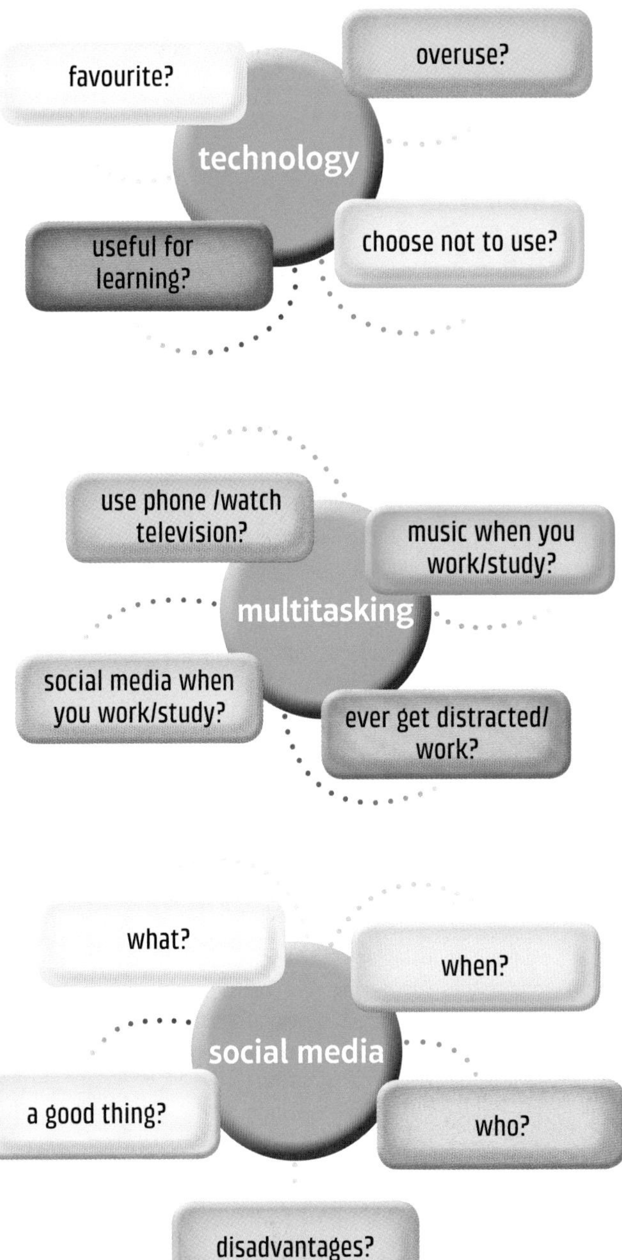

B Work in pairs or groups. Ask and answer your questions from Exercise 7A.

A: Do you think social media is a good thing?
B: Yes, I use it all the time.

C Work in small groups. Answer the questions.

1 Do you think technology has changed your generation? If so, how and is this a good thing?
2 Does your generation use social media differently from other generations? If so, how and why?

D Summarise your group's discussion for the class. Use these phrases.

- It has been suggested that our generation has …
- It is claimed that …
- It is thought that …

VOCABULARY PLUS

COMMONLY CONFUSED WORDS

8 Look at the pairs of commonly confused words in the box. Do you know the difference between the words in each pair?

accept/except advice/advise
economic/economical experience/experiment
possibility/opportunity principal/principle
right/rightly sensible/sensitive
complement/compliment stationary/stationery

9 A Complete the sentences with words from Exercise 8.

1 Use of mobile phones is ________ banned during examinations, in my opinion.
2 **A:** That's a beautiful necklace. Where did you get it?
B: My mother gave it to me. Thanks for the ________!
3 The ________ reason for the failure was poor communication, although there were other factors.
4 We were lucky to have had the ________ to explore the area.
5 **A:** I'm worried about Aisha. I don't know where she can be.
B: Don't panic. She'll turn up soon. She's a very ________ girl.
6 The printer has run out of paper and I can't find a pen that works. I need some new ________.
7 **A:** I really think you should take this opportunity.
B: Thanks for the ________.
8 People struggle to ________ that the world is changing.
9 I couldn't accept the offer on a matter of ________.
10 It's a great car, and very ________.

B Work in pairs. Act out these situations. Student A: follow the instructions for each situation. Student B: give a natural response. You only have thirty seconds for each situation. Then swap roles.

Student A

- Give your partner a compliment.
  A: That shirt really suits you.
  B: Thanks for the compliment!
- Suggest three pieces of advice about technology use.
- Describe an enjoyable experience.
- Describe an opportunity you shouldn't miss.

Student B

- Think of a crazy experiment.
- Describe the most economical holiday.
- Give your partner advice on how to cure internet addiction.
- Describe the most sensible person in your family.

▷ page 123 **VOCABULARYBANK**

F hedging
V internet words/phrases
P hesitation devices

VOCABULARY

INTERNET WORDS/PHRASES

1 A Work in pairs. Discuss the questions.

1 Is it possible to delete yourself from the internet?
2 How would you do this?
3 Why do you think people might choose to delete themselves from the internet?
4 Would you consider doing this? Why/Why not?

B Complete the article with the words/phrases in the box.

click of a button digital footprint social media posted updates delete email account profiles screenshots online search engine google cyberbullying

C Work in pairs and discuss. How easy would it be for you to delete yourself from the internet? What potential problems might you have in doing this successfully?

FUNCTION

HEDGING

2 A 4.4 Listen to people discussing the questions in Exercise 1A. For each conversation (1–3), circle the correct answer, a) or b).

1 The speakers think that a website like Deleteme
  a) could be useful as we have so many different internet accounts, and some are difficult to deactivate.
  b) isn't useful because people can easily deactivate their own internet accounts if necessary.
2 The speakers think that cyberbullying
  a) is such a problem that social media sites should be avoided altogether.
  b) may be an issue, but deleting yourself from the internet isn't the solution.
3 The man believes that
  a) face-to-face interaction is much more satisfying than social media.
  b) social media is a useful tool for social interaction.

B 4.5 Listen to conversation 1 again. Circle the sentence you hear, a) or b).

1 **a)** Presumably you can do that, right?
  b) You can do that, right?
2 **a)** That's a problem.
  b) That might be a problem.
3 **a)** You can delete most of them.
  b) I guess you can delete most of them.
4 **a)** So maybe a website like this would be useful after all.
  b) So a website like this is useful after all.

So they say the internet never forgets, but a new website, deleteme.com, promises to erase your [1]__________ at the [2]__________. You might ask why you would want to do that.

Figures suggest that eighty percent of employers [3]__________ you before inviting you to an interview. And almost ninety percent of people research new contacts using an [4]__________.

So, if you've been a victim of [5]__________, online abuse or you're just not happy with your online presence (maybe you've [6]__________ and information online in the past which you would now like to remove), then this could be the web service for you.

However, things are rarely as simple as they sound. The website relies on the fact that you've used a Google account to set up your networks. If you have used various [7]__________ to set up [8]__________ accounts, for example on Instagram or Snapchat, then you'll need to remove these separately. Also, people can take [9]__________ of images and posts, and save things that were said, so it can be hard to remove your digital traces completely.

You may have to accept that there are some things you can never [10]__________ from the internet.

C Look at the words/phrases in the table and underline the correct alternatives to complete the rule below.

hedging
I guess/I suppose presumably may/might/could perhaps/maybe/possibly (not) particularly/ really
vague language
kind of/sort of just … or something

RULE	We use hedging and vague language to soften what we say, to make it *more/less* direct. This makes you sound *more/less* polite.

D ▶ 4.6 **Listen to conversations 2 and 3 again and complete the extracts.**

1 I ________ one reason ________ be that you've experienced some kind of bullying, I mean cyberbullying or ________.
2 Yes, I ________ that's possible.
3 … the idea that you can ________ disappear from the internet.
4 … it's ________ of the same on the internet.
5 I ________ avoid social media in the first place.
6 I just don't think it's ________ interesting.

3 **Change the sentences to make them less direct. Use the words in brackets.**

1 I'm not happy about this. (particularly)
2 We should have asked him first. (suppose)
3 We have a problem. (may)
4 It's not my favourite. (really)
5 I thought you should know. (just)
6 We could buy her some flowers. (or something)

▷ page 110 **LANGUAGEBANK**

LEARN TO

USE HESITATION DEVICES

4 **Read the sentences from the conversations in Exercise 2. If you remove the underlined parts, does it change the meaning of the sentence? What do you think the function of the underlined language is?**

1 OK, so, umm … let me see … I guess I would start with the obvious sites.
2 I think you can, you know, deactivate the account.
3 Oh hold on, I didn't think about YouTube.
4 Well, I guess one reason might be that you've experienced some kind of bullying – I mean cyberbullying or something.
5 I don't really understand it – you know, the idea that you can just disappear from the internet.
6 The thing is, if I want to talk to someone, I arrange to meet up.
7 Hmm … but you see, I just don't think it's particularly interesting.

speakout TIP

We use hesitation devices (*umm, ah, well, let me see*, etc.) in conversation to give us time to think. They tell the speaker that we have understood the question and we are thinking about our answer. They are very common in spoken English and using them can help you sound more fluent. Look at audio script 4.4 on page 137 and underline the hesitation devices.

5 A **Match questions 1–6 with responses a)–f).**

1 What did you do on Saturday?
2 Where shall we go to eat?
3 Have you decided whether to take the job?
4 Have you got her phone number?
5 Do you want to come with us to the cinema?
6 Have you bought the tickets?

a) Well, we could try the new restaurant on Oxford Street.
b) Hmm … that would be great, but the thing is I really need to finish that report.
c) Er … hold on, I think I might have it here.
d) Umm … let me see … I was working.
e) Umm … no. You see, the problem is I don't have enough money.
f) The thing is, you know, I'm not sure that I'm really qualified.

B ▶ 4.7 **Listen and check your answers.**

C **HESITATION DEVICES** **Listen again and notice how the speaker slows down their speech and pauses when they use the hesitation device. Then listen again and repeat.**

Umm … [pause] let me see … [pause] … I was working.

6 ▶ 4.8 **Listen to the questions. Use the prompts in the box to come up with your own responses.**

Umm … Er … Hold on … Let me see …
Well … The thing is … You see …

SPEAKING

7 **Work in groups. Play *Just a minute*. Take turns to speak about one of these topics. You have to keep speaking for a minute. Use hedging and hesitation devices to help you. If you stop speaking for more than five seconds, you are out.**

- your mobile phone
- your favourite social network
- your last holiday
- whether you like/dislike technology
- the food you eat
- a hobby you have
- a good friend

OK, well, let me see … This is my phone and I bought it … err … about three months ago because …

4.4 SCIENCE LOVER?

DVD PREVIEW

1 A Work in pairs. Can you name three famous scientists? Why are they famous? Tell other students.

B Look at the words/phrases in the box. Check you understand their meaning. Do you associate the words with science (S), arts (A) or both (SA)?

biology chemistry English Lit equations experiments formulas geology innovation inventors medical advances practical/hands-on quantum mechanics space split the atom string theory theatre director theory of relativity

C Work in pairs and compare your ideas. Do you agree with each other?

DVD VIEW

2 A Watch Part 1 of the interviews. Are the speakers more sciency (S) or artistic (A)?

Samantha ________
Juliet ________
Anthony ________
Caitlin ________
Atri ________

B Watch Part 1 again. Answer the questions.

1 Who was hopeless at science subjects at school?
2 Who works in physical therapy?
3 Who couldn't get their head around all the equations and formulas?
4 Who did their best to study a few science subjects at school but found it didn't go so well?
5 Who is currently training to be a theatre director?
6 Who enjoys English literature, theatre and music?
7 Who can think quite logically but has to be quite innovative in their logic?

C Work in pairs and discuss. What about you? Are you more sciency or more artistic?

3 A Watch Part 2 of the interviews. Complete what the speakers say.

1 There were a lot of ________. It was very hands-on.
2 I can remember being supremely ________ at Chemistry, so I dropped out of that very early on.
3 I completed O level ________ but I didn't take it any further.
4 There's many different ways to get to a certain conclusion with ________.
5 I was surprised at how much I used to ________ and how little I actually remember now.

B Work in pairs. Answer the questions.

1 What does Errol mean when he says 'there were a lot of practicals'?
2 What does it mean to be 'supremely bad' at something?
3 If you 'drop out of something', do you continue to study it?
4 Do you know what an O level is?
5 Why was Caitlin reading through her old science books?

C Work in groups and discuss. What can you remember about science lessons at school? Did you enjoy them?

4 A Watch Part 3 of the interviews. Match the scientists 1-5 with what the speakers say about them a)-e).

1 Stephen Hawking
2 Albert Einstein
3 Ernest Rutherford
4 Antonie van Leeuwenhoek
5 Max Planck

a split the atom
b string theory of multiple realities/ theory of quantum mechanics
c something to do with blood
d theoretical scientist
e theoretical scientist/invented the theory of relativity

B Watch Part 3 again to check your answers. Which of these scientists did you already know about?

Sunny and Errol

David

Kathryn

Roxanne

5 A Watch Part 4 of the interviews. Tick the items in the box which are mentioned.

antibiotics bicycles cars iPad laptop medical advances microscopes phone/telephone planes trains

B Number the quotes in the order they are heard in the interviews.

a) 'I couldn't live without my laptop, I don't think, or my mobile phone.'
b) 'The medical advances that have been made in the last century or two are the most important.' *1*
c) 'I could live without most other things.'
d) 'I think I'd be stranded without both those things.'
e) 'I think without a telephone I think I would be really lost.'
f) 'My phone, my laptop and my iPad.'
g) 'Just hearing someone's voice on the other end is always a nice thing to hear.'

C Watch Part 4 again to check your answers.

D Work in pairs. Which scientific inventions could you not live without?

speakout famous scientists

6 A Work in groups. You are going to find out more about the scientists that were mentioned in the interviews. Make notes in the table for the scientist you read about.

Student A: read about Antonie van Leeuwenhoek on page 128.
Student B: read about Stephen Hawking on page 130.
Student C: read about Ernest Rutherford on page 132.
Student D: read about Albert Einstein on page 133.

Name	Where and when was the scientist born?	What scientific work are they famous for?	Other interesting facts/ information
Antonie van Leeuwenhoek			
Stephen Hawking			
Ernest Rutherford			
Albert Einstein			

B In your groups, tell each other about the scientist you researched. Make notes to complete the table.

C Do you think it's interesting that all the speakers talked about scientists who were men? Why do you think this is?

writeback a short biography

7 A Read the article. What is its main focus? Do you know any famous female scientists?

Female scientists you should know about

It has always been harder for women to succeed in science than for men. Historically, women had limited access to education and suffered discrimination in the science world. However, despite the difficulties, there are many brilliant female scientists who made important discoveries in a variety of fields. Many of their contributions have been hugely influential. When it comes to talking about women in science, Marie Curie is usually at the top of people's list. Here are a few others you should know about.

Dorothy Hodgkin (1910–1994)

Dorothy Hodgkin studied Chemistry at Oxford University and later worked at Cambridge, studying X-ray crystallography. Much of her work focused on the structure of penicillin, Vitamin B12 and insulin. She is the only British woman scientist to win a Nobel Prize in Chemistry, which she was awarded in 1964.

Emilie du Chatelet (1706–1749)

Emilie du Chatelet studied mathematics, and then physics. She collaborated with the philosopher Voltaire, who was also interested in science, and they worked together from a laboratory which she set up in her home. She also translated Isaac Newton's work *Principia* into French, in a version which is still used today.

B Research a female scientist and write a short paragraph about her to include in the article above (80–100 words).

V SCIENCE

1 A Put the letters in brackets in the correct order to complete the sentences.

1 She studied chimpanzees in their ________ (aihtbtas).
2 She did ________ (peermxtiens) that led to the discovery of certain brain cells.
3 She ________ (miteoonrd) the environment and wrote important books about environmental damage.
4 He ________ (aalydsen) bacteria, which led to the discovery of penicillin.
5 His study of ocean ________ (oanigrmss) and his TV series revolutionised marine biology.
6 He ________ (maueserd) the movements of the stars, which led to the idea of black holes.

B Work in pairs. Match sentences 1–6 in Exercise 1A with scientists a)–f).

a) Jacques Cousteau
b) Jane Goodall
c) Alexander Fleming
d) May-Britt Moser
e) Subrahmanyan Chandrasekhar
f) Rachel Carson

C Turn to page 129 and check your answers.

G ZERO, FIRST AND SECOND CONDITIONALS

2 A Work in pairs. Student A: use an *if* clause with the phrases in your box. Decide if the situation is real or unreal. Student B: complete your partner's conditional sentence using the phrases in your box.

Student A

~~I / have / more time~~
I / have / chance / travel
my car / break down
I / go / to restaurant / today
I / not go / to bed early tonight
learn / new instrument
not do / my homework

Student B

not eat / meat
feel tired / tomorrow
teacher / get / angry
be / violin go / Australia
~~not need / rush~~ take / taxi

A: If I had more time, …
B: … I wouldn't need to rush!

B Write true sentences about you using the *if* clauses in box A in Exercise 2A. Then work in pairs and share your answers.

If I had more time, I'd read more.

G PASSIVE REPORTING STRUCTURES

3 A Complete the sentences with the words in the box.

reported is be have to been it that

1 Every person is thought to ________ a unique pattern of connections in their brain.
2 It has been suggested ________ in the future 'brainprints' may be used instead of fingerprints.
3 It has been ________ that people who are paralysed can be trained to walk again.
4 It ________ claimed that virtual reality can help patients learn to use robotics.
5 Listening to music has ________ claimed to help people concentrate.
6 Special headphones are reported ________ be able to block out all sound.
7 ________ has been suggested that lack of physical exercise is a serious health threat.
8 The number of minutes of exercise we need to do in a week is estimated to ________ 150.

B Work in pairs. Discuss the sentences in Exercise 3A. Do you find any of the information surprising?

V REPORTING VERBS

4 Put the letters in brackets in the correct order to make words.

1 A study has ________ (camdiel) there will be no more seafood by 2048 due to overfishing.
2 Research ________ (sgesgust) we are born to dance. Dancing is in our DNA.
3 A report has ________ (merdfoinc) that mobile phones are killing gorillas. Mining for minerals in the Congo is destroying their natural habitat.
4 Scientists ________ (eblevie) that many animals are capable of creative problem-solving.
5 Researchers have ________ (toderper) that children who go to nursery have better social skills.
6 Listening to poetry has been ________ (wonsh) to trigger positive feelings in listeners' brains.

G HEDGING

5 A Match questions 1–5 with responses a)–e).

1 Do you think perhaps you could turn the music down?
2 Don't you like the food?
3 Do you want to meet up on Saturday?
4 Do you want to go to a classical music concert on Wednesday? I've got spare tickets.
5 Do you think you could possibly help me?

a) It's fine, thanks. I'm just not particularly hungry.
b) Of course. What sort of help do you need?
c) I suppose that might be a good idea. We don't want to annoy the neighbours.
d) I'm afraid I'm kind of busy this weekend.
e) Actually, it's not really my kind of thing. Perhaps you could ask Jean.

B Work in pairs. Practise the conversations in Exercise 5A.

5 explore

JOURNEYS p56

MY UTOPIA p59

MY PERFECT COUNTRY p62

CARRIBBEAN p64

SPEAKING **5.1** Describe a travel destination **5.2** Discuss your idea of utopia **5.3** Discuss different policies **5.4** Talk about stereotypes

LISTENING **5.2** Listen to people discussing their dream island **5.3** Listen to a conversation about policies **5.4** Watch a BBC programme about Haiti

READING **5.1** Read a book review of *The Lost City of the Monkey God* **5.3** Read about a radio programme: *My Perfect Country*

WRITING **5.1** Write a book review **5.4** Write a story

G quantifiers
P connected speech: *of*
V nature

A

B

C
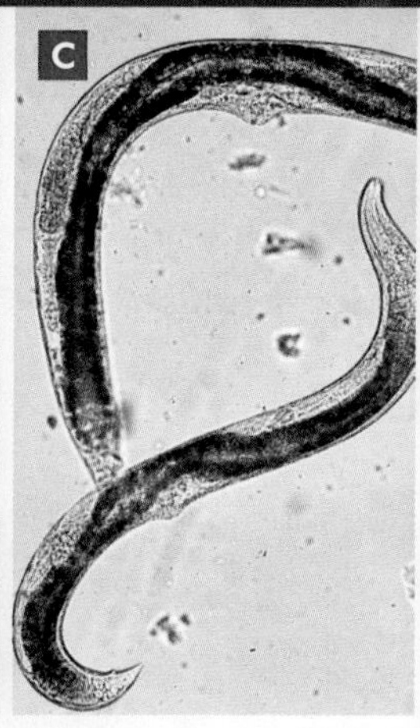

D

VOCABULARY

NATURE

1 A Work in pairs. Read the paragraph. Which of the words in bold can you see in the photos? What do the other words in bold mean?

Walk through a **rainforest** and you are protected from the weather by a huge **canopy** of trees. You see all kinds of **vegetation**. Because of all the rain, this vegetation can be enormous: some trees grow hundreds of feet high. There are also all kinds of **creatures**. These range from jaguars to **venomous snakes** to tiny **parasites** that carry **tropical diseases**. There are other dangers, such as **flash floods** that can put your camp under water in minutes. All of this is why some say the rainforest is the last place in the world that is truly wild.

B Work in groups. Discuss the questions.

1 What is the most geographically interesting/ extreme place you have travelled to?
2 What was it like?
3 Did it include any of the words in bold in Exercise 1A?

▷ page 124 **VOCABULARYBANK**

READING

2 A Work in pairs. You are going to read a book review. The book describes an adventure in a rainforest. The words in the box are in the review. What do you think happens in the book?

500-year-old	mystery	ancient civilisation	
explorers	expedition	parasite	tropical disease

B Read the review and check your ideas.

3 Read the review again and answer the questions.

1 What is hidden under the Honduran rainforest?
2 Why does Douglas Preston go to the rainforest and does he achieve his goal?
3 Who are the characters described in the book?
4 What dilemma do the explorers have concerning objects at the site?
5 What is the potential killer that gets them in the end?
6 How do we know Preston is a brave man?

The Lost City of the Monkey God

by Douglas Preston ★★★★★

Douglas Preston's new book is part memoir, part adventure, all action. The tale concerns his search for a 500-year-old mystery in the Central American country of Honduras. For half a millennium, there have been rumours of the ruins of an ancient civilisation hidden under the rainforest. These ruins are called the Lost City of the Monkey God. Preston tells the stories of the explorers who looked for it and then describes his own 2015 expedition to the Honduran rainforest, where he was involved in an astonishing discovery.

This non-fiction book combines archaeology, anthropology, adventure travel and a quite wonderful cast of characters. Preston has written many thrillers, but he's probably never invented more colourful people than these cheats, bullies and strongmen. One archaeology professor is a real-life Indiana Jones. The largest of the characters (in all senses) is a foul-mouthed, Hawaiian-shirt-wearing American, who sadly doesn't live to see the biggest discoveries. The toughest are the British soldiers whose job is to keep everyone alive. Early on, one of them traps and chops the head off a six-foot snake as if he's shelling a peanut.

GRAMMAR

QUANTIFIERS

4 A Read the review again. Write *T* (true), *F* (false) or *DK* (we don't know) next to these statements.

1 Douglas Preston has written **many** other books.
2 **Several** explorers had found the lost city previously.
3 Preston and his team didn't have **enough** time to find the lost city.
4 The story has **lots of** interesting characters.
5 They see **a large number of** dangerous creatures.
6 **A few** American soldiers kept the explorers safe.
7 **Few** people in the west know about leishmaniasis.
8 The book gives us **a little** information about the parasite.
9 The author goes to the rainforest **a couple of** times.
10 A flash flood causes them **a great deal** of trouble.
11 The expedition costs an enormous **amount of** money.
12 The reviewer thinks the book has **too much** information about the jungle.

The jungle, of course, is another central character. Preston describes the beauty of untouched nature and even starts to enjoy the screams of the monkeys that wake him every morning. However, the magnificent canopy that hides its treasures also has its dangers: jaguars, mosquitoes, flash floods and, scariest of all, the *fer-de-lance*, a vicious, venomous snake. But in the end, it isn't the biggest killers that get them; it's the smallest: a parasite.

Once they've found the lost city – an incredible experience for them all – Preston and the team discuss whether to remove objects from the site. But in the end they bring home nothing but a tropical disease. Few people in the west know about it, but it's existed since the time of the dinosaurs and it's killed millions.

A section in the second half of the book describes exactly what the leishmaniasis parasite can do to your body. While getting treatment for it, Preston documents the destruction caused worldwide by this parasite. Remarkably, he later returns to the jungle to complete his story.

The Lost City of the Monkey God is a page-turner. From his observations on the disaster of colonialism to the descriptions of disease, Preston is always entertaining and informative, and this tremendous book is full of truths that will outlive us all.

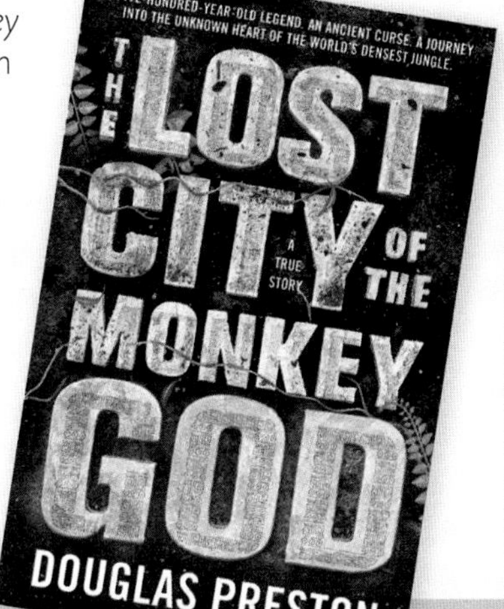

B Look at the quantifiers in bold in Exercise 4A. Underline the nouns that follow the quantifiers. Then answer the questions.

1 Which quantifiers are used with countable nouns and which with uncountable nouns? Are any used with both?
2 Which are used with small numbers? Which with large numbers?
3 What's the difference between *few* and *a few*? Which emphasises the fact that it's a very small number?

5 A 5.1 **CONNECTED SPEECH: *of* Listen to the phrases. How is *of* pronounced in connected speech?**

1 lots of people
2 an amount of money
3 a number of times
4 a few of us

B Listen again and repeat. Copy the pronunciation of *of* (/əv/).

6 Underline the correct alternatives to complete the sentences.

1 Typically, a large *amount/number/deal* of trees forms a canopy above the rainforest.
2 There isn't a great *couple/deal/number* of information about that unexplored area.
3 Realistically, we won't have *little/several/ enough* time to visit everything.
4 It costs too *much/few/many* money to go there in the summer, so we go in winter.
5 She was in the Amazon for *much/several/ a great deal* of months.
6 *Much/A bit of/ Few* people have caught this rare tropical disease.
7 The creatures have been seen in their natural habitat only a *little/couple of/loads* times.
8 There were too *little/much/many* people, and they undoubtedly scared off the animals.

▷ page 112 **LANGUAGEBANK**

SPEAKING

7 A Think of a place you have travelled to or know well (e.g. a town, city, natural habitat, holiday resort). Think of sentences to describe it using quantifiers. Describe these features.

- nature
- parks
- trees
- traffic
- people
- noise
- mosquitoes
- pollution
- peace and quiet
- crime

There's too much traffic and too many people. In the evening there's lots of noise.

B Work in pairs. Listen to your partner's sentences. Which place is he/she describing?

WRITING

A SHORT BOOK REVIEW; LEARN TO OFFER PRAISE AND CRITICISM

8 A Work in groups and discuss.

1 How many types of review can you think of (e.g. hotel reviews, film reviews)?
2 Which of these do you sometimes read? Why? Where do you find these reviews?
3 Have you read any book reviews recently?

B Which of the features in the box does a book review usually NOT contain?

title author where to buy the book
genre (fiction, non-fiction, biography, poetry, etc.)
style (academic, humorous, literary) main idea(s)
assessment (whether you like the book) subject

Three Daughters of Eve
by Elif Shafak

Great book!
Review by JAC

This powerful novel begins with a car journey. A Turkish woman is driving to a dinner party in Istanbul when a thief snatches her handbag from the back seat of the car. She chases him and a photo drops out of the bag. The photo is of the same woman, Peri, years earlier, with two friends and a professor, and it reminds her of the time she spent as a student at Oxford University.

The novel switches between Peri's past – her childhood and her time at Oxford with the two friends and the charismatic Professor Azur – and the present: the dinner party. She is on a journey to discover her identity, but it doesn't always run smoothly.

Peri grew up in a warring household, her mother representing traditional values while her father was a progressive unbeliever. Peri is saved from this conflict by her love of books, and this leads to her getting a place at Oxford. But there is a mystery concerning her time at Oxford: something terrible happened, which caused her to abandon her life in England.

Three Daughters of Eve has several contrasting ideas and themes: friendship and rivalry, religion and doubt, modernity and tradition. It also contains magical elements – Peri is haunted by an image of a child's face – something we have seen before in Shafak's novels, especially in *The Architect's Apprentice*. Overall, I found the work compelling and original, and would highly recommend it to adult readers of literary fiction.

9 Read the book review on the left. What is the book about and what does the reviewer think of it?

10 Read about the four As of book reviews. Does the review in Exercise 9 mention all of these?

The four A's of book reviews >>

Author – Who is he/she? What else has he/she written? Is this book typical of his/her style? How is his/her background relevant to the book?

Audience – Who is this book for? Children? Adults? People looking for information? Or is it just a good read?

Argument – What are the main ideas or themes of the book? What makes it different and new? Did the author convey the argument successfully?

Assessment – Do you like the book? All of it or parts of it? Why? Who would you recommend the book to?

11 A Look at the first and last paragraphs of the review in Exercise 9. Find three adjectives used to praise the book. Write them in the first column of the table.

praise	criticism

B Work in pairs. Write the phrases in the box in the correct place in the table in Exercise 11A. Use a dictionary to help you.

it's too slow it's well-written it's unconvincing
it's charming it's persuasive it's moving
it's difficult to follow it's dull

speakout TIP

Compound adjectives are common for describing books, films, etc. These use two words which are often hyphenated (e.g. *well-written*). The stress is usually on the second word (*well-written*). What do you think these compound adjectives mean? Do we use them to describe books/stories, authors/characters or both?

world-famous fast-paced slow-moving
badly-drawn well-researched old-fashioned

Find three compound adjectives in the second paragraph of the review in Exercise 2B.

12 A Write a short review (250 words) of a book you have read. Don't forget to include the four As from Exercise 10.

B Read other students' reviews and discuss the books in more detail. Would you like to read any of the books they reviewed?

MY UTOPIA

G -ing form and infinitive
V types of people
P connected speech: elision

A

B

C

D

How, where and with whom do you want to live your life?

If you could design your own utopia, an imaginary island filled with the community of your choice, what would you choose? Would it be an island filled with books, surfboards or gadgets? A foodie's heaven or a place for social-media-obsessed teenagers to hang out? What would your utopia look like? What would people do there? Would there be any rules?

TAKE PART IN SURVEY >

VOCABULARY

TYPES OF PEOPLE

1 A Work in pairs. Complete the phrases with the words in the box.

music teenager nerd worm junkie film addict

- book lover/ [1] book________
- foodie
- couch potato/telly [2]________
- techie/computer [3]________
- news [4]________
- sports fan/sports enthusiast
- beach bum
- [5]________ buff
- [6]________ fan
- rebellious [7]________

B Look at the phrases in Exercise 1A and follow these steps.

1 Mark the phrases *I* (informal) or *N* (neutral).
2 Some of the phrases could be considered rude/insulting. Mark them with (!), to remind you to be careful when you use them.

C Work in groups and discuss. What kind of person are you? Do you know anyone among your friends or family who fits one of the descriptions above? Tell your group about them.

I'm a real telly addict – I think I spend about five hours a day watching the latest crime dramas on Netflix. My brother is a computer nerd …

▷ page 124 **VOCABULARYBANK**

LISTENING

2 A Read the text. Which islands can you see in the pictures?

B ▶ 5.2 Listen to four people answering the questions in the text. Complete the table for each speaker.

	island	what people do there	what is not allowed
Speaker 1			
Speaker 2			
Speaker 3			
Speaker 4			

3 A Listen again. Are the statements true (T) or false (F)?

1 On Book Lovers' Island there is no television.
2 E-books are popular on Book Lovers' Island.
3 The only problem on Gadget Island is that the wi-fi signal is sometimes weak.
4 On Gadget Island robots cook the food.
5 Adults are allowed on Teenager Island.
6 The teenagers might enjoy a bit of sport.
7 On Foodie Island people enjoy growing and preparing food as well as eating it.
8 Some pre-packaged food, like sliced bread, would be allowed on the island.

B Work in pairs and discuss. Would you enjoy visiting any of these islands? Which one would you choose? Why? Is there an island you would definitely choose NOT to visit? Which one? Why?

GRAMMAR

-*ING* FORM AND INFINITIVE

4 A Check what you know. Underline the correct alternatives to complete the sentences.

1 I **fancy** *to spend/spending* time on Book Lovers' Island.
2 I love cooking. I **look forward to** *prepare/preparing* the meal as much as to eat/eating it.
3 I think I could **manage** *to spend/spending* all day *to lie/lying* around in hammocks doing nothing.
4 I **can't stand** *to wait/waiting* around when you have a piece of technology that doesn't work and you have to take it somewhere to get it fixed.
5 **I'm not very keen on** *to eat/eating* pre-packaged food. I'd rather cook everything from scratch.
6 I **tend** *to spend/spending* a lot of time *listen/listening* to music or just to *chill/chilling*.
7 I think I'd **miss** not *to watch/watching* television, although I **enjoy** *read/reading* the books.
8 **Imagine** never *to have/having* a problem with technology or the internet. That really would be a utopia!

B Look at the verb patterns in the table. Find another example of each pattern in the sentences in Exercise 4A. Add the examples to the table.

***-ing* form**
Verbs followed by an *-ing* form include *like, love, hate, enjoy, fancy, mind, miss, imagine, can't stand.* *I really **enjoy cooking**.* *I don't **mind not watching** television.* 1 ___________
Use an *-ing* form after fixed phrases ending in a preposition, e.g. *look forward to, be keen on, give up.* *I'm **not very keen on running**.* 2 ___________
Use an *-ing* form as a subject or object (i.e. as a noun). *I love **reading**.* ***Eating** good food is one of my passions.* 3 ___________
infinitive with *to*
Verbs followed by the infinitive with *to* include *seem, want, tend, promise, agree, manage, decide, refuse.* *He **promised to contact** me.* *She **refused to switch** her phone off.* 4 ___________
Use infinitive with *to* to express purpose. *I'm going to the library **to get** a book.* *We came **to listen to** the author talk about her new book.* 5 ___________

C 5.3 **CONNECTED SPEECH: elision Listen and complete the phrases.**

1 We're not ___________ to do anything.
2 I ___________ to spend time just chilling.
3 I'm ___________ very keen on running.
4 I think I ___________ manage to get there.
5 He ___________ to contact me.
6 I ___________ mind not watching television.

D Listen again. Notice how in connected speech sometimes the /t/ or /d/ sound is lost through elision, especially when there are several consonants together. Listen and repeat the phrases.

expecte(d) to
ten(d) to
jus(t) chilling

5 A Complete the sentences with the correct form of the verbs in brackets.

1 We tend ___________ (go) to the mountains in the summer months.
2 I love ___________ (listen) to really loud music and ___________ (dance) around the kitchen.
3 I can't stand ___________ (have) to get up early on a Sunday.
4 ___________ (surf) is one of my favourite hobbies.
5 I'm not very keen on ___________ (swim).
6 I'm looking forward to ___________ (see) my family at the weekend.
7 We often travel to the coast ___________ (swim) in the summer.
8 I've decided ___________ (try) and learn Mandarin.

B Change two or three of the sentences in Exercise 5A so they are true for you or write new sentences using some of the verb forms in Exercise 4B. Then work in pairs and compare your sentences.

6 Choose one of the personality types in Exercise 1A (book lover, rebellious teenager, etc.). Think of sentences to describe how these people like to live. Try to use verb forms from Exercise 4B.

Book lovers tend to read a lot. They always look forward to finding a new book.

▷ page 112 **LANGUAGEBANK**

SPEAKING

7 A Plan your own private utopia. Make notes.

- Where would it be?
- What would be special about it?
- What would it look like?
- What kind of people would be there?
- How would you spend your time?
- Would there be any rules?

B Present your ideas to other students. Ask and answer questions about each island. Who do you think has the best idea for a private utopia?

VOCABULARY *PLUS*

FORMAL VS INFORMAL REGISTER

8 A Match sentences 1–10 with responses a)–j).

1 Have you met Rebecca's new man? He's really attractive.
2 She never stops talking. It drives me crazy!
3 We're never going to get there on time at this rate. What are we going to do?
4 Anne-Marie is very ambitious, isn't she?
5 The house was a real mess. I can't believe how lazy they are.
6 Danny's parents are going to pay for the holiday. They've got plenty of money.
7 The problem is that he's always trying to impress people.
8 I need to finish both of these essays by tomorrow.
9 What's the matter with you?
10 What do you feel like doing later? Do you want to go out?

a) I know. They're **loaded**.
b) Yes, she's a real **go-getter**.
c) That's a bit of a **hassle**.
d) Yes, he's a bit of a **try-hard**.
e) I had an argument with my boss so I'm a bit **hacked off**.
f) Yes, I saw them on Saturday. You're right. He's really **fit**.
g) We'll be fine. Just **chill**, will you?
h) I agree. She can be a bit **chatty**.
i) I know. They are a bunch of **slobs**.
j) To be honest, I'd rather just stay at home and **veg out**.

B Match six of the phrases in bold in Exercise 8A with definitions 1–6.

1 relax and stop worrying *chill*
2 annoyed
3 lazy, unclean people
4 very rich
5 sit around doing nothing productive
6 be very attractive (or be in good physical shape)

C Write the correct part of speech (adjective, noun or verb) next to each phrase in Exercise 8A.

9 A Work in pairs. Study the phrases in Exercise 8A and then cover them so you can't see them. Using one of the phrases you have studied, what might you say in these situations?

1 Your teenage son invites his friends to your house and they laze around and leave a horrible mess everywhere.
2 You take a taxi from the airport and the driver tells you all about how he grew up in this city, asks you about your holiday, tells you different places you should visit, etc.
3 Your partner suggests going out on a Friday night, but you are tired and would rather stay at home and watch TV.
4 You're angry because you have just spent an hour trying to get through to your internet service provider on the telephone but you keep being put on hold.
5 Your younger sister likes to set herself ambitious goals and then achieve them.
6 You are a teenage girl and you want your mother to stop worrying about everything and just relax.

B Choose a situation from Exercise 9A and write a short conversation (3–4 lines) including some of the phrases in Exercise 8A. Then work in pairs and act out your conversations to the class.

5.3)) MY PERFECT COUNTRY

F express your opinion
V society
P word stress

VOCABULARY

SOCIETY

1 A Work in pairs. List three things you think your country does well and three things it could do better. Show your lists to other students.

B Are any of the things in the box problems in your country? Which are the biggest issues at the moment? Can you add any more to the list?

unemployment   violent crime   child poverty access to clean water/sanitation   terrorist threats media manipulation   road/rail networks   tax evasion power cuts   housing   healthcare   freedom of speech

2 A Read the text. Which issues from Exercise 1B are referred to?

B Work in pairs. Discuss what your perfect country would be like.

FUNCTION

EXPRESSING YOUR OPINION

3 A Look at the photos. What policies do you think they represent?

B 5.4 Listen to three people discussing different policies. Make notes about each policy in the table.

	policy
Bermuda	
Japan	
Estonia	

C Work in pairs and compare your notes. Would you include any of these policies in your perfect country? Why/Why not?

My Perfect Country

In a world where so much is going wrong, perhaps it's worth looking at what's going right. What if you could build a country with policies that actually worked? From systems for teaching maths in Shanghai and ideas for clean energy in Costa Rica, to policies to help reduce smoking in Australia, Fi Glover and Martha Lane Fox look at innovative policies from across the world that have been truly successful. So, what would your perfect country look like?

There would be room for everyone. Borders would be meaningless. People would be allowed to live and work wherever they want.

Everyone would have their own house with a nice garden.

No children would go to bed hungry. In my perfect country there would be no child poverty and enough food for everyone to eat healthily.

In my perfect country everyone can trust each other. The government can trust the people and the people can trust the government. You can believe what you read in the media because you trust the people writing the news.

There would be no prisons or violent crime. People would respect each other and each other's property.

4 A Listen again and complete the speakers' opinions.

Bermuda white roofs

A: Well, if you ask me, it's a really [1]________. In Bermuda they have no natural water resources, right?

B: Personally, I'm not [2]________. Don't you think it would be better if the government was responsible for making sure that everyone has access to clean water and sanitation?

Japanese martial arts

A: As I [3]________ it, karate isn't much good to you when you're standing in front of an armed criminal, surely?

B: I'm absolutely convinced that kind of [4]________ can really work.

Estonian digital revolution

C: Well, in my [5]________, the country is one of the best examples of how a country can run online.
It seems to [6]________ that this one is working pretty well.

B Look at the phrases for expressing opinion. Which ones did you hear? Check in audioscript 5.4 on page 139.

1 Well, if you ask me, ...
2 Personally, I'm convinced/Personally, I'm not convinced ...
3 As I see it/The way I see it, ...
4 It seems to me that ...
5 I'm absolutely convinced that ...
6 I have the feeling that/I feel that ...
7 You can take it from me that ...
8 I think that/I don't think that ...
9 In my opinion, ...

C WORD STRESS Underline the stressed syllables in the phrases in Exercise 4B.

D ▶ 5.5 Listen and check your answers. Then listen again and repeat. Copy the stress patterns.

▷ page 112 **LANGUAGEBANK**

5 A Put the words in brackets in the correct order to complete the sentences. Add commas where necessary.

1 ________ (convinced / power / not / solar / I'm) is the answer to all our problems.
2 ________ (see / I / need / it / as / we) to deal with the threat of terrorism.
3 ________ (you / if / me / ask) free healthcare is essential.
4 ________ (opinion / in / my / unemployment) is the biggest problem.
5 ________ (absolutely / that / convinced / I'm) digital is the future.
6 ________ (that / to / it / me / seems) tax evasion is the issue.

B Do you agree with the statements in Exercise 5A? Why/Why not?

LEARN TO

EXPRESS DOUBT/QUESTION AN OPINION

6 A ▶ 5.6 Listen and underline the alternative you hear to complete the phrases for expressing doubt and questioning an opinion.

1 Don't you *think/suppose* it would be better if ...?
2 What *about if/when* ...?
3 That may be *true/right*, but I still feel that ...
4 I'm not *sure/convinced* about that.
5 Shouldn't we *consider/think about* ...?
6 That's a *fair/good* point, but ...

B Listen again and repeat. Copy the polite intonation.

7 Work in pairs. Take turns to say a sentence and give a response. Student A: start by saying one of the sentences from Exercise 5A. Student B: respond using phrases from Exercise 6A.

A: *I'm not convinced solar power is the answer to all our problems.*
B: *That may be true, but using more solar power would reduce the need for nuclear power stations.*

SPEAKING

8 Work in groups. Plan your perfect country. You are going to consider which policies to include. Follow the instructions.

1 Read about a possible policy. Make some notes about how it would work.
- Student A: read about a Shanghai policy on page 129.
- Student B: read about an Australian policy on page 131.
- Student C: read about a policy in Peru on page 132.

2 Tell your group about your policy. The other students ask the speaker about any problems with it. Decide together if this policy should be included in your perfect country. Are there any other policies which should be included?
3 Tell the class about the policies you agreed on and why.

5.4 CARIBBEAN

DVD PREVIEW

1 A Work in pairs. Discuss the questions.

1 What do you know about the Caribbean? Have you been there?
2 How many Caribbean countries can you name? What do you know about the history of the area?

B Read about the programme. What might Simon Reeve discover in Haiti?

Caribbean

BBC

In this BBC series, Simon Reeve explores the Caribbean. With its thousands of diverse islands, rich history, and stunning golden beaches, the Caribbean is one of the world's great treasures. In this episode, Reeve visits Haiti. Haiti is the poorest country in the Americas.

Besides many political problems and a high crime rate, it had a terrible earthquake in 2010 that killed thousands of people and destroyed most of the capital's infrastructure. But Reeve finds that the public perception of Haiti is wrong. He travels around the country and discovers some of its wonderful and lesser-known history.

DVD VIEW

2 A Watch the programme. According to the presenter, what do people generally think of Haiti, and how is the reality different?

B Circle the correct answer, a) or b).

1 How does Jean-Daniel, the guide, describe Haiti's street life?
a) busy **b)** beautiful
2 What does Jean-Daniel say about Haiti?
a) It isn't as bad as people say.
b) The country is becoming more dangerous.
3 Which country colonised Haiti in the 1700s?
a) the UK **b)** France
4 What was Haiti's financial state at that time?
a) extremely poor because of wars
b) rich because of sugar, coffee, cotton, etc.
5 What is special about the fortress?
a) It's the biggest in the Americas.
b) It's the oldest in the Americas.
6 What is extraordinary about Haitian history?
a) Haitians fought for Napoleon.
b) It's the only country formed after a successful slave rebellion.

C Watch again to check your answers.

3 A Simon, the presenter, uses the adjectives in Box A to describe the words in Box B. Match the words in Box A with those in Box B.

A

astonishing breathtaking colossal exotic extraordinary fertile long-suffering negative sturdy

B

as the mountain itself climate Haiti island of Hispaniola place structure tale of struggle the view view of the country

B Watch again to check your answers. Then write the adjectives from Box A next to the correct definition.

1 _astonishing_: very surprising
2 __________: able to produce good crops (vegetables, fruits, etc.)
3 __________: bad or harmful
4 __________: strong and not likely to break
5 __________: has had problems for many years
6 __________: unusual or exciting because it's from a foreign country
7 __________: very impressive or surprising to look at
8 __________: extremely large
9 __________: very unusual or special

4 Would you like to visit Haiti? Why/Why not?

speakout looking beyond stereotypes

5 Read about *Hidden Stories* documentaries. What is their purpose?

Hidden Stories

This documentary series looks at the sides of towns and cities that the public don't see. It looks beyond the stereotypes to find out more about places. Every programme in the series involves visiting a town or city and discovering stories, traditions, little-known neighbourhoods, and deep secrets. So what's the hidden story of your town?

6 A 5.7 Listen to a woman describing the hidden history of her city. What does she say about the city's image today and its less well-known side?

B Listen again. Tick the key phrases you hear.

KEYPHRASES

The stereotype of [place] is that it's ...
When people talk about [place], the first thing they say is ...
The city is famous for ...
People associate my city with ...
There's a side people don't know about.
You may never have heard of [it/them], but ...
The most interesting thing about [place] is ...
That's the hidden side of [place].

7 A Read the questions and think about your answers.

1 What are the stereotypes about a town or city you know well? What is it famous for? Are there any negative things people say about it?
2 Is there anything that outsiders generally DON'T know about the town (history, people, customs, neighbourhoods, etc.)?
3 Your town/city has been chosen to appear on Hidden Stories with you as the presenter! What aspect will you focus on?
4 Which of the key phrases will you use?

B Work in groups and discuss the questions in Exercise 7A.

writeback a hidden story of a town/city

8 A You are going to write a 100-word summary of your *Hidden Stories* idea. Read the example.

Detroit: the hidden story

There's nowhere in the USA more associated with the inner-city blues than Detroit. The city went from boom to bust in one hundred years. With the car industry collapsing, Detroit became known for poverty, crime, and abandoned neighbourhoods. But it's just this kind of situation that has always inspired musicians, and Detroit's music scene has remained strong. Historically, Detroit was at the forefront of musical styles ranging from jazz to techno to rap to hip-hop. That hasn't changed. If you want to hear cutting edge new music, live or recorded, Detroit is still the place to be.

B Write your summary.

C Read other students' summaries. Did you learn anything new? Which places sound interesting?

5.5 ((LOOKBACK

V NATURE

1 A Add the missing vowels to make nature words.

1 rnfrst
2 cnpy
3 vgttn
4 crtrs
5 vnms snks
6 prsts
7 trpcl dsss
8 flsh flds

B Work in pairs. Describe one of the words in Exercise 1A for your partner to guess.

G QUANTIFIERS

2 A Circle the correct answer, a), b) or c), to complete the sentences.

1 I've taken ________ international flights.
a) much **b)** a lot **c)** several

2 I've also been on ________ of long boat trips.
a) a couple **b)** many **c)** a little

3 Before travelling, I always spend a ________ of time preparing.
a) amount **b)** lots **c)** great deal

4 I read ________ guidebooks about my destination.
a) enough of **b)** a few **c)** a great deal of

5 If I'm going abroad, I learn ________ words to communicate basic ideas.
a) amount of **b)** a little **c)** enough

6 These days, ________ places are completely untouched by tourism.
a) a lot **b)** few **c)** too much

7 I don't think you need a large ________ of money to enjoy travelling, but you need time.
a) amount **b)** number **c)** deal

8 A ________ knowledge of local customs and traditions is important when you travel.
a) few **b)** couple of **c)** little

B Which of the sentences in Exercise 2A are true for you? Change the others to make them true. Then work in pairs and share your ideas.

V TYPES OF PEOPLE

3 A The words in bold are in the wrong sentences. Replace them with the correct words.

1 My mother is a real **foodie**. She's read every book in the library!
2 He's never going to get a job. He loves being a beach **techie**.
3 The kid is a telly **bum**. He never does anything else.
4 I love it when we eat at Sara's, because she's such a **bookworm**.
5 Your laptop's not working properly? Ask Chris to help you; he's a real **addict**.
6 He never does what I ask him to. He's going through a rebellious **enthusiast** stage.
7 If's he's not playing rugby or cricket, he's watching it. He's a sports **teenager**.

B Choose one of the types of people in Exercise 3A. Write three questions to ask a partner, to find out if they match that description.

sports enthusiast:
Do you think of yourself as a sporty person?
Do you ever go to matches or see any live sports?
What sports do you watch on TV?

C Work in pairs. Ask and answer your questions from Exercise 3B.

G -ING FORM AND INFINITIVE

4 A Underline the correct alternatives to complete the sentences.

1 I managed *spending/to spend* all my money in the first week.
2 We miss not *to be/being* able to go to the beach every day.
3 I'm not very keen on *to watch/watching* television.
4 They promised *to call/calling* us when they got there.
5 I've given up *to wait/waiting* to hear from them.
6 The service was so bad they refused *to pay/paying* the bill.
7 They tend *to argue/arguing* all the time.

B Use the prompts to make sentences which are true for you.

- At the weekends I tend …
- Something I'm really looking forward to …
- I don't mind …
- I'm not very keen on …

F EXPRESSING YOUR OPINION

5 A Complete the conversations with the words in the box.

see convinced think opinion me seems absolutely feeling

1 **A:** I think we should take the motorway.
B: Personally, I'm not ________ it will be quicker.

2 **A:** We need a change of government.
B: Well, if you ask ________, that will only make things worse.

3 **A:** I have the ________ that the situation is going to get worse.
B: The way I ________ it, it can only get better.

4 **A:** In my ________, the Spanish team are stronger.
B: Yes, I'm ________ convinced that they're going to win.

5 **A:** I don't ________ that we should decide yet.
B: It ________ to me that's the best idea we've had.

B Work in pairs. Practise the conversations in Exercise 5A.

6 goodness

GOOD OR BAD? p68 | KIND DEEDS p71 | THE GOOD LIFE p74 | A HELPING HAND p76

SPEAKING **6.1** Discuss good or bad behaviour **6.2** Discuss a news story **6.3** Decide on the rules for a happy life **6.4** A group discussion

LISTENING **6.2** Listen to a news story **6.3** Listen to a conversation about the rules for a happy life **6.4** Watch people talking about helping others

READING **6.1** Read an article about good vs bad **6.3** Read about the happiest people on the planet

WRITING **6.2** Write a thank you message **6.4** Write a short essay

6.1 GOOD OR BAD?

G modals of deduction
V extreme adjectives; two-part phrases
P intonation: emphasis

SPEAKING

1 A On a scale of 1 to 3, how would you rate your behaviour in these situations (3 = really bad, 2 = bad, 1 = not really that bad)?

1. A shop assistant gives you too much change. You say nothing and don't return the money.
2. You borrow a friend's book and accidentally spill coffee on the inside pages. You return it without telling her.
3. You scrape another car while trying to park. You drive away immediately and pretend it didn't happen.
4. A friend of a friend needs a lift. You're tired and busy. You lie, saying you have a doctor's appointment.

B Work in pairs and discuss. What would you do in these situations?

1. You are at an ATM and find twenty euros in the machine.
2. Your boss comes to a meeting with food on his cheek. (You don't like him very much.)
3. You see an old man struggling to cross the street. (It's raining and you are rushing to get to a meeting.)
4. You see a couple arguing loudly in the street. (The man looks aggressive and the woman looks distressed.)

READING

2 A Read the first part of an article. What examples of good and bad behaviour does it mention?

B Work in pairs. Student A: read the second part of the article on page 128 and answer the questions. Student B: read the third part of the article on page 132 and answer the questions.

C Work in the same pairs. Tell your partner about your section of the article.

GOOD VS EVIL

Is it better to be good or bad?

It's good to be good!

Remember that boy at nursery who wouldn't share his toys? How about that flatmate who never did the washing-up? We've all encountered **selfish** people but thankfully, there are also plenty of people who are kind and behave generously.

Our history of warfare suggests we might be programmed to behave selfishly and aggressively towards each other. However, there are many stories of people doing all kinds of **spectacular** altruistic acts, like diving into the paths of cars to push children aside or into icy waters to save drowning babies.

Millions of others do quiet acts of giving that rarely feature in newspapers. According to a survey, three-quarters of people in the UK gave money to a good cause, one-third gave their time and two-thirds helped a stranger. The proportion of people who reported doing **altruistic** acts increases every year.

Sometimes it's good to be bad!

Our ability to be friendly towards other people and care about them has helped to make us the humans we are today. This may be the reason why all through our childhoods, we're told that we need to be good: kind, considerate, respectful of others, etc. Why, then, do so many adults **abandon** these principles? One explanation is that being bad, i.e. not caring about your fellow human and focusing only on your own needs, could have **genuine** benefits. It might even help you to become more successful.

For example, if you're around people who all share the same idea about an important issue, then if you're being 'good' and respectful of others, you're more likely to agree with it. You'll either say you agree, even if you don't, or you'll become genuinely **convinced** that it's correct. However, if you deliberately try not to be concerned with the views and opinions of others, you can reach more valid and accurate decisions and conclusions.

3 A Try to guess the meanings of the words in bold in the article.

B Check your ideas. Match the words in bold in the article with definitions 1–6.

1. real, authentic
2. showing a selfless concern for the welfare of others
3. forget about
4. people who think only about themselves
5. completely certain about something
6. amazing, impressive

C Work in groups. Which argument do you agree with: that it's better to be good or that it's better to be bad? Why? Use the phrases in the box in your discussion.

I'm convinced that …
I think that …
My opinion is that …
I would/wouldn't abandon the principles of …
It's more important to be altruistic/selfish because …

GRAMMAR

MODALS OF DEDUCTION

4 A Check what you know. Underline the correct alternatives to complete the sentences.

1. He's sleeping on the street and it's minus 4 degrees! He *should/must/can't* be freezing, so I've brought him a blanket and a hot drink.
2. You've charged us thirty euros for the service, but we waited over an hour for our meal. You *can/may/can't* be serious!
3. It's cloudy now, but it *may/shall/shouldn't* be sunny later.
4. Don't worry. I'll pick you up from the hospital. It *can't/shouldn't/will* be a problem.
5. You can ask him, but I'm sure he *might/can't be/won't* agree
6. I've just read this self-help book and it *could/shall/will* be the best thing I've ever done.

B Look at the examples in the first column of the table. Then complete the second column with *really certain*, *very likely* or *possible*.

modal	how the speaker feels about the situation
will/won't His train just arrived. He **won't be** long.	1 *really certain*
must/can't There **must be** a better way of dealing with this. Twenty percent service charge? You **can't be** serious!	2 ________
may/might/could If you look inside the book, you **might be** lucky. It ***could be*** our best option in the circumstances.	3 ________
shall/shan't No more coffee for me or I **shan't** sleep tonight.	4 ________
should/shouldn't We're nearly there. It **shouldn't be** long now. Chelsea are playing well. They **should win** today.	5 ________

5 A Underline the correct alternatives to complete the conversations.

1 **A:** I can't find my phone. I left it on my desk.
B: Don't worry. It *might/must* be here somewhere. (There is nowhere else it can be.)

2 **A:** Thank you so much for agreeing to look after Oliver for me.
B: It's not a problem. I'm sure he *won't/can't* be any trouble at all. (Oliver is a very good boy.)

3 **A:** I can't remember what Jo's studying at university.
B: It *must/could* be psychology or it might be sociology.

4 **A:** Do you know where Samantha is?
B: I'm not sure. She *may not/should not* be at work today.

5 **A:** We only have half an hour to get to the airport. Is that enough time?
B: It should be fine. There *should/shouldn't* be too much traffic at this time.

6 **A:** Is that Akihiro?
B: No, that *might/can't* be him. He's got a beard.

B ▶ 6.1 Listen and check your answers.

C ▶ 6.2 Cover the conversations in Exercise 5A. Listen to speaker A from each conversation and try to say the response.

6 A Write sentences expressing your opinion or suggesting solutions for each problem. Use the phrases in the box.

must be could be can't be won't be
should be may not be might be

1. unhealthy lifestyles (no exercise, bad food choices, etc.)
2. increased numbers of homeless people
3. more individualistic/selfish behaviour in western cultures

Making fruit and vegetables cheaper could be a way to improve peoples' health. Governments shouldn't tell people how they should live their lives.

B Work in small groups. Compare your ideas from Exercise 6A. Do you agree with the other students' opinions/suggestions?

VOCABULARY

EXTREME ADJECTIVES

speakout TIP

Overusing the word *very* can be boring for the listener. For example: *We were very hungry, but the restaurant was very crowded*. Try using extreme adjectives like *brilliant*. Can you think of extreme adjectives for *very hungry* and *very crowded*?

7 A Match extreme adjectives 1–8 with definitions a)–h).

1 astonished	a) very scary
2 spotless	b) very old
3 packed	c) very ugly
4 filthy	d) very clean
5 starving	e) very hungry
6 ancient	f) very shocked/surprised
7 hideous	g) very dirty
8 terrifying	h) very crowded

B Complete the sentences with the extreme adjectives in Exercise 7A.

1 We were interested in the history of the place, so we went on a tour through the __________ streets of the old city.
2 I spent all morning cleaning because the flat was __________.
3 We travelled during rush hour and the train was __________. There were so many people we had to stand for the whole journey.
4 We stood at the top of the tower, but I was too scared to look down. It was __________!
5 I was __________ when I won. I couldn't believe it.
6 Can we get lunch soon? I'm __________.
7 I spent all day cleaning the kitchen. Now it's absolutely __________!
8 I can't believe she wore that ugly dress. It looked __________ on her.

▷ page 114 **LANGUAGEBANK**

C 6.3 **INTONATION: emphasis Listen and check your answers. How do the speakers emphasise the extreme adjectives with their voice? Listen again and repeat.**

SPEAKING

8 A Prepare to talk about one or two of the following using extreme adjectives. Make notes.

- something you have done which you found scary
- somewhere you love because it has beautiful views
- somewhere you have been that was dirty/crowded

B Tell other students about your experiences.

I went bungee jumping in New Zealand. It was absolutely terrifying.

VOCABULARY *PLUS*

TWO-PART PHRASES

9 A Read the texts. What do they have in common?

on and on	fair and square	bright and early

Pay it forward

A chain of people buying each other's drinks at a Starbucks in Florida reached nearly 400 people, until one person decided to ruin it. It all started [1]__________ in the morning when someone offered to pay for the person behind her as an act of kindness. The situation went [2]__________. For eleven hours, people voluntarily offered to pay for the next customer, until customer 379 refused. She appeared not to understand and wanted to pay for her own coffee [2]__________, and not for anyone else's.

hustle and bustle	again and again
sick and tired	round and round

Can I help you with anything?

Joe, a London-based maths tutor, decided to spend a day doing things for people he didn't know. [4]__________ of watching people's selfish behaviour, he wanted to be kind and help as many people as possible. He went out into the [5]__________ of a London street and asked people if they needed any help. He made a video of the results. He wanders [6]__________, but at first, people seem suspicious. Many people turn him down. Eventually, a girl at a bus stop suggests that he buys the bus ticket for the next person in the queue, so he does. The clip was filmed for the charity Kindness.org, which encourages people to take part in acts of kindness and share them online. The video was shared [7]__________ and reached 6 million views in under twenty-four hours on Facebook.

ups and downs	give and take	wine and dine

Random Acts of Kindness

Life is supposed to be about [8]__________, but sometimes people take more than they give. The website Random Acts of Kindness encourages people to give more by doing simple things to help others. Here are a three easy things you could do:

- Offer to do some shopping for a neighbour.
- Cook a special meal and invite your friends over and [9]__________ them.
- Buy flowers and send them to someone you love.

Small acts of kindness like these can help us to cope with the [10]__________ of life.

B Complete the texts in Exercise 9A with the phrases in the boxes.

10 Work in pairs. Discuss the questions.

1 Do you think Random Acts of Kindness offers an effective way to encourage more kindness in the world? Why/Why not?
2 Can you think of some examples of possible random acts of kindness?

KIND DEEDS

G third and mixed conditionals
P connected speech: elision
V money

6.2

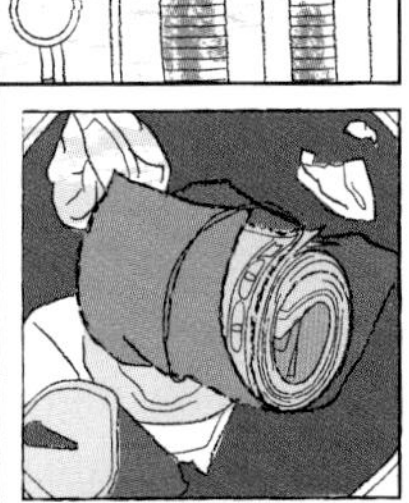

LISTENING

1 A Work in pairs. Look at the picture story. What do you think happened?

B 6.4 Listen and check your ideas.

2 A Answer the questions.

1 Why did Bruno have so much money in his car?
2 Who threw away the money?
3 Where did Bruno look for the money?
4 What was João's job?
5 What did João do when he found the money?
6 Who is Gabriel?
7 What did Gabriel do for João? Why?
8 What was 'the second happy ending'?

B Listen again and check your answers.

SPEAKING

3 Work in small groups. Discuss the questions.

1 Who did the kindest thing in this story: João (the garbage sorter), Bruno (the owner of the money) or Gabriel (the singer)?
2 Why do you think João's story was on the Brazilian news?
3 Do you agree with these comments about the story?
   - 'Often, it's the poor people who are more honest than the rich.'
   - 'The guy who lost his money was lucky enough to find a rare species: an honest person.'
   - 'He only gave the money back because it was dollars, which he couldn't spend in Brazil.'

VOCABULARY

MONEY

4 A Complete the sentences with the words in the box.

reward salary donations poverty

1 As a garbage sorter, João didn't earn a big ___________ – he made just 600 reais a month.
2 This meant that João lived in ___________, with barely enough money to raise a family.
3 The singer Gabriel thought João deserved a ___________ for being so honest.
4 Gabriel asked his friends for ___________ of money.

B Read the paragraph. What do the words in bold mean?

João's **income** was 600 *reais* a month. The *real* is the **currency** of Brazil. Even in countries with great **wealth**, there are millions of poor people. Many can't even **afford** to feed their families. Buying things like houses and cars is just a dream because it's impossible to have **savings** when you earn so little. It's also easy to get into **debt** when you need to borrow money frequently. One solution is for governments to **fund** housing projects and food banks for the poor, but this too is just a dream in many countries.

C Match the words in bold in Exercise 4B with definitions 1–7.

1 a large amount of money, property, etc. a person/country owns
2 a sum of money a person or organisation owes
3 the money you earn from your work or receive from the government, investments, etc.
4 money you have saved and not spent
5 have enough money to buy or pay for something
6 provide money for an activity, organisation or event.
7 the type of money a country uses

speakout TIP

Silent letters: *debt* is pronounced /det/. Which letter is silent?

What are the silent letters in these words from this lesson: *character*, *government*, *honest*, *heart*?

▷ page 125 **VOCABULARYBANK**

GRAMMAR

THIRD AND MIXED CONDITIONALS

5 A Read sentences 1–4 about João's story and underline the verb forms. Then answer questions a)–d below).

1 If João hadn't been so honest, he would have kept the money.
2 If he'd kept the money, no one would have known his story.
3 If no one had known his story, he wouldn't have been on the news.
4 If he hadn't been on the news, Gabriel wouldn't have collected money for him.
5 If he hadn't returned the money, João would still be a garbage sorter today.

a) Are these sentences about the past or present? Which sentence is a mixed conditional – about both the past and the present?
b) Which tense comes after *if*?
c) Which verb form comes after *would/wouldn't* + *have*?
d) How is the grammar of sentence 5 different from 1–4?

B Complete each sentence in two different ways: one referring to the past and the other to the present. Use the prompts in brackets.

1 If he'd eaten his food, he (not be / hungry).
If he'd eaten his food, he wouldn't have been hungry.
(He didn't eat his food. He was hungry at a time in the past.)
If he'd eaten his food, he wouldn't be hungry.
(He didn't eat his food. He is hungry now.)
2 If you'd practised the piano more, you (be / a professional).
3 If he hadn't met Juan, he (not be / so happy).
4 If we'd planned the schedule better, we (not have / problems).
5 If I'd remembered my keys, I (not be / locked out).

▷ page 114 **LANGUAGEBANK**

6 A Complete the third conditional sentences with the correct form of the verbs in brackets.

1 If I <u>had sold</u> the merchandise, I <u>wouldn't have got</u> into debt. (sell, not get)
2 I ________ the work if I ________ time. (do, have)
3 If he ________ some savings, he ________ the car. (have, buy)
4 We ________ the data if they ________ the project. (not collect, not fund)
5 If you ________ me about the meeting, I ________. (tell, come)
6 The day ________ easier if you ________ to your routine. (be, stick)
7 I ________ the experiment if I ________ long hours. (not finish, not work)
8 If Johnny ________ sick, he ________ us. (not feel, visit)

B Write one mixed conditional sentence (past situation with present result) for each pair of sentences.

1 She stopped for a snack. She isn't hungry now.
If she hadn't stopped for a snack, she'd be hungry now.
2 I went to the party. I'm friends with Erdem.
3 I didn't miss my flight. I'm not still in New York.
4 They didn't stay late. They aren't tired today.
5 She met Professor Lindley. She's doing her PhD.

7 A ▶ 6.5 CONNECTED SPEECH: elision Listen and notice how sounds are joined together in connected speech.

would /wʊd/
would have /wʊdəv/
would have been /wʊdəvbɪn/
I would have been late.

B Listen again and repeat.

SPEAKING

8 A Think about two or three of the following that have been important to you. Prepare to explain how life would be or would have been different without them.

- something you did
- someone you met
- a course you took
- a place you visited
- something you bought
- something you read or saw

If I hadn't moved to Istanbul, I wouldn't have such a good job.
If I hadn't moved to Istanbul, I wouldn't have met my husband.

B Work in groups and share your ideas.

WRITING

A THANK YOU MESSAGE; LEARN TO USE FORMAL/INFORMAL EXPRESSIONS

9 A Work in pairs and discuss. When was the last time you wrote a message to say thank you? Was it formal or informal? Why?

B Read the messages below and answer the questions.

1 Why is the writer thanking the recipient of the message?

2 Are the messages formal or informal? Which words/phrases tell you this?

To vkoch8@fastmail.com From adrianaklein@king.com

Hi Vincent,

Thanks a lot for yesterday. It was great to hang out with you and I really enjoyed the National Museum. I'll be back next month, so let's get together again.

Good luck with your exams!

Best wishes,

Adriana

To townsendk@glg.com From appleton19@creavy.com

Dear Ms Townsend,

Thank you very much for all your help in planning our annual conference. We greatly appreciated your expertise in handling the logistics and the travel arrangements. Everyone at Creavy Associates feels that the conference was a success and this is, in no small part, due to your efforts. Please send us your invoice at your earliest convenience.

I look forward to hearing from you.

Yours sincerely,

Mark Appleton

To lcahoun49@cahoun.com From deaverl@wireless.com

Hi Auntie Liz,

Thank you ever so much for the gift, which arrived today. It was really kind of you. I'll use the money for a trip to France this summer after graduation!

I hope you and Uncle Dave are well.

Love,

Lou

10 A Complete the table with phrases from the messages in Exercise 9B.

	formal	informal
starting the message		Hi … ,
expressing thanks		Thanks a lot for …
adding more information	We greatly appreciated …	
signing off	Yours sincerely,	

B Write the phrases in the box in the correct place in the table in Exercise 10A. Which phrases could be either formal or informal?

I was delighted to receive … All the best,
I had a great time. Warm regards, See you soon,
I am very grateful for your help with …
Thank you very much indeed for … Kind regards,

11 Read the scenario and write an informal thank you message to the taxi driver.

You are going home in a taxi late at night. You accidentally leave your bag in the taxi. The bag contains many important personal items. Hours later, you realise what has happened and you cannot remember anything about the taxi. Two days later the bag arrives at your home, with an informal note:

Hi. You left this bag in my taxi on Saturday. I found your address on two envelopes in the bag.

Haluk

HGF Taxi Service
645 Morton Way
TD56NG
HGF

You check the bag and everything is there. Your taxi driver has saved the day!

6.3 THE GOOD LIFE

F asking for and expressing agreement/disagreement
V happiness
P intonation: showing agreement/disagreement

A

B

C

D

VOCABULARY

HAPPINESS

1 A Work in pairs. Discuss the questions.

1 Do any of the situations in the photos make you happy? Why/Why not?
2 What things made you happy in the last twenty-four hours? Compare with your partner.

B Read the article. Why are the Danish so happy?

The happiest people on the planet?

Denmark has frequently been ranked the happiest nation on the planet in world happiness reports. It seems that the Danes really **are on top of the world**, despite living in a country that has sixteen hours of darkness in winter, depriving them of that vital ingredient to happiness: sunshine. So how come the Danes always manage to **look on the bright side**? What are their secrets? What keeps the world's happiest people smiling through the winter months?

One secret seems to be the idea of Hygge (pronounced Hoo-gah). This Danish concept of living cosily incorporates the idea of coming inside to the warm and enjoying a hot chocolate or some kind of treat. It's about **taking pleasure in** the small things, being nice to yourself. It's about **having a good time** with family and friends. The true essence of Hygge is the pursuit of everyday happiness by **living in the moment**. The Danish seem to **be contented** with their lives – they trust one another, have a better work-life balance and are less stressed. No wonder they're so happy.

C Match the phrases in bold in the article with definitions 1–6.

when someone:

1 always tries to see the positive side of a situation ________
2 feels like things couldn't get any better ________
3 likes to focus on the present ________
4 enjoys (doing) something ________
5 is enjoying themselves in a particular situation ________
6 is generally happy ________

D Work in pairs and discuss. What do you think of the ideas in the article? Is it possible to measure a nation's happiness? Are there other reasons the Danes might be happy?

page 125 **VOCABULARYBANK**

FUNCTION

ASKING FOR AND EXPRESSING AGREEMENT/ DISAGREEMENT

2 A 6.6 Listen to two people discussing their golden rules for a happy life. Number the ideas in the box in the order they mention them. Which idea do they NOT mention?

preparing and eating good food	spending time in nature
getting eight hours of sleep	living in the moment
focusing on the simple things in life	listening to music
going out with good friends	

B What do the speakers say about each topic? Do you agree?

3 A Listen again. Who says the following, the man (M) or the woman (W)?

1 Oh that scenery must be just breathtaking!
2 I felt this real stillness.
3 Music is one of my keys to happiness.
4 It's all about living in the moment.
5 I have to change something about my lifestyle.
6 I never cook for myself.
7 To be happy, you've got to put good food into your system.

B Look at how speakers use tags to ask for agreement. What tags could you put at the end of statements 1–5 below?

asking for agreement
That's definitely one of the keys, **isn't it**? Getting eight hours of sleep, **right**? It's so important, **isn't it**? You like listening to music, **don't you**?

1 It's all about living in the moment, ________?
2 Getting enough sleep is really important, ________?
3 You have to put good food into your system, ________?
4 It's about having the right work-life balance, ________?
5 You enjoy cooking, ________?

speakout TIP

We use question tags to encourage interaction in a conversation. We say, 'You remember …, don't you?' and 'It's beautiful here, isn't it?' Sometimes we use shorter tags like 'right?' 'yes?' 'no?' and 'OK?'. For example, 'You're coming back, right?' or 'You're hungry, yes?' Which shorter tags could you use to complete the statements in Exercise 3B?

C Do the responses in the box show agreement (A) or disagreement (D)?

Yes, definitely. Really? I don't think so. It really does! Absolutely. I (totally) agree. That's right./You're so right. No way! Not necessarily. No doubt about it. Totally! Tell me about it! I'd say the opposite. That's so true./That's probably true.

▷ page 114 **LANGUAGEBANK**

4 A ▶ 6.7 **INTONATION: showing agreement/disagreement** Listen to the responses in Exercise 3C. Notice how the speakers use intonation to emphasise their opinion. When the speaker agrees, is their voice high or low? How about when they disagree?

B Listen again and repeat the responses. Copy the intonation.

C ▶ 6.8 Listen to some statements/questions. Respond using phrases from Exercise 3C.

5 A Complete the conversations with the words in the box.

opposite isn't necessarily it totally true right way

A: Being active is really important, [1]________ it?
B: Yeah, I [2]________ agree. I run to make myself feel good. Running is fantastic, [3]________?
A: No [4]________! It's so boring.

A: Having good friends is one of the most important things, isn't [5]________?
B: Yeah, that's so [6]________.

A: Eating chocolate is a great way to be happy.
B: Not [7]________. In fact, I'd say the [8]________. I don't really eat chocolate.

B Work in pairs. Practise the conversations in Exercise 5A.

LEARN TO

AGREE USING SYNONYMS

6 A In a conversation, we often use synonyms to agree with someone. Underline the synonyms in these conversations.

1 **A:** Oh that scenery must be just breathtaking!
B: Oh it's incredible!
2 **A:** Yes, definitely.
B: Absolutely.

B Match sentences 1–6 to responses a)–f). Underline the synonyms which helped you.

1 This music's got great rhythm.
2 The traffic is crazy today.
3 It's hot in here, isn't it?
4 You're busy, right?
5 I've never seen such a huge painting.
6 There were so many people at the concert.

a) You're right. It was enormous.
b) Yes, it's boiling.
c) It was absolutely packed.
d) Definitely. I really like the beat.
e) Yeah, I'm in a bit of a hurry.
f) I know. It's really mad.

SPEAKING

7 A Think about your own golden rules for a good life. Write them in a circle.

B Work in pairs and compare your ideas. Decide on the five most important rules and write them in a new circle.

C Work in groups. Compare your ideas again and decide on the five most important rules from your group. Share them with the class.

6.4 HELPING HAND

DVD PREVIEW

1 A **Work in pairs. Tell your partner about three good things you have done for other people this week.**

B **You are going to watch some street interviews. The interviewer asks about helping others, being helped and making the world a better place. Who is the most helpful person you know? What does he/she do to help others?**

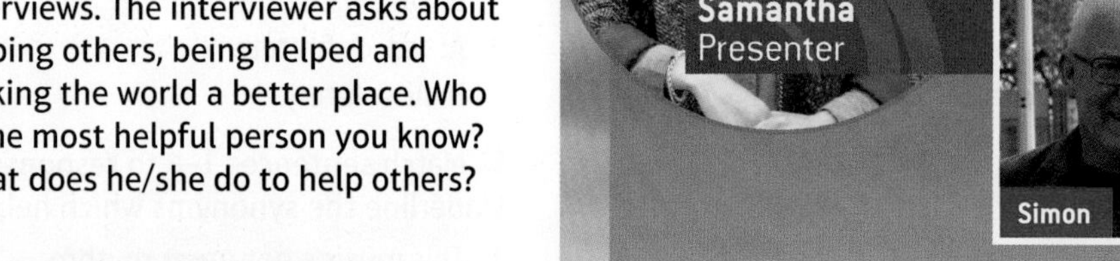

DVD VIEW

2 A **Watch Part 1. Samantha helped her neighbours. Who did Chris, Simon and Russell help? Write the name of the speaker next to the correct answer.**

1 a woman on a bus __________
2 people in the community __________
3 a colleague __________
4 refugees __________

B **How did the speakers help these people?**

C **Complete the lines from the video with one word in each gap. Watch again to check your answers.**

1 I try and __________ **a hand** whenever they need something done.
2 But it was **for a** __________ **cause** and worth it.
3 I **was** __________ **to help** her buy the ticket.

D **What do the phrases in bold in Exercise 2C mean? Match them with a)–c).**

a) could assist
b) help
c) for an important and worthwhile reason

E **Complete the sentences with your own ideas. Compare your sentences with other students.**

1 I might lend someone a hand if …
2 If it's for a good cause, I'm happy to …
3 I'm always glad to be able to help …

3 A **Watch Part 2 and answer the questions.**

1 What did Simon receive?
2 How did a singing teacher help Juliet 'for three years'?
3 What was the big change in Roxanne's life and who helped her?

B **Work in pairs. What other details can you remember? Tell your partner. Watch again to check.**

4 A **Watch Part 3. Number the issues in the order you hear about them.**

a) diversity in the arts
b) refugees
c) mental health issues
d) social justice for children/trafficking

B **Complete the lines from the video with one word in each gap. What do the phrases in bold mean?**

1 People who **are** __________ **need of** support and help … need those who will listen to them.
2 Children and trafficking … that's really __________ **to my heart**.
3 … to not **put on a** __________ and pretend that everything's OK when it's not.
4 I'm **very passionate** __________ diversity in the arts.

C **Work in pairs and compare your answers. Watch again to check your answers.**

5 A **Watch Part 4. Who says these things: Chris, Juliet or Roxanne?**

1 'Kindness goes a long way.'
2 'Be open about things people are passionate about.'
3 'Just smile.'
4 'Being respectful is something everyone should practise.'
5 'Say nice things to each other.'
6 'Get active around those causes.'

B **Watch again to check your answers . Which statement from Exercise 5A (1–6) do you think is the best answer to the question? Work in pairs and discuss.**

speakout a group discussion

6 A Read the questions and think about your answers.

1 Can you remember a time when someone helped you? When? What did they do?
2 When people are in need, who should help them: governments, charities, family? Why?
3 Are there any causes that are important to you?
4 What could people do to make the world a better place?

B Work in groups and share your ideas from Exercise 6A.

writeback a short essay

7 A Read the essay. What cause does the writer support? Why is he so passionate about one particular organisation?

A good cause

A cause that is close to my heart is medical aid for people who are desperately in need. With this in mind, I want to describe the incredible work done by Médecins Sans Frontières (MSF). This organisation provides doctors, medicine and medical equipment wherever it's urgently needed.

The organisation was founded in 1971 and it has offices in twenty-eight countries. It employs 35,000 people. These aren't all doctors and nurses; MSF needs managers to deal with the logistics of serving so many people. And the number of patients? According to MSF's website, they've served over 100 million people. And all for free.

The thing I like most about MSF is that it's apolitical. It brings aid after natural and man-made disasters: earthquakes, hurricanes, epidemics, wars and refugee crises, and provides assistance regardless of the race, colour, gender, or religious beliefs of the people. I think this is rare in the world today. For me, the doctors and nurses who work for MSF are real heroes, and the organisation fully deserved its 1999 Nobel Peace Prize.

Jean Belfort-Ferly

B Write a short essay about a good cause (150–200 words). Say what it is and why it's important to you.

G MODALS

1 A Complete the sentences with the words in the box.

might be	could	must be
won't be	can't be	should

1 I'm sure it ________ necessary but bring your passport, just in case.
2 Being a fireman ________ an incredibly difficult job. You have to be so brave.
3 If he gets good results in his exams, he ________ able to get a job at the university.
4 **A:** Is that Sylvia over there?
B: No, it ________. She's gone to Malta on holiday.
5 We'd better get ready. The guests ________ be here in about an hour.
6 A swim in the sea? That ________ be the best idea you've had all day!

B Work in pairs. Discuss the following.

1 a job you think could be interesting
2 something that can't be good for you
3 a holiday that must be one of the best you ever had

V EXTREME ADJECTIVES

2 A Underline the correct alternatives to complete the sentences.

1 We were really scared. The film was *gigantic/terrifying*.
2 The views from the villa were absolutely *spotless/stunning*.
3 There were loads of people at the exhibition. It was *astonished/packed*.
4 It's the ugliest building in the city. It's *stunning/hideous*.
5 We looked at the wedding photos; the bride looked *gorgeous/terrifying* in her lovely dress.
6 It's a very dirty place. The streets around there are *gorgeous/filthy*.
7 I couldn't believe my eyes. I was *ancient/astonished*.

B Work in pairs. Answer the questions.

1 Where is the most ancient place you have been? OR What is the most ancient building in your town/city?
2 Describe somewhere in your town/city that is usually packed.
3 What do you think councils should do about streets which are filthy?
4 Think of a time when you were astonished.
5 Is your house/bedroom usually spotless or filthy?
6 Have you ever seen a terrifying film?

V MONEY

3 A Find ten words connected with money in the word square.

r	e	w	a	r	d	a	s	c	f
s	a	v	i	n	g	s	a	e	a
d	s	v	a	w	e	a	l	t	h
a	d	g	w	q	d	i	a	l	l
s	n	f	e	u	i	n	r	j	e
c	u	r	r	e	n	c	y	f	i
d	o	n	a	t	i	o	n	u	d
e	c	v	r	e	u	m	k	n	o
b	a	i	p	o	v	e	r	t	y
t	a	f	f	o	r	d	o	j	l

B Work in pairs and take turns to do the following. Student A: describe one of the words in the word square. Student B: guess which word your partner is describing.

G THIRD AND MIXED CONDITIONALS

4 A What would the situation be now? Write sentences about these situations.

1 if money hadn't been invented
2 if the internet had been made illegal
3 if television hadn't been invented

B What would or wouldn't have happened in the past? Write sentences about these situations.

1 if Europeans hadn't colonised other continents
2 if electricity hadn't been discovered
3 if someone had discovered a cure for cancer
4 if private cars had been banned seventy years ago

C Work in groups and compare your ideas. Would the world be a better place if these ideas were real?

F ASKING FOR AND EXPRESSING AGREEMENT/ DISAGREEMENT

5 A Put the words in the correct order to complete B's responses.

1 **A:** It's a good idea to start work early, isn't it?
B: right / you're / so
2 **A:** You can only fight war with war, right?
B: say / opposite / I'd / the
3 **A:** If you want to improve, you just have to practise.
B: true / probably / that's
4 **A:** German grammar is so difficult, isn't it?
B: about / me / tell / it!
5 **A:** You have to be really dedicated to want to work here.
B: doubt / about / no / it
6 **A:** It feels like summer today.
B: does / really / it

B Work in pairs. Practise the conversations in Exercise 5A, focusing on your intonation.

7 arts

OUTSIDER ART p80

THE POWER OF MUSIC p83

LIFE HACKS p86

GRAFFITI p88

SPEAKING **7.1** Discuss art and creativity **7.2** Talk about music **7.3** Tell someone about a skill **7.4** Talk about a cultural experience

LISTENING **7.2** Listen to someone talking about their musical tastes **7.3** Listen to a conversation about life hacks **7.4** Watch a BBC news report about Taiwanese street artists

READING **7.1** Read about outsider art **7.3** Read about life hacks

WRITING **7.2** Write an essay **7.4** Write a review

7.1 OUTSIDER ART

- **G** making comparisons; *so/such*
- **P** connected speech: *schwa* in comparatives
- **V** visual arts; multi-word verbs

A

B

C

GRAMMAR

MAKING COMPARISONS; *SO/SUCH*

1 Look at the pictures. Do you like any of these artworks? Which is your favourite and why? Which do you like the least? Do you have a favourite artist or artists?

2 A In your opinion, which sentences describe which artwork?

This artwork is:

1 more realistic than the others.
2 the most abstract.
3 as good as a Picasso!
4 almost as famous as the artist who painted it.
5 so strange I don't know if it's really art.
6 such a beautiful picture that it must be worth a lot.

B Underline the phrases we use for comparing/describing in sentences 1–6 in Exercise 2A.

more realistic than the others

C Check what you know. Complete the rules with the words in the box.

such so *as* + adjective + *as* more the most/the least

RULES

1 Comparatives use *-er* with short adjectives and ________ with long adjectives.
2 Superlatives use *-est* with short adjectives and ________ with long adjectives.
3 Use ________ + article (+ adjective) + noun to describe something that leads to a result or to show strong feelings about something. An adjective often comes before the noun.
4 Use ________ + adjective/adverb to describe something that leads to a result or to show strong feelings about something.
5 Use ________ to say something is equal to another thing. We can use *nearly* or *almost* to say the two things are not exactly the same.

▷ page 116 **LANGUAGEBANK**

3 A ▶ 7.1 CONNECTED SPEECH: *schwa* in comparatives
Answer the questions. Then listen and check.

1 In connected speech, how do we pronounce *as* in *as good as*?
2 How do we pronounce *than* in comparatives?

B ▶ 7.2 Listen and repeat.

4 Complete the second sentence so that it means the same as the first, using the word in bold.

1 The weather was beautiful, so we went for a picnic.
It was ________ day that we went for a picnic. **beautiful**
2 Marissa has more friends than anyone else.
Marissa is ________ person. **popular**
3 Behir was brilliant at football – a professional club wanted to sign him.
Behir was ________ at football that a professional club wanted to sign him. **good**
4 This was the most boring presentation I've seen.
This was the ________ presentation I've seen. **interesting**
5 It's a lovely necklace, but the other one is more beautiful.
It's lovely, but it's not ________ the other necklace. **gorgeous**
6 The Metropolitan Museum of Art is huge, but the Louvre in France is slightly bigger.
The Metropolitan Museum of Art is nearly ________ the Louvre in France. **big**
7 Maya danced brilliantly and won.
Maya was ________ dancer that she won. **brilliant**
8 He was growing too fast and they thought something was wrong with him.
He was growing ________ that they thought something was wrong with him. **quickly**

5 Make sentences about the artworks in Exercise 1. Use the structures in the Rules box and the adjectives in this box. Then work in pairs and share your sentences.

beautiful ugly interesting strange famous good

I think the first piece of art is the most beautiful.

READING

6 A Work in pairs and discuss. Which statement best matches your opinion of modern art? Why?

1 I love it.
2 I like some of it.
3 I can't stand most of it.
4 I don't know much about it.

B You are going to read about *outsider art*. What do you think this term means? Read the article to find out.

7 A Read the article again. These statements are all false. Why? Underline the parts of the article that tell you.

1 Outsider art is produced by people who went to art school.
2 Outsider art usually consists of oil paintings.
3 William Edmondson is a recent outsider artist from the USA.
4 Guo Fengyi made art out of rubber.
5 The Venice Biennale refuses to show outsider art.
6 There is less interest in outsider art now than in the past.

B Work in groups. Discuss the questions.

1 'Modern art can be strange.' Some people think modern art looks like children's art and anyone could do it. Do you agree? Why/Why not?
2 Do you think outsider art is 'real art'?

Outsider art: how it found its way in

Modern art can be strange. Here's some of the work that's turned up in galleries: a sliced-up shark, a video of a wall falling down, a **self-portrait** made of wire and string, lights going on and off. No wonder someone said about the modern art scene, 'The lunatics have taken over the asylum.'

And there's also the rise of outsider art. What exactly is it? It's art produced by people who are on the edges of society: prisoners or people with mental illness, who are untrained as artists.

They often have a history of institutionalisation (orphanage, asylum, prison), little or no education and an obsession with art-making. Their work tends to show fantasy worlds and extreme mental states, and it's made of anything that comes to hand.

In the past, art meant **oil paintings** and **watercolours**. These were painted using a **canvas** that was placed on an **easel**. The artist would do a **sketch** first, using a pencil or perhaps **charcoal**. Then he or she would apply the paint with a **paintbrush**. In contrast, outsider art can mean **sculptures** of gorillas made of tin foil, plastic *Star Wars* figures glued to boards, chairs made of chicken bones and stuffed squirrels fitted with angels' wings.

William Edmondson

So what's happening now? It seems that outsider art is becoming insider art. At a recent Venice Biennale, one of the world's biggest art exhibitions, the main attraction was an **installation**: *Il Palazzo Enciclopedico*. This was a copy of a 1950s work by self-taught Italian Marino Auriti (1891–1980). According to the Biennale's artistic director, Auriti had built 'an imaginary museum that was meant to house all worldly knowledge – from the wheel to the satellite'.

Why is outsider art suddenly popular? For several years there's been a growing interest in 'alternative' art: graffiti, **collage**, handmade objects, digital photography and **multimedia** works. As a result, major museums and galleries are starting to exhibit the work of self-taught artists and art dealers are capitalising. Among today's finest outsider artists are the Dutchman Huub Niessen, whose drawings are in permanent collections all over Europe, and the Brazilian Marilena Pelosi, who says, 'If I didn't draw, I would die.'

One of the earliest outsider artists was William Edmondson (1874–1951). The son of former slaves, Edmondson was a self-taught sculptor and the first African American to have an exhibition at the Museum of Modern Art, in 1937.

Another outsider artist was Guo Fengyi (1942–2010), from China, who made ink drawings. She had worked in a rubber factory but retired at thirty-nine because of ill health. Later she began to have visions – for example, of imaginary beasts and angels – which she included in her work.

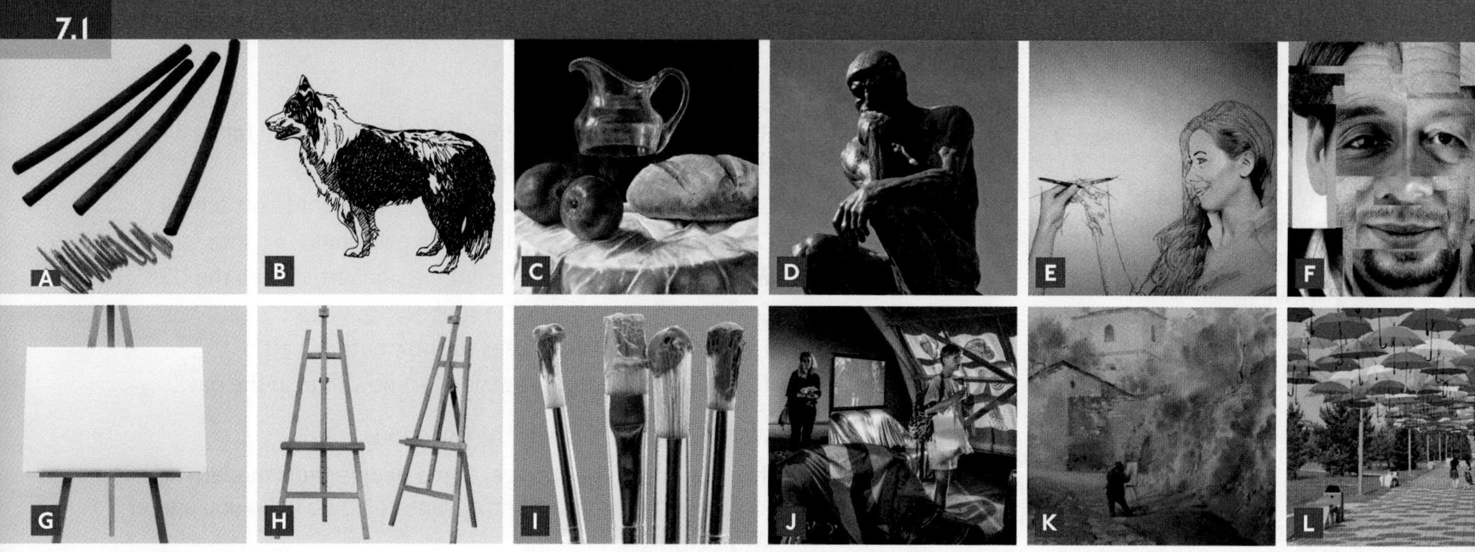

VOCABULARY

VISUAL ARTS

8 A **Look at the words in bold in the article on page 81. Which of the items can you see in the photos?**

B **Work in pairs. Discuss the questions.**

1. Have you, or has anyone you know, created the types of art above (paintings, sculptures, etc.)?
2. Have you been to any art galleries? If so, which? What did you see that you liked/disliked?
3. What sculptures are in your town/city? What are they like?
4. Has anyone ever made a portrait of you? When? What did you think of it?

▷ page 126 **VOCABULARYBANK**

VOCABULARY PLUS

MULTI-WORD VERBS 2

9 A **Find and underline twelve multi-word verbs in the quiz below. What do they mean? Use a dictionary to help you.**

B **Do the quiz. Then work in pairs and compare your answers. Check your answers on page 130. Are the results accurate about you?**

▷ page 126 **VOCABULARYBANK**

speakout TIP

Here are some ways to use creativity to help you learn English:

1. Make up sentences, conversations and stories that use new vocabulary.
2. Keep a journal in English. Describe your day but invent one imaginary thing every day.
3. Use illustrations instead of words to explain the grammar you learn.

Have you tried any of these? Try doing one for a week. Report back to other students on how effective it is.

How creative are you?

Choose a), b) or c).

1 You're looking after your friend's three small children. What do you do with them?

a) make up stories and have the kids perform with costumes
b) take the children for a walk in the park
c) turn on the TV and find the cartoon channel

2 A machine breaks down. You spend the day trying and failing to fix it. What do you do next?

a) read a novel or poetry, sleep and try again the next day
b) call a friend for help
c) give up and throw away the machine

3 A relative is celebrating her 100th birthday! What do you do?

a) make her a collage with images of the last 100 years
b) shop around for the most beautiful gift you can afford
c) buy a card with a birthday message

4 A friend asks you to design a logo for her new business. What do you do?

a) spend a day sketching until you come up with a perfect design
b) copy something from the internet (no one will notice)
c) turn her down and tell her to find a real designer

5 Ten foreign students are visiting your city. You must arrange a programme. What do you do?

a) make three programmes – they choose their favourite
b) arrange visits to the city's four most famous attractions
c) put them on a tour bus – you can count on a tour guide to do the job

6 You organise a celebration picnic for a friend. It starts raining heavily. What do you do?

a) make a canopy between two trees – and still have the picnic
b) invite everyone to your house instead
c) call it off – there's no way to have a picnic in the rain

THE POWER OF MUSIC

G *be/get used to* vs *used to*
V music
P the letter *A*

SPEAKING

1 Work in pairs or groups. Do the questionnaire.

Let's talk about music

1. What kind of music do you enjoy listening to?
2. When/Where do you usually listen to music?
3. What was the last piece of music you listened to? Why?
4. What was the first song/musician you can remember really enjoying?
5. Do you play music when you work/study? Why/Why not?
6. Do you have a particular song that makes you happy/sad? What is it?
7. Is there any music you really cannot stand?
8. Have you ever been to see your favourite musicians live? Where? When?
9. Have your musical tastes changed over the last 5–10 years? How?
10. Do you believe music has the power to change people? How important do you think music is to society in general?

VOCABULARY

MUSIC

2 A Match the words in the box with definitions 1–12.

album rhythm lyrics track rave download rap techno speakers number one fan dance music

1. electrical devices used to allow you to hear sound or music ________
2. a collection of songs or pieces of music recorded together ________
3. a huge party involving dancing, often in a big space with hundreds of people ________
4. the words to a song ________
5. the beat of the music ________
6. a type of electronic music which is intended for dancing to in clubs ________
7. the most popular song in the charts (with the most sales) ________
8. a way to access music which is stored online ________
9. one of several pieces of music on a CD or musical recording ________
10. someone who particularly likes a type of music ________
11. a type of popular music with a heavy beat and a vocalist speaking over the top ________
12. a form of electronic dance music that began during the 80s ________

B 7.3 **THE LETTER *A*** How is the letter *a* pronounced in the words in the box? Write them in the correct place in the table. Then listen and check your answers.

favourite class party fan album shake last tape track

/eɪ/	/æ/	/ɑː/
rave	rap	dance

C Choose two or three words from Exercise 2A. Use them to write questions to ask other students.

Do you have a favourite album?
What was the last track you downloaded?

D Work in groups. Ask and answer your questions.

LISTENING

3 A 7.4 **Listen to Anya talking about her musical tastes. Are the statements true (T) or false (F)?**

1 Anya likes listening to lots of different types of music.
2 In the past Anya listened to music in the car with her mum.
3 Anya didn't enjoy dance music when she was younger.
4 She's a massive fan of country music.
5 Anya's mother had a wide taste in music.
6 Anya's **musical** tastes have changed a lot since she was a child.

B Match 1–10 with a)–j) to complete Anya's sentences. Then listen again and check.

1 I've always been a
2 My mum used to have so many
3 I used to listen to
4 We'd listen to a tape, or whatever,
5 She had such an eclectic
6 I've always listened to
7 It started when
8 I used to go to, like, raves
9 One thing I can't get into is
10 It's the sort of music that

a) that we'd chosen from the supermarket at the weekend.
b) makes my toes curl.
c) for young people when I was at school.
d) I was about thirteen years old.
e) massive fan of music.
f) CDs and tapes and records.
g) country and western.
h) all sorts of things.
i) taste in music.
j) electronic music and dance music.

C Answer the questions.

1 What do you think it means to be a 'massive fan' of something?
2 If you have 'an eclectic taste in music', do you like lots of different types of music?
3 If you 'can't get into' something, have you tried to enjoy it or not?
4 If something 'makes your toes curl', do you think that's a positive or negative reaction?
5 Can you think of something that 'makes your toes curl', something you 'can't get into' and something you are 'a massive fan' of? Work in pairs and tell your partner about them.

GRAMMAR

BE/GET USED TO VS USED TO

4 A Read the sentences. What is the difference in meaning between the underlined forms (*used to*, *get used to* and *be used to*)? Which form is followed by an infinitive without *to*? Which are followed by a noun/*-ing* form?

1 I <u>used to</u> go to raves when I was younger.
2 I cannot <u>get used to</u> country and western music.
3 I'<u>m used to</u> singing in front of an audience.

B Complete rules 1–3 with phrases a)–c).

RULES

1 ________ is for talking about something you are accustomed to doing; it's usual for you to do this.
2 ________ is for talking about something you become accustomed to; it is no longer unusual or strange.
3 ________ is for talking about a habit or state in the past, which you don't do now.

a) *get used to* + noun/*-ing* form
b) *used to* + infinitive without *to*
c) *be used to* + noun/*-ing* form

▷ page 116 **LANGUAGEBANK**

5 Circle the correct answer, a) or b) to complete the sentences.

1 I ________ play the piano, but I stopped when I left home.
a) get used to **b)** used to
2 I can't ________ used to the taste of this coffee. It's too bitter.
a) be **b)** get
3 She ________ paint but then she started working on sculptures.
a) got used to **b)** used to
4 Remember to drive on the left. It's tricky at first but you'll ________ used to it.
a) get **b)** be
5 I really can't ________ waking up so early. I'm tired all the time.
a) get used to **b)** used to
6 Don't worry. He's a journalist, so he ________ people disagreeing with him.
a) used to **b)** is used to
7 When I was younger, I ________ a lot of basketball.
a) used to play **b)** get used to playing
8 He used to ________ a long distance runner when he was at school.
a) being **b)** be

6 Work in pairs. Talk about these things.

1 something you used to do as a child but you don't do any more
2 a hobby that you started. Was there anything that was difficult to get used to?
3 things you are used to doing every day (drinking tea, sitting in traffic, etc.)
4 music that your parents used to listen to
5 something you will never get used to

WRITING

AN ESSAY; LEARN TO USE PARALLELISM

7 A Work in pairs. Complete the essay writing tips with the words in the box.

conclusion topic sentence introduction paragraph main idea quotations

Essay writing tips

1 **Introduction:** the purpose of the introduction is to present your [1]________ on the topic. The essay should begin with a 'hook'– something to grab the reader's attention and make them want to read on. Examples of good hooks are relevant [2]________ or surprising statistics. You can also use a strong descriptive image or statement. The introduction should also tell us what to expect from the rest of the essay.

2 **Body paragraphs:** Each [3]________ should exemplify a different point. Begin the paragraph with a [4]________ that expresses the main idea of the paragraph. Then give some supporting details or examples of what you're talking about.

3 **[5]________:** the concluding paragraph should repeat the ideas you mention in your [6]________, even using the same language sometimes, to reinforce the message.

B Read the essay below. Find an example of each of the ideas mentioned in the tips in Exercise 7A.

C Do you agree with the points in the essay? Is there anything that you find surprising/interesting?

The power of music

Music is an integral part of our lives. We carry it in our pockets and blast it from the rooftops. It controls our emotions and our behaviour and it can even help us to make friends. As Henry Wadsworth Longfellow said, 'Music is the universal language of mankind'.

Music affects our memories and our emotions. We remember the music that was playing at weddings and funerals or during a special holiday together. We can use music to change our mood. Just think about how your emotions are affected by the soundtrack when you watch a scary scene in a movie.

Our brains are also affected by music. Music can help to relieve stress and depression, and even helps people to sleep better. Music affects our behaviour in other ways too. When calming music is played in shopping centres, people tend to walk more slowly and buy more. When we listen to loud music in the gym, we tend to work faster and do more exercise. Music can even make us more intelligent. People who listen to Mozart before doing an IQ test perform better. This is known as the 'Mozart effect'.

Lastly, music has an incredible power to bring people together, even when they don't speak the same language. Music and singing have been used by societies all around the world to help social groups to bond more strongly. Think about the way football fans sing and chant. There's no doubt about it, music has always been a fundamental part of our society, for all of these reasons, and perhaps for others we don't even know. The power of music is simply magical.

8 Read the sentences. Which sounds better, a) or b)? Why?

1 a) Writing essays takes time and you have to be careful and you have to think a lot.
 b) Writing essays takes time, care and a lot of thought.

2 a) I enjoy cooking, jogging and I like to read books.
 b) I enjoy cooking, jogging and reading books.

3 a) When people get together, they like to sing and enjoy dancing and having a good time.
 b) When people get together, they like to sing, dance and have a good time.

speakout TIP

Parallelism is the use of a repeated grammatical structure in a sentence to add rhythm and balance, e.g. *I listen to music when I'm working, studying and driving.*
Find examples of parallelism in the essay in Exercises 7B and 8.

9 Circle the best answer, a) or b), to complete the sentences from an essay on the power of love.

1 When you feel loved,
 a) you feel sure of yourself and you are protected and have confidence in yourself.
 b) you feel secure, protected and confident.

2 I think love is more important than
 a) money, cars or other material possessions.
 b) how much money you have or if you have a big car or other things you can buy with lots of money.

3 Everybody needs
 a) love and everybody needs to be happy, and to feel secure.
 b) love, happiness and security.

10 Write an essay with the title *The power of ...* . Follow these steps.

1 Choose one of the topics from the box or another of your choice.

love politics money exercise meditation sport literature art conversation education

2 Do some research and plan your essay. Think about the writing tips in Exercise 7A.
3 Write a first draft of the essay (400 words).
4 Check your work. Can you improve your writing by using parallelism?

7.3 LIFE HACKS

F responding to suggestions
P intonation: sounding positive or negative
V everyday objects

A
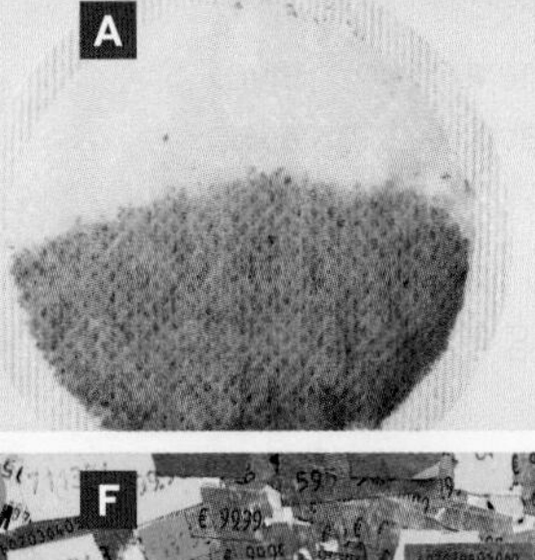
B
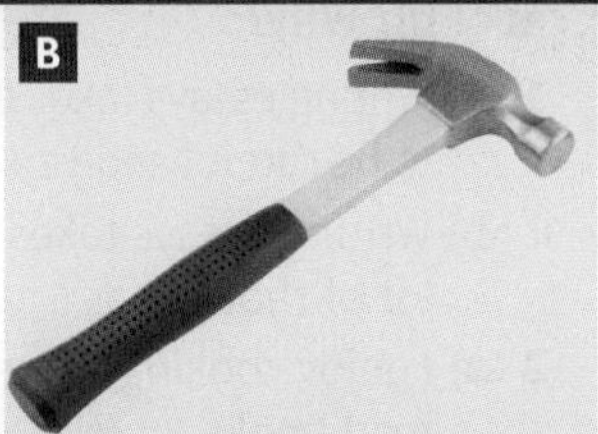
C

D
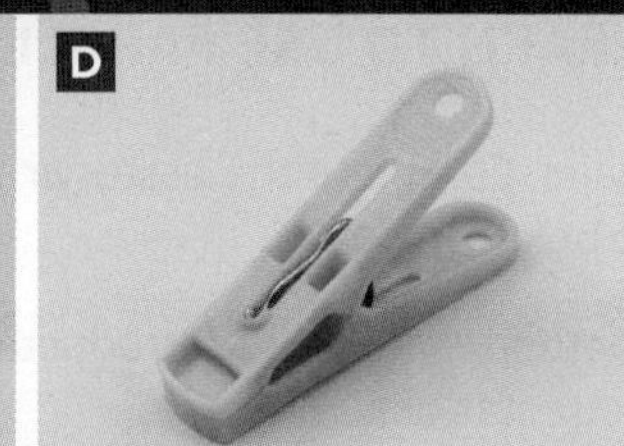
E
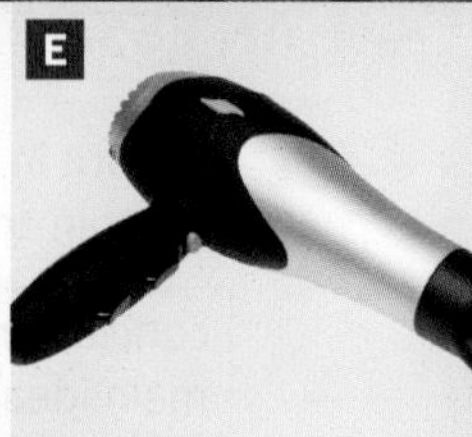
F

G

H

I

J

VOCABULARY

EVERYDAY OBJECTS

1 Match the words in the box with photos A–J.

sponge wrapping paper tea bag price tag hairdryer electric fan hammer watering can paper towel clothes peg

2 Read about some life hacks (creative ideas to make everyday life easier). Which of these ideas do you like? Which do you think are the most useful?

10 Life hacks

1 Smelly shoes? Put dry tea bags in them to absorb the smell.

2 After washing the dishes, put the sponge in the microwave for two minutes. This kills germs.

3 If a metal object is rusting, soak it in salt and vinegar overnight.

4 If someone spills ink, use milk to clean it. To remove grass stains, use vinegar. To remove make-up, use shaving cream.

5 Need to remove a sticky price tag without making a mess? Use a hairdryer to blow warm air on it. The glue will melt, making it easy to remove.

6 If you burn yourself, put yellow mustard on the burn and then wash the area with cold water.

7 Cut open old toilet rolls and use them as a cuff to hold wrapping paper.

8 Worried about burning your fingers when lighting candles? Use a lighted piece of spaghetti instead of a match.

9 No watering can for watering the plants? Put holes into the top of a plastic bottle and fill it with water.

10 Need to make your drink colder? Wrap a wet paper towel around the bottle and put it in the freezer. It will be ice cold in fifteen minutes.

FUNCTION

RESPONDING TO SUGGESTIONS

3 A 7.5 Listen to a conversation about life hacks. What life hacks does the woman mention?

B Answer the questions. Then listen again and check your answers.

1 How can you stop your clothes from wrinkling in a suitcase?
2 How can you stop dirty clothes from smelling in a suitcase?
3 What should you do if a mosquito bites you?
4 What should you do if mosquitoes are buzzing around you?
5 What container can you make to stop your valuables from being stolen at the beach?
6 What can you do if you're caught in the rain and you're on the street?

4 A 7.6 Complete the extracts from the recording. Use one word in each gap. Then listen again and check your answers.

1 **A:** If you're travelling and you have dirty laundry, keep it in a separate plastic bag, but put a bar of scented soap in the bag as well.
B: To stop the clothes from smelling bad?
A: Yep.
B: That's a good ________.

2 **A:** Lick your finger and dip it in salt. Then rub the mixture of salt and saliva on the bite. It heals after a few minutes.
B: Oh wow – **that** ________ **so easy**! I'll try it.

3 **A:** You switch on a fan and sit in the breeze. Mosquitoes are very light and can't fly in the wind.
B: Oh, ________**'s good**.

4 **A:** First, you clean it out. Then you cut the top off so you can fit your phone, keys and money in it. Then you fit the top back on. If it looks old and nasty, people are much less likely to steal it.
B: I get it. **That's** ________ **a good idea**.

B The man in the recording responds to suggestions in different ways. Look at the phrases in bold for responding to suggestions in Exercise 4A. Write them in the correct place in the table.

questions	*To stop the clothes from smelling bad?*
a *so* or *such sentence*	
***that sounds/that's* + adjective (e.g. *great, amazing, interesting, terrible*)**	
***how* + adjective**	
one-word comment	

C Write the phrases in the box in the correct place in the table in Exercise 4B.

Brilliant! You're so clever! How awful! Is it really?
That's wonderful! That sounds terrible!
Congratulations! Excellent! How interesting!
That sounds amazing! That's unfair! Are you serious?
That's such a nice thing to do. Great!

▷ page 116 **LANGUAGEBANK**

5 A Underline the correct alternatives to complete the conversations.

1 **A:** To get rid of a cold, you should rest and drink hot tea with honey.
B: *How awful!/Congratulations!/That sounds good.*

2 **A:** Use the sticky part of a Post-it note to clean between the keys on your keyboard.
B: *Is it?/You're so clever!/Does it really?* I've been trying to clean my keyboard for ages!

3 **A:** If you're feeling miserable, clean out your cupboards. Getting rid of old stuff will cheer you up.
B: *That's a good idea./That sounds terrible!/Do they really?*

4 **A:** If you often forget where you parked in a multi-storey car park, take a photo of the floor number.
B: *That sounds amazing!/That's such a kind thing to do./ Brilliant!*

5 **A:** If you run out of shaving cream, use olive oil. It works just as well.
B: Olive oil on my face? *Are you serious?/How sweet!/ That's very nice of you.*

6 **A:** I've been eating carrots to improve my eyesight, but now my skin has turned orange!
B: Oh no. *Is it really?/That sounds terrible!/That's unfair!*

B ▶ 7.7 **INTONATION: sounding positive or negative** Listen to the conversations from Exercise 5A and repeat B's responses. Copy the intonation.

LEARN TO

AGREE USING *ME TOO/ME NEITHER*

6 Read conversations 1 and 2 and complete rules a) and b).

1 **A:** Mosquitoes love me.
B: Me too.

2 **A:** I don't think this plan will work.
B: Me neither.

RULES
a) To agree with a positive statement, use *me* ________.
b) To agree with a negative statement, use *me* ________.

7 A ▶ 7.8 Listen to people reacting to ten statements. In which conversations (1–10) does the second speaker disagree?

B Read the sentences. Put a cross next to the ones that are NOT true for you.

1 I drink coffee every morning.
2 I don't write in a notebook.
3 I sometimes wash the dishes.
4 I don't like mustard.
5 I work long hours.
6 I don't listen to classical music.
7 I like DIY.
8 I don't have a sedentary lifestyle.
9 I water the plants at home.
10 I don't own an umbrella.

C Work in pairs. Take turns to read the sentences from Exercise 7B which are true for you. Your partner responds using *me too* or *me neither*.

A: I drink coffee every morning.
B: Me too.

D Work in pairs. Think of three true sentences each about things you do regularly. Then tell your partner, who should respond with *me too* or *me neither*.

SPEAKING

8 A Work in groups of three. Think of a skill you are good at or something you know about. What creative advice can you give to someone who wants to learn it? If you need help, Student A: turn to page 129. Student B: turn to page 130. Student C: turn to page 133. Plan what you will say to your group.

B Share your 'hacks' with your group. As you listen, respond to the suggestions.

I'm going to talk about 'exercise hacks'. These are ways to …

7.4 GRAFFITI

DVD PREVIEW

1 A Work in pairs. Discuss the questions.

1 Do you think graffiti should be legal or illegal? Why?
2 Is there any street graffiti that you like? Where? What can you remember about it?

B Read about graffiti artists in Taiwan. What has changed for Taiwanese street artists?

Taiwan opens up to graffiti artists

BBC

Walk around many cities in Europe or the US and you won't be surprised to find colourful graffiti sprayed across its walls. Graffiti used to be considered vandalism, but many countries now support and encourage street artists. In Asia, however, street artists still often face fines or even prison sentences.

In Taipei, the capital of Taiwan, new legislation means that penalties for street art are low, and artists are being given spaces to legally create their art.

The BBC team went to meet Jimmy Cheng, long-time graffiti artist and founder of the Taipei Alliance for the Advancement of Multi Art Culture Youth Center

DVD VIEW

2 A Watch the programme. Answer the questions.

1 How are attitudes to graffiti changing in Taiwan?
2 Why are they changing?
3 Do you think this change is a good thing?

B Are the statements true (T) or false (F)?

1 When Jimmy Cheng started spraying graffiti twenty years ago, Taiwanese people already had a good understanding of graffiti as a form of public art.
2 In Ximending graffiti has been legalised, with spaces for people to spray, practise or exhibit their art.
3 Before the graffiti artists arrived it was mostly vagrants and drug addicts who occupied the space.
4 At first, the artists only used Chinese, but now they include English words.
5 The fine for spraying graffiti in Taiwan is very high, so foreigners don't like to go there.
6 Taiwanese public acceptance of graffiti is higher than that in Europe or America.
7 Foreign graffiti artists exchange ideas with local Taiwanese artists.

C Watch again to check your answers.

3 Work in groups. Discuss the questions.

1 What kinds of messages or ideas do you think graffiti artists try to represent in their work?
2 Do you think graffiti art is a good way for a city to improve the look of run-down areas? What else could be done?

speakout a cultural experience

4 7.9 **Listen to Marcella talking about an art experience. Answer the questions.**

1 What does Marcella like to do when she visits a new city?
2 What was the art experience?
3 What is special about the Barranco district in Lima?
4 What did Marcella enjoy about the tour?

B Listen again and underline the alternative you hear to complete the key phrases.

KEYPHRASES

It's no secret that I [1]*love/adore* street art …
Whenever I travel to a new city, it's one of *the* [2]*first things I see/my favourite things to see* …
I love the vibrant colours and the [3]*exciting/interesting* atmosphere …
I'm always on the lookout for good [4]*art/restaurants* …
I was so [5]*thrilled/excited* when a friend told me about …
The area is [6]*inhabited/frequented* by artists, photographers and musicians.
It was really [7]*fascinating/fantastic* to hear about their history.
[8]*Undoubtedly/Unfortunately,* I would not have discovered …
To [9]*finish/top* it all, we had a wonderful lunch …
The best thing about the [10]*exhibition/tour*?

C Choose a cultural experience from the box to talk about. Before you talk, think about the questions below.

going to a music festival/gig   seeing a theatre show
visiting a place with interesting architecture
seeing interesting art

1 Where were you and who were you with?
2 What was special about the experience?
3 Would you recommend it to others? Why/Why not?

D Work in groups. Take turns to tell each other about the experience you chose. Would you be interested in trying some of the cultural experiences you heard about?

writeback a review

5 A Read the review. Would you enjoy this art experience? Why/Why not?

Shoreditch Street Art Tours

This has to be one of the best things to do in London! I went with my fourteen-year-old niece and we really enjoyed getting off the tourist trail and taking photos of the amazing art. The tour takes place in Shoreditch, an area which used to be a working-class industrial neighbourhood, but after the Second World War, fell into disrepair. Its factories and warehouses were abandoned until groups of young artists started to move in, looking for cheap studio space. Over the past twenty years, the area has been transformed and it's now an open-air gallery for some of the world's best known street artists and muralists, including Banksy and Deface. The tour takes you around the colourful and vibrant streets near Brick Lane, where you will see murals, markets, cafes, bars and galleries. You'll learn all about street culture, meet some of the artists and hear the stories that have made this area one of the world's epicentres for street art. Don't miss it.

B Write an online review of one of the cultural experiences you talked/heard about in Exercise 4C (150–200 words).

V VISUAL ARTS

1 A Add the missing letters to complete the comments by people who make art.

A 'My mother gave me a set of [1]paintb_ _ _ _es for my tenth birthday. I painted my family, using [2]water_ _ _ _urs. Then I started doing oil [3]pai_ _ _ _gs. Now I'm working on a series of [4]self-po_ _ _ _its.'

B I paint in a traditional way. I begin by making a [5]sk_ _ _ _ of my subject, using [6]ch_ _ _ _al. Then I place the [7]c_ _ _ _s on my [8]e_ _ _ _ and begin.'

B What do you remember about making art when you were younger? Do you make art now?

G MAKING COMPARISONS; *SO/SUCH*

2 A Put the words in the correct order to make sentences.

Who was the greatest: Picasso or Michelangelo?

1 Michelangelo was / that he was / a great artist / known as 'the divine one' during / such / his lifetime

2 As a sculptor, architect / greater range / and painter, / Michelangelo had a / of artistic interests / than Picasso

3 Art critic Robert / not even Michelangelo, / Hughes wrote, / had been as famous / 'No painter or sculptor, / as Picasso in / his own lifetime'

4 highest price ever paid / More of / been stolen than / and a Picasso picture also holds / Picasso's paintings have / any other artist's, / the record for the / for a painting

B Write sentences comparing people, things, places, etc. Use the words in the box. Then work in pairs and compare your ideas.

such	so	as + (adjective) + as
more	the most/the least	

G *BE/GET USED TO* VS *USED TO*

3 A Complete the texts with the words in the box.

get used to	am used to
used to do	used to be
used to it	used to

Tell us about the things you [1]__________ as a child that you don't do anymore.

Be creative. I [2]__________ so imaginative. I would draw things all the time. Now I find it really hard. My new job is in marketing though, and we have to come up with new ideas, so I'm going to have to [3]__________ thinking creatively again.

I [4]__________ play a lot of sport, so I was really fit. Nowadays, I [5]__________ sitting around all day in an office. I never do exercise. I'm really weak, so I've started to train again. It's hard, but I'm getting [6]__________.

B Work in pairs. Tell your partner about something you used to do as a child that you don't do now. Does it affect your life now?

V MUSIC

4 A Underline the correct alternatives to complete the sentences.

1 I love this new *lyrics/album*. It's got some really great *tracks/speakers* on it.
2 I'm not really a *fan/number* one of *download/dance* music. I generally don't like *techno/album*.
3 Have you heard that new *track/speakers* by Ed Sheeran? I must *techno/download* it.
4 You need to move the *number one/speakers* so they face this way. I can't hear the *rave/rhythm* properly.
5 You haven't heard of Jay Z?! He's a *rhythm/rap* artist, with several *number one/speakers* albums.

B Work in pairs. Tell your partner about these things.

1 the last piece of music you downloaded
2 whether you like techno, rap or dance music
3 what kind of music you were a fan of when you were younger

F RESPONDING TO SUGGESTIONS

5 A Complete the conversations with the words in the box.

such	idea	so	it
serious	sounds		

1 A: If you're stressed, try painting big circles. It clears your mind.
B: Are you ________?
2 A: You should exercise more. I used to run up a mountain at 6a.m. every morning.
B: That ________ terrible!
3 A: You can't sleep? Try drinking herbal tea before bed.
B: That's a good ________.
4 A: Before exams I'd always go swimming. It helped me relax.
B: That's ________ a nice thing to do.
5 A: 4a.m. is the best time to see wild animals here.
B: Is ________ really?
6 A: I just fixed the air conditioning. You should always check the filter.
B: You're ________ good at fixing things!

B Work in pairs. Read situations 1–5. Take turns to make a suggestion for each situation. Your partner responds.

Your partner:
1 can't sleep.
2 has an English exam tomorrow.
3 has a broken TV.
4 needs to find a good restaurant.
5 wants to try a new sport.

A: *I can't sleep!*
B: *You should read a boring book for thirty minutes.*
A: *That's a great idea!*

8 knowledge

ONS FROM THE PAST p92

BIG DATA p95

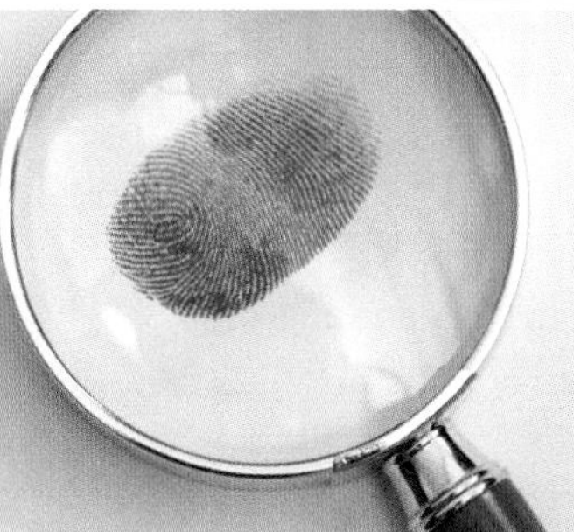

IDIOMS AND ORIGINS p98

FINDING OUT p100

SPEAKING **8.1** Tell an anecdote **8.2** Discuss big data and future predictions **8.3** Discuss some idioms **8.4** A group discussion about information and knowledge

LISTENING **8.2** Listen to a radio programme about big data **8.3** Listen to people discussing the origins of some idioms **8.4** Watch people talking about information and knowledge

READING **8.1** Read about knowledge and power **8.2** Read some facts about big data

WRITING **8.1** Write an anecdote **8.4** Write a response to a proposal

G relative clauses
P stress on lexical chunks
V lexical chunks with *make, do, take*

SPEAKING

1 Discuss with other students. Do you recognise any of the people in the pictures? If so, what do you know about them? Who are the greatest historical figures in your country?

READING

2 A Read four stories about the people in the pictures. Which do you like best?

B Each of the stories can teach us a lesson. Read stories 1–4 again and match them with lessons a)–d).

a) Work with people who have the same goals as you.
b) Know how to sell yourself.
c) Let powerful people feel important.
d) Listen to criticism.

C What do you think of these four lessons? Have any applied to you?

VOCABULARY

LEXICAL CHUNKS WITH *MAKE, DO, TAKE*

3 Find phrases with *make, do* and *take* in the stories. Match them with 1–12.

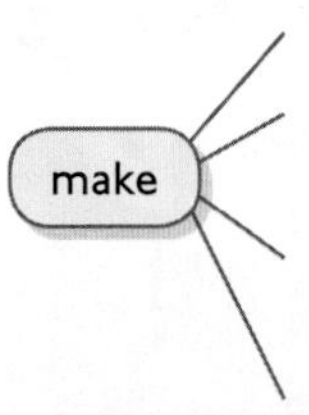

1 change things (story 1) __________
2 make an agreement or arrangement (especially in business or politics) (story 3, title) __________
3 make a formal agreement between two groups/people (story 3) __________
4 earn (story 3) __________

do

5 cause physical harm (story 1) __________
6 make a mistake (story 2) __________
7 do an important task (story 4) __________
8 do everything possible (story 4) __________

9 pay attention to someone and/or their opinion because you think it is important (story 2) __________
10 use a situation for your benefit or gain (story 3) __________
11 be in charge or become the boss of something (story 4) __________
12 accept without questioning or assume something (story 4) __________

4 A 8.1 **STRESS ON LEXICAL CHUNKS** Listen to sentences with the phrases from Exercise 3. Which words are stressed?

B Listen again and repeat.

▷ page 127 **VOCABULARYBANK**

Knowledge and power

four lessons from historical figures

1 Michelangelo pretends to sculpt

In 1502 Piero Soderini, the mayor of Florence, commissioned Michelangelo to build the statue of David. When the piece was nearly finished, Soderini, who thought he was an expert, told Michelangelo the nose was too big. The sculptor climbed a ladder with a handful of dust and a chisel. He then pretended to make alterations, tapping the chisel gently against the stone, careful not to do any damage, while dropping dust from his hand. 'Look at it now,' he said. Soderini replied, 'I like it better. You've made it come alive.'

The lesson: __________

2 Churchill paints a sheep

British prime minister William Churchill was a talented painter. Once, when visiting publisher Henry Luce in Luce's New York office, Churchill saw one of his own paintings on the wall. Luce commented, 'It's good, but I think it needs something in the foreground – a sheep, perhaps.' He didn't expect Churchill to take him seriously. However, a few days later, Churchill's secretary called, asking for the painting to be sent to England. Luce panicked, thinking he'd done something wrong and offended Churchill. He sent the painting anyway, and shortly afterwards, the work was returned with a sheep newly painted in the foreground.

The lesson: __________

*governess = a woman who tutors the children of wealthy families

GRAMMAR

RELATIVE CLAUSES

5 A Underline the relative clauses in these sentences from the stories.

1 Marie Curie, whose achievements in science won her Nobel prizes in physics and chemistry, did not have an easy childhood.
2 Soderini, who thought he was an expert, told Michelangelo the nose was too big.
3 She had carvings made that showed her as the daughter of the god Amun.
4 The person who helped her to get an education was her sister.

B Which two relative clauses in Exercise 5A are essential to the sentence? Which two add extra information?

C Read the rules. Underline the correct alternative and cross out the incorrect one. The first has been done for you.

RULES	
	1 For essential information, use a *defining/~~non-defining~~* relative clause. 2 For extra information, use a *defining/non-defining* relative clause. 3 Use commas to separate *defining/non-defining* relative clauses from the rest of the sentence. 4 We can use *that* instead of *who* or *which* in *defining/non-defining* relative clauses. 5 Use *who's/whose* to show possession.

3 Curie sisters make a deal

Marie Curie, whose achievements in science won her Nobel prizes in physics and chemistry, did not have an easy childhood. When she was young, her family was too poor to take advantage of her obvious intelligence and send her to university. The person who helped her to get an education was her sister, Bronisława. The sisters, who were very close, made a pact. Marie would work as a governess*, making enough money to pay for Bronisława's medical studies. Then, after starting her career, Bronisława would finance Marie's studies. The deal worked perfectly. They paid for each other's education and the rest is history.

The lesson: ______________

4 Hatshepsut builds for glory

In Ancient Egypt, when King Thutmose I died, his daughter Hatshepsut became queen and took control of the country. But the real power always belonged to men, so she declared herself 'king'. She then did various deeds to demonstrate her power: she commissioned hundreds of statues of herself, restored important monuments, had carvings made that showed her as the daughter of the god Amun (some depicted her with a long false beard) and finally, she built a massive burial temple to ensure that her reputation would survive after death. Hatshepsut understood that male rulers took their power for granted, but she had to do her utmost to gain respect.

The lesson: ______________

D Read the statements about relative clauses. Which one is false?

1 Relative clauses are useful for giving essential or extra information.
2 They are common when we try to define something (place, person, object).
3 They are common when we want to describe something in more detail.
4 Relative clauses are not used frequently in writing.

▷ page 118 **LANGUAGEBANK**

6 Join the sentences using non-defining relative clauses. Use the underlined sentence for the relative clause.

1 Eben joined our company last month. He was my best friend at school.
Eben, who was my best friend at school, joined our company last month.
2 My father is staying with me. He lives in New Zealand.
3 I visited Lagos. My mother is from there.
4 The castle was owned by the royal family. It was built in 1684.
5 My friend Jo will come over later. I borrowed her guitar.
6 Sunil moved to Delhi. He went to university there.
7 He studied physics. He loved it.

7 Join the sentences using defining relative clauses.

1 That's the shed. I keep my tools there.
That's the shed where I keep my tools.
2 This is the place. We grew up here.
3 The taxi was yellow. We took it.
4 Was that the girl? Her father went to prison.
5 The nightclub is the best in town. It has four dance floors.
6 It's that man. I spoke to him yesterday.
7 Is this the restaurant? You ate here last night.
8 The lady later became famous. We bought her house.

SPEAKING

8 A You are going to tell an anecdote that taught you something. Think of true endings to these sentences and add details: where and when did these things happen? Who was involved and what did you learn?

1 I learned something important when …
2 I travelled to … , where …
3 I met … , who …
4 I learned to … , which …

B Share your anecdote with other students.

WRITING

ANECDOTE; LEARN TO SET THE SCENE

9 A Read the anecdote. Why do you think the writer gave it this title? What was/were the lesson(s)?

B Complete the useful phrases with words from the text.

anecdote – useful phrases	
setting the scene: time	The story took place one winter. In those days, … When I was [1]__________, …
setting the scene: place	This happened in a big city … I was living in a town by the sea. I grew up in a [2]__________
setting the scene: people	She was larger than life. She would (give us treats/take us to the river/ hug us daily). She was the greatest [3]__________.
describing a sequence of events	At first, I … Years later, … Inside it was the letter my teacher had sent home all those [4]__________.

10 Are the statements about anecdotes true (T) or false (F)?

Anecdotes:

1 often use emotion or humour.
2 often have a lesson or a moral.
3 are informal – written in the same style as speech.
4 include details to 'set the scene'.
5 are divided into short sections with subheadings.
6 can use dialogue to bring the scene to life.

11 A Think of an anecdote or use the one you told in Exercise 8B. Write the story (250–300 words). Try to use some of the useful phrases in Exercise 9B.

B Work in pairs. Read your partner's story and think of one question to ask. Then ask your partner your question.

A lesson from my mother

I grew up in a windy little town with one school, one shop and no future. When I was eight years old, my teacher sent home a note for me to give to my mother. She opened it and began to read aloud. 'Dear Mrs Boujayen, your daughter is a genius. She is too gifted for this school. You will need to teach her yourself.' My mother smiled at me, returned the letter to its envelope and said, 'Come, my little genius, now your real education begins,' and gave me a hug.

I never set foot in that school again. Even though my mother was alone with three children and had to work, she somehow taught me for the next ten years. She was the greatest teacher imaginable. We did our lessons at the flimsy kitchen table or, when it wasn't freezing outside, in the fields near our tiny bungalow. She taught me to think logically and to ask questions. Every day after studying, we'd finish off with our favourite hobby: a game of chess.

Perhaps because she'd had a hard life, her health began to fail in her late fifties. My brothers and I looked after her and we played chess right up until her final days. She died at the age of sixty-four – the same number of squares as on a chess board.

When I was going through her things, I found an envelope. Inside it was the 'genius' letter that my teacher had sent home all those years ago. As I began reading it, I learned something new about my mother. The letter said, 'Dear Mrs Boujayen, your daughter is a difficult child. She is too wild for this school. You will need to teach her yourself.'

Soumaya Boujayen
surgeon, chess champion, writer

SPEAKING

1 A Look at the photo. What do you think it shows?

B Read the article and answer the questions.

1 Can you think of examples of how your everyday activities are tracked?
2 Are you concerned about governments and big businesses monitoring and collecting data about you? Why/Why not?

Data is everywhere

We're living in an era where data is everywhere. As we walk around every day, our phones and devices track our location. Apps and websites we visit are tracked. When we walk along a street or into a shopping centre, our movements are tracked by surveillance cameras. If we get into a car with GPS, we are tracked. If we drive too fast or go through a red light, there's a camera. If we wear a medical device, information about our activities and our health is tracked. It's known as 'digital exhaust', the trail of data that we leave behind us, and now all this information is being collected and analysed. From business to science, from government to the arts, 'big data' is everywhere and it's about to change our lives forever.

LISTENING

2 A 8.2 Listen to an interview about 'big data'. Tick the topics in the box the speakers mention.

healthcare education news	
crime prevention online dating	
farming/agriculture traffic	
politics/elections sports	

B What does the man say about each topic?

3 A Circle the correct answer, a) or b). Then listen again and check your answers.

1 In the future big data will be used in healthcare to cure diseases like cancer by
   a) developing new and more effective drugs and predicting the progress of the disease.
   b) matching patients to exact treatments and increasing monitoring to help prevent the disease.
2 Police are using data to
   a) predict where a crime is likely to happen.
   b) identify criminals.
3 Online dating websites can use
   a) information shared on social networks to understand your personality and find a match.
   b) location tracking from social network apps to help people find a partner who lives near them.
4 Professional sports players have their performance tracked
   a) so that their pay can be tracked according to their performance.
   b) both when they play the sport and in their free time.
5 In the future traffic jams in big cities
   a) will be a big problem as there are more and more driverless cars.
   b) should decrease as data analytics helps drivers to choose a better route.

B Work in groups and discuss. Do you agree that big data analytics is going to change the world for the better? What do you think the downsides might be?

GRAMMAR

FUTURE FORMS

4 A Work in pairs. Underline the future forms in the sentences. Then discuss why you think each form is used.

1 Big data is everywhere and it's about to change our lives forever.
2 Experts try to work out where the disease is going to spread to.
3 In the future it will be used to cure diseases like cancer.
4 Data in healthcare enables us to predict when there might be a problem.
5 They use the data to help predict where crime is likely to occur.
6 In the future you'll probably never get stuck in a traffic jam.
7 You won't be driving your own car either; it'll be driving itself.
8 There are bound to be problems.
9 Big data is due to change the world. I think it will be for the better.

B Match sentences 1–9 in Exercise 4A with rules a)–h). You need to match one of the rules with two sentences.

RULES	
	1 Use *going to* + infinitive for a prediction based on evidence. **2** Use *will/won't* to make general predictions. **3** Use *probably will/won't* to make a prediction less certain. **4** Use *may/might* for predictions which are less certain. **5** Use *be about to* for something that is going to happen soon. **6** Use *be likely to* when a prediction is probable. **7** Use *be due to* for something that is expected to happen. **8** Use *be bound to* for a prediction that is very likely.

▷ page 118 **LANGUAGEBANK**

5 A Underline the correct alternatives to complete the article.

The problems with big data

So big data [1]is *going/might* to transform how we live, work and think. But is there a dark side to big data? Big data analysis will [2]*probably/due to* improve our lives in some ways but there [3]*will/are* bound to be problems too.

Robocop

If you're [4]*about to/bound* commit a crime in Dubai, you [5]*might/might to* get stopped by a robotic police officer. Robocop uses big data to identify offenders. One problem is that if we have technology that can predict what people [6]*are about/are about to* do, then in the future [7]*will/are* we going to punish people for crimes before they even commit them? Also, in Dubai the police department [8]*is about/is due to* replace a quarter of its officers with robots by 2030. In the future many jobs done by people today will be performed by robots using big data.

Ice cream

It's also important to consider how we interpret this data in order to get the best outcomes. For example, big data tells us that in summer deaths from drowning [9]*going to/will* increase, and so [10]*will/likely* the amount of ice cream people eat. Data analytics [11]*might/bound* suggest that if you eat ice cream, you're more [12]*likely/about* to die from drowning. But the reason the two activities increase is because it's summer. If big data [13]*going/is going* to help us, [14]*we'll have/we might* to become better critical thinkers.

B Do you think robotic police officers are a good or bad idea? Do you think it's important that we become better critical thinkers?

VOCABULARY

CRITICAL THINKING

6 A Match the words in bold in sentences 1–10 with definitions a)–j).

1 That seems like a **plausible** explanation.
2 It's a **reliable** source of information.
3 The media coverage during the election was **biased**.
4 The article contains a number of **misleading** statements.
5 Unfortunately, their business strategy was fatally **flawed** and they went bankrupt.
6 We need **accurate** information about the spread of the disease.
7 That seems like a **reasonable** solution to the problem.
8 I'm sure there's a perfectly **rational** explanation.
9 Doctors nowadays are more **open-minded** about alternative medicine.
10 She's very **well-informed**. She obviously knows her subject.

a) that can be trusted or depended on
b) fair and sensible
c) having a lot of knowledge or information about something
d) believable
e) having a weakness or imperfection
f) designed to be deceptive
g) explained using facts and logic rather than emotion
h) willing to try new things or consider new ideas
i) correct in all details; exact
j) unfairly preferring one person or group over another

B Work in pairs. Discuss the questions.

1 Can you believe everything you read? Why/Why not?
2 Do you know any news websites that you think are reliable/unreliable?
3 How can you be sure that the information you receive is accurate? How can you stay well-informed?
4 'Statistics can be misleading.' Do you agree?

SPEAKING

7 A Look at these topics and the questions below. Make notes.

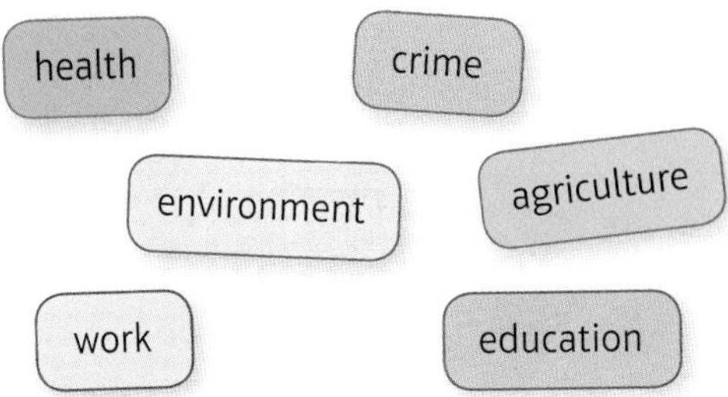

- Within the next fifty years, what do you think will be the major problems in each area?
- What will be the consequences of these problems?
- Can you think of any possible solutions?
- Do you think big data will have an influence on this?

Health:
Problem: Antibiotics will no longer work.
Solution: …

B Work in groups and compare your ideas. What do you think are going to be the greatest challenges in the next fifty years? Can you think of any plausible solutions?

VOCABULARY PLUS

NUMBERS AND STATISTICS

8 A Read the facts on the right. Do any of them surprise you? If so, why?

B Try reading the facts out loud. Do you know how to say the numbers?

C 8.3 **NUMBERS** Listen and check.

9 Match the numbers in the box with how we say them.

10%	3.2	276,000 km	-10°C	50 m²
10:1	150 kg	1,800,000		

1 one point eight million/one million, eight hundred thousand
2 two hundred and seventy-six thousand kilometres
3 ten percent
4 fifty square metres
5 minus ten degrees Celsius
6 three point two
7 one hundred and fifty kilograms
8 ten to one

10 A Work in pairs. Ask and answer questions to complete a list of crazy statistics.

Student A: turn to p132. Ask Student B questions to complete your statistics. Then answer his/her questions.

Student B: turn to p133. Answer Student A's questions. Then ask him/her questions to complete your statistics.

B Do you find any of the statistics in Exercise 10A surprising/unbelievable? Can you check the information to see if it is accurate?

Eight amazing facts

about big data that everyone should know

1 **Every 2 days** we create as much data as we did from the beginning of time until **2013**.

2 Over **90%** of all the data in the world was created in the last two years.

3 Every minute we send **204 million** emails, generate **1.8 million** Facebook likes, send **278,000** tweets and upload **200,000** photos to Facebook.

4 Google processes on average over **40,000** search queries per second, which amounts to **3.5 billion** in a single day.

5 Around **100** hours of video are uploaded to YouTube every minute. It would take you around **15 years** to watch every video uploaded by users in one day.

6 If you burned all of the data created in just one day onto DVDs, you could stack them on top of each other and **reach the moon (384,400 km) – twice**.

7 **570** new websites spring into existence every minute of every day.

8 The number of bits of information stored in the digital universe is thought to have **exceeded the number of stars** in the physical universe in **2007**.

8.3 IDIOMS AND ORIGINS

F guessing and estimating
P intonation in short responses
V idioms

A

B
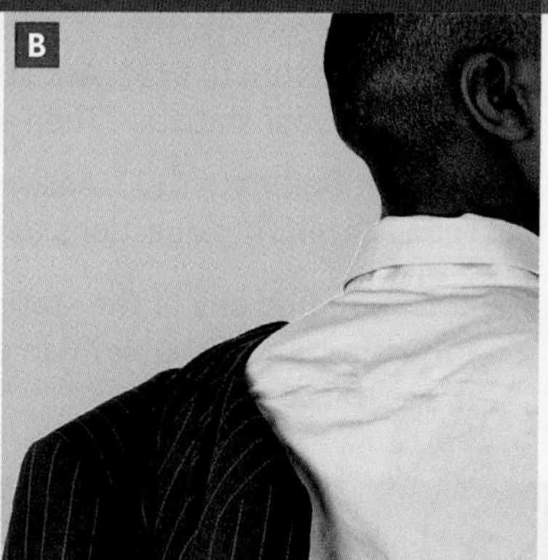
C

D
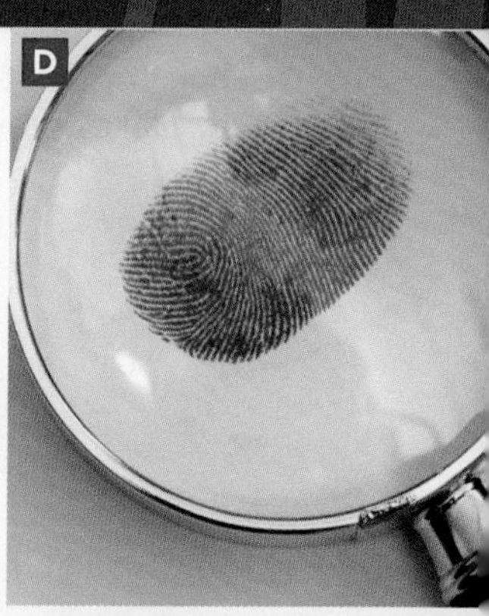
E
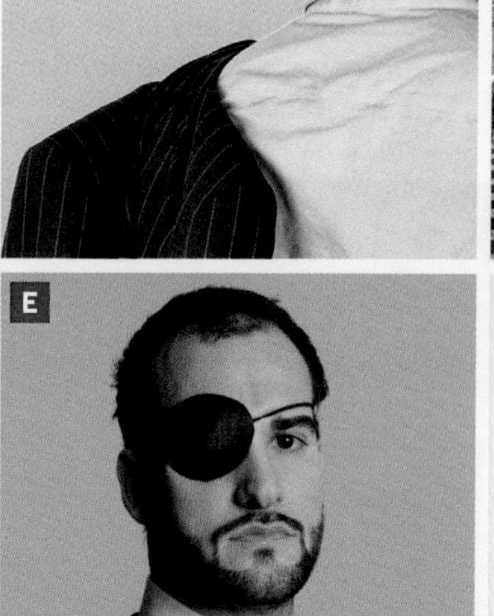
F
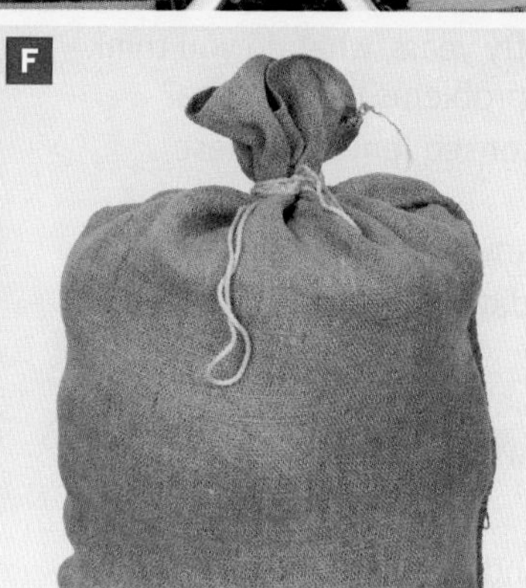
G

VOCABULARY

IDIOMS

1 A Read the sentences. What do you think the idioms in bold mean?

1 What's the big secret? Oh go on, **spill the beans**!
2 Let's not **get side-tracked**. We need to make a decision today.
3 I like my teacher. She always **turns a blind eye** to my bad behaviour.
4 I have to work. I can't afford to **miss my deadline**, which is on Monday.
5 I hope I don't **get the sack**. I need this job!
6 These shoes are **brand new**.
7 I don't think she likes me. That's why she **gives me the cold shoulder**.
8 He's hopeless at maths. He **doesn't have a clue**.
9 Whether you're tired or not is **beside the point**. We were talking about your grades!
10 Politically, I'm **left-wing**, but my family is **right-wing**.

B Match the idioms in sentences 1–9 in Exercise 1A with the definitions in the box. Do you have any similar idioms in your language?

not relevant *9* fail to submit work on time deliberately not see something lose your job recently made start discussing something unrelated liberal or conservative doesn't know anything is unfriendly or ignores (someone) tell the secret

C Which idioms are related to which photos?

2 A Complete the conversations with the idioms in Exercise 1A.

1 **A:** I'll get up early. My essay is due by noon.
B: Yes, you don't want to ________.
2 **A:** Who wrote the lyrics to that 1943 song?
B: 1943?! I ________.
3 **A:** I can't tell you – it's a secret.
B: Oh go on! ________!
4 **A:** I'm sick and tired of her behaviour!
B: It's not that bad! Can't you just ________?
5 **A:** I know I stole the money, but I'm usually honest!
B: That's completely ________.
6 **A:** Was he friendly?
B: Not at all. He ________.
7 **A:** Sorry, but I lost the coat that you lent me.
B: Oh no! It was ________.
8 **A:** That politician's a liberal, isn't she?
B: Yes, she's definitely ________.
9 **A:** What if I can't fix the machine?
B: It's your job. If you can't do it, you'll ________.
10 **A:** Then he changed the subject and we wasted twenty minutes.
B: I know. He's always ________.

B Work in pairs. Look at Exercise 2A and take turns to read A's turn. Your partner responds.

▷ page 127 **VOCABULARYBANK**

FUNCTION

GUESSING AND ESTIMATING

3 **Look at the idioms in Exercise 1A. Is it possible to guess what they mean by looking at the words? Read the Speakout tip.**

speakout TIP

The meanings of idioms in English are usually impossible to guess. This is because idioms often refer to very old customs, traditions and uses of language. Some idioms were first used hundreds of years ago. The traditions have changed but the language has kept the idiom. This means you have to learn the meaning of idioms.
What do the actual words in the idioms in Exercise 1A mean (the literal meaning)?
'Spill the beans' means you accidentally drop beans!

4 **A** 8.4 **Listen to two people discussing the origins of some of the idioms in Exercise 1A. Which idioms do they mention?**

B **Listen again. What are the origins of the idioms the speakers mention? Work in pairs and check your answers.**

5 **A** **Read the extracts from the recording. Underline the phrases the speakers use to make guesses.**

1 **A:** Where do you think the expression *get the sack* comes from?
B: I have no idea. Perhaps it's something like Father Christmas …

2 **A:** What about *brand new*?
B: I'd imagine it's connected to the word *brand*.

3 **A:** Why do we say *left-wing* and *right-wing* for political views?
B: Is it something to do with where people sat in parliament?

B **Here are eight more phrases for guessing or estimating. Match the phrases in box A with phrases with a similar meaning in box B.**

A

approximately … it might be …
I'm not sure, but I'd estimate … there's no way it's …

B

at a rough guess, I'd say … more or less …
it could be … it can't be …

C 8.5 **Listen and check your answers.**

▷ page 118 **LANGUAGEBANK**

6 **Put the words in brackets in the correct order to complete the conversation. Add punctuation.**

A: How many languages does he speak?
B: [1]________ (guess / say / a / rough / I'd / eight / at)
A: Eight?! [2]________ (no / there's / that / way / many / it's)
B: [3]________ (could / it / be). He's lived in a lot of places.
A: Has he? How many? [4]________ (be / six / can't / more / it / than). He's only twenty.
B: [5]________ (estimate / not / but / I'd / sure / I'm / ten / countries)
A: [6]________ (as / more / that's / the / or / same / less / me)
B: Yes, and you only speak English!

LEARN TO

GIVE SHORT RESPONSES TO NEW INFORMATION

7 **A** **Read these two-word responses to new information and answer questions a)–d).**

1 I see.
2 Oh wow!
3 Kind of.
4 No idea.
5 No way!
6 You're kidding!

a) Which responses show surprise?
b) Which response shows understanding?
c) Which response shows you don't know?
d) Which response says the other person is partly, but not completely, correct?

B 8.6 **INTONATION IN SHORT RESPONSES Listen to the phrases in Exercise 7A and repeat. Copy the intonation.**

SPEAKING

8 **Work in pairs. Student A: turn to page 130. Student B: turn to page 133. Explain to your partner where two of the idioms in Exercise 1A come from.**

8.4 FINDING OUT

Simon

DVD PREVIEW

1 Read the quotes. Do you agree? Why/ Why not?

1 'Google can bring you back 100,000 answers. A librarian can bring you back the right one.' *Neil Gaiman, writer*

2 '[Because of the internet], the level of intelligence has been tremendously increased. Much of the real action is taking place in cyberspace.' *Timothy Leary, writer*

DVD VIEW

2 Watch Part 1. Number the answers in the order you hear them.

a) colleagues, school books and online research

b) blog posts, bloggers and news channels

c) newspapers and radio

d) a variety of sources

3 A Watch Part 2. Answer the questions.

1 What does David say about the modern world?

2 What does Anthony say about googling?

3 Does Marie believe what she reads on the Internet?

4 What does Julian say about research and sources?

B Underline the correct alternatives to complete what the speakers say. Watch again to check your answers.

1 You have to learn to *filter/fill* the information so you understand where it's coming from.

2 Does it have a trusted *sort/source*?

3 I take what I read from the internet with a *punch/pinch* of salt.

4 It's important to see if you can come to *a lone/your own* conclusion of what the real story is.

C Work in pairs. Answer the questions.

1 What is a filter, e.g. a coffee filter? What does *filter information* mean?

2 What is a source, e.g. the source of a river? What does a *trusted source* mean?

3 If you *take something with a pinch of salt*, do you believe it completely or not?

4 If you *come to your own conclusion*, are you thinking for yourself or agreeing with someone else?

4 Watch Part 3. Are the statements true (T) or false (F)?

1 Simon thinks the internet has good and bad things.

2 Isabelle says it's full of fake news.

3 Sophie says it makes you smarter if you use it to educate yourself.

4 Anthony thinks it wastes our time.

5 A Complete the extracts with one word in each gap.

1 I think the internet is **a** __________ **blessing**.

2 You need to be **a** __________ **user** of it.

3 We don't feel like we need to **learn** as many things **by** __________ any more.

4 We've got **so much** __________ now to knowledge.

B Watch Part 3 again to check your answers.

C Match the phrases in bold in Exercise 5A with their definitions.

a) memorise

b) chances to experience or get something

c) something that is both good and bad

d) someone who is able to make good judgments

D Work in pairs and discuss. Do you agree that the internet is a mixed blessing? Do you think it stops us learning things by heart?

Isabelle

6 A Watch Part 4. Number the answers in the order you hear them.

a) believe in people
b) values
c) a love of history
d) a love of books

B Answer the questions.

1. Simon mentions his mother's reading habits. What did she teach her children about books?
2. Juliet says she learned how to 'live life well'. What does she say was NOT important?
3. According to Julian, who exactly should you believe in?
4. Which two people exposed Atri to history? How?

C Watch again to check.

speakout a group discussion

7 A Read the questions and think about your answers.

1. How do you usually get information?
2. Which websites do you trust? Which don't you trust? Why?
3. Do you think the internet is making us smarter or more stupid?
4. What knowledge would you like to pass on to younger members of your family? Why?

B Work in groups. Discuss the questions in Exercise 7A.

writeback a response

8 A Read the proposal for an internet-free day and a response. Does Mary-Lou like the idea?

ACTIVITY

Unplug!

Can you survive a day without the internet? Why not find out? Join us for Internet-free Day on 5 January this year.

The idea is inspired by the 5th Street Café. This café has wi-fi, but it also has an Unplugged Hour every day. During this hour, which is called Coffee-and-Conversation, the owners offer free coffee on one condition: that you sit with a stranger and chat.

The owners tell us the hour has been extremely popular and that having a break from the web has restored the ancient art of conversation.

Mary-Lou
@mary-lou

I think Internet-free Day is an absolutely terrible idea. For a start, I get my news from the net. Secondly, unless EVERYONE does it, it'll be a disaster. All those work emails will be unread and your colleagues will be wondering what's going on. As for the 'evidence' from 5th Street Café, well, of course people like it! They're getting free coffee! As soon as the hour is up, I bet you everyone's back on Facebook.

Mary-Lou, Texas

B Write your own response to the proposal in Exercise 8A (70–100 words).

8.5 LOOKBACK

V LEXICAL CHUNKS WITH *MAKE, DO, TAKE*

1 A Complete the sentences with the words in the box.

damage control granted alterations seriously utmost deal advantage

1 The dress was too big, so we made some ________ to make it smaller.
2 I find it hard to take this report ________ when it has so many mistakes.
3 The companies made a ________ worth 100,000 euros.
4 The storm did a lot of ________ to our house.
5 Not everyone goes to university, so you have to take ________ of this opportunity.
6 When the boss died, his daughter Jennifer took ________ of the company.
7 These days it's taken for ________ that people have mobile phones.
8 The exam is difficult but I'll do my ________ to pass it.

B Choose six phrases with *do*, *make* or *take* and write three true and three false sentences about yourself. Read your sentences to other students. Can they guess which are true?

G RELATIVE CLAUSES

2 A Underline the correct alternatives to complete the story.

Wise words

Henry David Thoreau was a writer [1]*whose/who* was famous for leaving society to live in the woods. One day, Thoreau took a group of friends to pick berries. He knew [2]*the places where/what the places* every type of berry grew. These friends included young Edward Emerson, [3] *whose father/who's father* was another writer, Ralph Waldo Emerson.

At [4]*the moment of/the moment when* they were turning to go home, Edward tripped and dropped his basket. The [5]*berries what/berries that* he'd picked fell onto the ground and were ruined. Everyone offered to share theirs, but Edward, [6]*whose basket/the basket which* was now empty, was extremely sad. Thoreau, [7]*whose seen/who had seen* the incident, put his arm around the boy and explained that for berries to keep growing, nature had made sure that little boys would trip sometimes and drop their pickings. When he came back next year, Edward would find lots of berries in [8]*the place where/where* he'd dropped them. On hearing this, Edward smiled.

B Work in pairs. Read the story again and discuss. What lesson can we learn from it? Then work in groups and compare your ideas.

G FUTURE FORMS

3 Find and correct the mistakes in the sentences. There is one mistake in each sentence.

1 The train is due arrive at 14.30.
2 I was just about telephoning you.
3 Unfortunately, we're not likely seeing them again soon.
4 I'd take an umbrella. It might to rain later.
5 We don't need to buy any food. They bound to have lots already.
6 I'm not convinced we'll to be finished by lunchtime.
7 We haven't seen each other for over a year. We're going have a brilliant time.
8 They'll probably arriving just before the start.

V CRITICAL THINKING

4 Add the missing letters to complete the adjectives relating to critical thinking.

1 He had no pl_ _ _ _ _ _ _ reason for leaving the country.
2 We need more ac_ _ _ _ _ _ statistics regarding the rate of unemployment.
3 The information we have received has not come from a re_ _ _ _ _ _ source.
4 We encourage members to be as we_ _ -i_ _ _ _ _ _ _ as possible.
5 The article contained many mi_ _ _ _ _ _ _ _ statements.
6 The judge's decision was bi_ _ _ _.
7 He put forward a perfectly re_ _ _ _ _ _ _ _ argument.
8 He was very op_ _ -m_ _ _ _ _ about other people's work.
9 Unfortunately, the system is fl_ _ _ _ and it fails many people.
10 I don't understand his behaviour. It just wasn't ra_ _ _ _ _ _.

F GUESSING AND ESTIMATING

5 A Read the conversations about three quiz questions. Cross out the option which is not possible.

1 **A:** Where is the world's biggest library?
B: *It could be/It guesses/It might be* the one in Alexandria in Egypt.

2 **A:** Where did the name *Google* come from?
B: *Perhaps it's something to do with/I'm not sure, but I think it's/There is definitely* the word for a big number.

3 **A:** Which is the world's most educated country?
B: *There's no way it's/It can't be/I don't estimate* my country, the UK!

B Work in pairs. Try to answer the quiz questions in Exercise 5A. Then turn to page 129 **and check your answers.**

IRREGULAR VERBS

Verb	Past simple	Past participle
be	was/were	been
beat	beat	beaten
become	became	become
begin	began	begun
bend	bent	bent
bet	bet	bet
bite	bit	bitten
bleed	bled	bled
blow	blew	blown
break	broke	broken
bring	brought	brought
broadcast	broadcast	broadcast
build	built	built
burn	burned/burnt	burned/burnt
burst	burst	burst
buy	bought	bought
catch	caught	caught
choose	chose	chosen
come	came	come
cost	cost	cost
cut	cut	cut
deal	dealt	dealt
dig	dug	dug
do	did	done
draw	drew	drawn
dream	dreamed/dreamt	dreamed/dreamt
drink	drank	drunk
drive	drove	driven
eat	ate	eaten
fall	fell	fallen
feel	felt	felt
feed	fed	fed
fight	fought	fought
find	found	found
fly	flew	flown
forbid	forbade	forbidden
forget	forgot	forgotten
forgive	forgave	forgiven
freeze	froze	frozen
get	got	got
give	gave	given
go	went	gone
grow	grew	grown
hang	hung	hung
have	had	had
hear	heard	heard
hide	hid	hidden
hit	hit	hit
hold	held	held
hurt	hurt	hurt
keep	kept	kept
know	knew	known
lay	laid	laid
lead	led	led
leap	leapt	leapt
lean	leaned/leant	leaned/leant
learn	learned/learnt	learned/learnt

Verb	Past simple	Past participle
leave	left	left
lend	lent	lent
let	let	let
lie	lay	lain
light	lit	lit
lose	lost	lost
make	made	made
mean	meant	meant
meet	met	met
mistake	mistook	mistaken
pay	paid	paid
put	put	put
read	read	read
ride	rode	ridden
ring	rang	rung
rise	rose	risen
run	ran	run
say	said	said
see	saw	seen
sell	sold	sold
send	sent	sent
set	set	set
shake	shook	shaken
shine	shone	shone
shoot	shot	shot
show	showed	shown
shrink	shrank	shrunk
shut	shut	shut
sing	sang	sung
sink	sank	sunk
sit	sat	sat
sleep	slept	slept
slide	slid	slid
smell	smelled/smelt	smelled/smelt
speak	spoke	spoken
spell	spelt	spelt
spend	spent	spent
spill	spilled/spilt	spilled/spilt
split	split	split
spread	spread	spread
stand	stood	stood
steal	stole	stolen
stick	stuck	stuck
sting	stung	stung
swim	swam	swum
take	took	taken
teach	taught	taught
tear	tore	torn
tell	told	told
think	thought	thought
throw	threw	thrown
understand	understood	understood
wake	woke	woken
wear	wore	worn
win	won	won
write	wrote	written

GRAMMAR

1.1 the passive; causative *have*

the passive

Form the passive with *be* + past participle.

	active	passive
present simple	Someone **cleans** the room every day.	The room **is cleaned** every day.
present continuous	They **are checking** his documents.	His documents are **being checked**.
past simple	The team **gave** the coach a present.	The coach **was given** a present by the team.
present perfect	No one **has told** us about a delay.	We **haven't been told** about a delay.
will	Someone **will explain** the rules to you.	The rules **will be explained** to you.
modals	No one **can help** her right now.	She **can't be helped** right now.

Use the passive:

- to talk about what happens to people/things.
  Sarah ***was taken*** *to the zoo.*
- when you don't know who does the action or their identity is not important.
  The painting ***was stolen****.*
  Those cars ***are made*** *in Japan.*
- when the identity of the doer of the action is obvious.
  He ***was sent*** *to prison.* (The action was done by a judge.)
- to sound more formal.
  The topic ***was discussed*** *at the forum.*
  Jackets ***must be worn*** *at all times.*

causative *have*

Form the causative *have* with *have* + object + past participle.

Use the causative *have*:

- to say when you arrange for somebody to do something for you.
  I ***had my hair done****.* (Somebody did my hair, not me.)
  We ***had our house painted****.* (Somebody else painted the house.)
- to talk about a bad experience that was caused by someone unknown or unnamed.
  I ***had my watch stolen****.*
  He ***had his house broken into****.*

1.2 present tenses

present simple

+	He works for a company that makes microchips.
-	He doesn't enjoy his job.
?	Does she know what she wants to do?

Use the present simple:

- to talk about habits and everyday actions.
  We usually ***have*** *lunch at about 1p.m.*
- for facts/things that are always true.
  Stress ***is*** *one of the main causes of insomnia.*
- for states or feelings (state verbs: *like, love, think, want, be, know*, etc.).
  Italians ***love*** *cooking and eating good food.*

present continuous

+	We're working on a new system.
-	They're not helping us.
?	Are you starting your course next month?

Use the present continuous:

- for actions happening now or around now.
  *We****'re trying*** *to fix the problem at the moment.*
  *The battery****'s not charging****.*
- to describe a situation that is in the process of changing.
  People in Bangladesh ***are eating*** *more fish than they did twenty years ago.*
- after words like *always, forever* and *constantly*, to describe repeated actions (that may be annoying).
  Our neighbours ***are constantly playing*** *loud music.*
- to describe a planned future action.
  *We****'re leaving*** *the country in August.*

Note: As a rule, we don't usually use state verbs in the continuous form. The following are some common state verbs.

love	*understand*	*seem*	*realise*
hate	*imagine*	*possess*	*suppose*
want	*mean*	*contain*	*need*
prefer	*see*	*include*	*matter*
believe	*hear*	*agree*	*prefer*
know	*sound*	*depend*	*forget*
remember	*appear*	*consist*	

However, there are exceptions to this. Sometimes people use the continuous form to focus specifically on the verb as an action.

*I****'m loving*** *this!*

*I****'m seeing*** *Adrian this afternoon.*

1.3 describing everyday objects

That's (definitely not) essential/vital/indispensable.	It's a bit impractical/heavy/pointless.	It's (no) good for telling the time.
You (can) use it to get online/cut …	You need it to prove who you are.	It's really special.
You (can) wear it.	It's made of wool/metal/plastic/leather.	It has sentimental value.

PRACTICE

1.1 **A Complete the article with the correct active or passive form of the verbs in brackets. Use the verb tenses in italics.**

The history of lemonade

No one knows when lemon juice, sugar and water [1]________ (mix, *past simple*) together for the first time, but we do know that lemonade [2]________ (enjoy, *present perfect*) for at least 1,000 years. It [3]________ (believe, *present simple*) that lemons [4]________ (introduce, *past simple*) to Egypt from Asia in AD700, and there is written evidence of the drink in Egypt dating from AD1000.

We also know that lemonade [5]________ (sell, *present perfect*) commercially since 1676, when Compagnie de Limonadiers was founded in Paris. The company [6]________ (send, *past simple*) its vendors onto the streets with tanks of lemonade on their backs, and the drink [7]________ (sell, *past simple*) in cups.

Compagnie de Limonadiers [8]________ (make, *past simple*) cloudy lemonade. The other type [9]________ (make, *present simple*) with carbonated water. Another variation, which mixes lemon juice, sugar, water and mint, [10]________ (drink, *present simple*) in the Middle East.

B Put the words in the correct order to make sentences. Use the causative *have*.

1 handbag / had / stolen / her / she
2 checked / have / by / I / doctor / blood / the / my / month / every
3 hair / his / he's / cut / having
4 walls / we'll / the / painted / have
5 broken / his / he / by / nose / opponent / his / had
6 dress / she / the / made / for / had / occasion / a
7 followed / we / a / by / him / had / private / investigator
8 had / repaired / they / roof / their

1.2 **A Complete the blog with the words/phrases in the box.**

think are always asking paint don't realise is 'm putting looking finish check have collect get up make 'm rebuilding spend

My life as an artist

People [1]________ me about my life as an artist. Artists [2]________ a bad reputation. I [3]________ people imagine that we just [4]________ our time sitting around and staring at canvases. Most people [5]________ how much work is involved. I usually [6]________ at sunrise. The light [7]________ golden and soft at that time. I [8]________ some tea and walk into my studio. I generally spend a bit of time [9]________ at yesterday's work, thinking about what needs doing. Then I [10]________ my website and deal with email enquiries. Currently, I [11]________ the website so people can buy from me directly. Then I spend most of the day painting. Some days I [12]________ until late at night. Other days I [13]________ early and go to visit the galleries I work with or [14]________ paintings from the framer. At the moment things are really busy as I [15]________ on an exhibition next month so there's a lot to organise.

B Underline the correct alternatives to complete the sentences.

1 It's a difficult month for Nina because *she's working/she works* hard for her exams.
2 I*'m not remembering/don't remember* exactly where I left my bag.
3 Good health *is depending/depends* on having a good diet and getting enough sleep.
4 It's wonderful to see you again. How long *are you staying/do you stay*?
5 The other boys play rugby at the weekend, but Sam *is preferring/prefers* to stay at home.
6 I*'m cutting down/cut down* on my coffee drinking at the moment.
7 The figures suggest that the economic situation *is improving/improves* slightly.
8 We*'re travelling/travel* around Northern Europe for three weeks, starting on Monday.

1.3 **A Complete the sentences with the words in the box.**

sentimental essential need leather use a good indispensable

1 It's an old suitcase, made of ________________. It's ________________ bit heavy.
2 Bring your licence – you ________________ it to prove you can drive.
3 A penknife is ________________ when camping. You can ________________ it to cut meat or fish.
4 My grandmother gave me this painting. It has ________________ value.
5 It's no ________________ for telling the time, but I still keep it.
6 Swimming trunks are not ________________, but they might be a good idea.

GRAMMAR

2.1 question forms; indirect questions

direct questions

Most direct questions use the following word order: (question word) + auxiliary verb + subject + main verb.

question word	auxiliary verb	subject	main verb (+ phrase)
Where	do	you	work?
When	does	he/she	finish?
Where	would	you	like me to put your things?
Why	haven't	they	invited me?

subject questions

When the question word is the subject of the sentence, use the affirmative form of the verb, without the auxiliary.

*Who **invented** the computer?* NOT ~~*Who **did invent** the computer?*~~

indirect questions

Use indirect questions to sound more polite. After the opening phrase (*Could you tell me …?, Can I ask you …?*, etc.) use the affirmative form.

Direct: *Where do I have to go?*

Indirect: *Could you tell me **where I have to go?*** NOT ~~*Could you tell me where do I have to go?*~~

*Can I ask you **what time the show starts**?* NOT ~~*Can I ask you what time does the show start?*~~

2.2 present perfect simple and continuous

Use either the present perfect simple or the present perfect continuous to talk about situations or repeated actions which started in the past and continue until now.

*Jack **has lived/has been living** here for a month.*

Form the present perfect simple with *have/has* + past participle.

Use the present perfect simple:

- for recent events, often with *just, yet* or *already*.
  *I**'ve just eaten** my lunch.*
- to emphasise actions that are short and complete.
  *I**'ve passed** my exam!*
- with state verbs (*know, love, like, understand*, etc.).
  *We**'ve known** her for two years.* NOT ~~*We've been knowing her for two years.*~~

Form the present perfect continuous with *have/has + been + -ing*.

Use the present perfect continuous:

- to emphasise ongoing, incomplete actions that began in the past and continue now.
  *I**'ve been learning** Japanese for two months.* (I haven't finished learning it.)
- to emphasise the length of time of an activity.
  *You**'ve been playing** video games for eight hours!*
- when there is present evidence of a recent activity.
  *You're wet. You**'ve been swimming**.* NOT ~~*You've swum.*~~

Do NOT use the present perfect continuous with state verbs.

~~*I've always been loving dogs.*~~ *I**'ve** always **loved** dogs.*

2.3 judging and evaluating ideas

asking for an evaluation of an idea	saying an idea is possible	saying an idea is very good
What do you think? How does that sound? Do you like the idea?	It has potential. That's a possibility. That might work.	That seems like a really good idea. I like the sound of that. That looks/sounds great!

saying an idea might not work	saying an idea is completely impossible
I'm not sure that'll work. I have my doubts about that. I'm not convinced about that.	That's a non-starter. That's out of the question. No way.

PRACTICE

2.1

A Circle the correct answer, a), b) or c), to complete the questions.

1 Do you know how expensive ____?
a) is it b) it is c) are they
2 Can you tell me where ____ born?
a) was he b) did he c) he was
3 Where ____ put the clean dishes?
a) I should b) should I c) I shall
4 Do you think ____ wait for her?
a) we should b) do we c) should we
5 Why ____ want to leave her job?
a) she does b) she would c) would she
6 Who ____ all the biscuits?
a) ate b) did eat c) would ate

B Rewrite the questions.

1 What time is the show?
Can you tell me ____________________?
2 Where did Marco put the luggage?
Do you know ____________________?
3 How old are you?
Can I ask you ____________________?
4 Have you ever seen one of these before?
Could you tell me if ____________________?
5 What do you think of the idea?
Can I ask ____________________?
6 What is the problem?
Do you know ____________________?

2.2

A Underline the correct alternatives to complete the text.

Thomas Dambo has always [1]*enjoyed/been enjoying* building things. As a child in Denmark, he built treehouses and boxcars. He now specialises in making sculptures from recycled materials. Dambo's first major work was a series of wooden birdhouses. Since he began these, he has [2]*built/been building* more than 3,000 of them. For his most recent project, Dambo has [3]*worked/been working* on a series of giants made from recycled wood, and so far he has [4]*completed/been completing* six of them. These sculptures have [5]*been hidden/being hidden* in the woods of Copenhagen, where people can search for them. When asked about his work, he says that over the last decade, as well as making beautiful art, he has [6]*been tried/been trying* to get people to take better care of the planet.

B Complete the sentences with the present perfect simple or continuous form of the verbs in the box.

work read watch finish wait write do plan speak rain

1 Bring your umbrella. It's ________ all day here.
2 You look exhausted! What have you ________?
3 The same film again? You've ________ it three times already!
4 I haven't ________ to Ali for ages.
5 We don't know where he is. We've ________ for him since 10 o'clock.
6 Have you ________ your essay? You need to hand it in today.
7 I'm not surprised he's tired. He's ________ in the garden for five hours.
8 I've ________ our music festival. It will involve 120 musicians.
9 He's a young author. He's ________ just two books so far.
10 I've already ________ that book. It's brilliant!

2.3

A Put the underlined words in the correct order to complete the conversations.

1 A: So that's my plan. ____________________ (idea / like / do / you / the?)
B: ____________________ (convinced / not / I'm / it / about)
2 A: We'll organise it. ____________________ (sound / does / that / how?)
B: ____________________ (seems / really / a / idea / that / like / good)
3 A: He said we can start the project tomorrow. ____________________ (possibility / a / that's)
B: ____________________ (about / my / have / that / I / doubts). We aren't ready.
4 A: That's her idea. ____________________ (has / I / potential / it / think)
B: ____________________ (of / out / it's / question / the). It's too expensive!
5 A: I finished the proposal. ____________________ (do / think / you / what?)
B: ____________________ (like / sound / it / the / I / of)
6 A: He gave me the plan. ____________________ (work / not / I'm / it'll / sure)
B: I agree with you. ____________________ (non-starter / a / it's)

3 LANGUAGE BANK

GRAMMAR

3.1 narrative tenses

Use the past simple to talk about completed actions or the main events of the story.

*She **got** up early and **went** out to surf.*

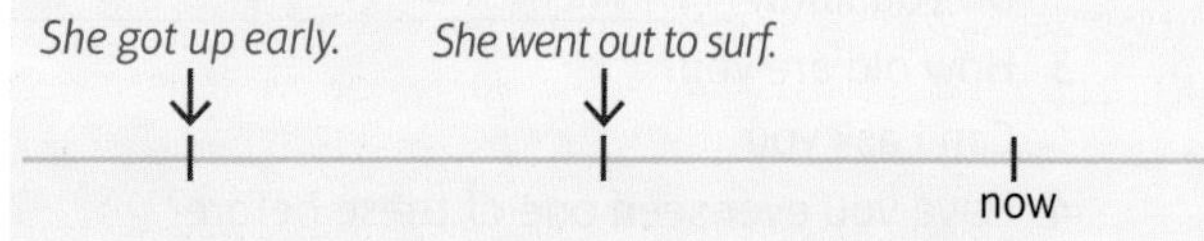

Use the past continuous (*was/were* + verb + *-ing*):

- to give background information or to focus on the duration of the activity.

  *They **were living** in Australia.*

- to talk about one or more actions which were in progress at the same moment in time.

  *She **was relaxing** and her arm **was dangling** in the water.*

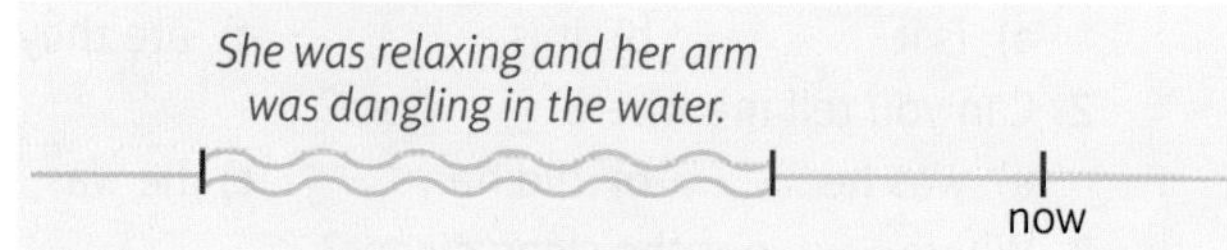

Use the past perfect (*had* + past participle) to talk about an action which happened before the main events.

*She **left** the house after she **had eaten** her breakfast.*

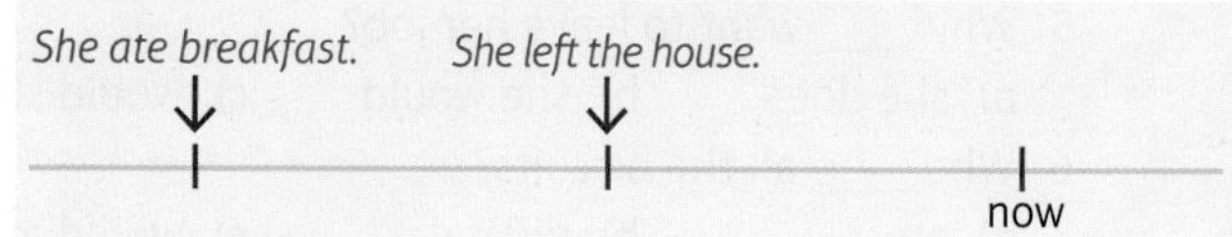

The past perfect links a past point (*she left the house*) to a point further back in time (*she ate breakfast*).

3.2 modals of obligation: present/past

	advice (present)	regret or criticism (past)	obligation (present)	obligation (past)	lack of obligation (present)	lack of obligation (past)
+	You **should call** him.	We **should have arrived** earlier.	You **must go** now. We **have to leave.**	She **had to leave** at six.		
-	You **shouldn't do** that.	You **shouldn't have done** that.	We **mustn't be** late.		You **don't have to wear** a suit.	You **didn't have to** bring food!
?	**Should** I **wait?**	**Should** we **have called** first?	**Do** I **have to pass** a test?	**Did** he **have to do** the exam again?		

should

Use *should* and *shouldn't* for advice and mild obligation.

*You **should** see that film! You **shouldn't** arrive late.*

should have

Use *should have* + past participle for regrets.

*I **should have left** home earlier.* (I missed my train.)

must* and *have to

Use *must* and *have to* for strong obligation. *Must* is often used when we decide something for ourselves.

*I **must** lose weight!*

Must is also used in written rules.

*All members **must wear** a tie.*

Have to is often used when we're talking about rules.

*You **have to buy** a ticket.* (It's the rule if you want to enter.)

had to

The past form of *have to* is *had to*. There is no past form of *must* or *mustn't*.

*Yesterday **I had to take** a test.* NOT

~~*Yesterday I must take a test.*~~

mustn't

Mustn't means something is not allowed.

*You **mustn't walk** on the grass.* (It's against the rules).

don't have to

Use *don't have to* to show that something is not necessary.

*You **don't have to bring** food.* (But you can if you want to.)

didn't have to

The past of *don't have to* is *didn't have to.*

*You **didn't have to bring** flowers!* (But it was kind.)

3.3 resolving conflict

preparing the other person for the conversation	introducing the subject	explaining the problem
Can I talk to you about something? There's something I need to talk to you about.	It's about … The problem/The thing is …	This is making it impossible to … I can't … because of this.

suggesting a plan of action	describing next steps
Would you be able to/Perhaps you could …? What if we …? What about …?	So for now, we'll (do this). We can just (do this).

PRACTICE

3.1

A **Complete the sentences with the past simple, past continuous or past perfect form of the verbs in brackets.**

1 At 5.30 I ________ (sleep) when the alarm ________ (go off).
2 We ________ (talk) about Jo when she ________ (walk) into the room.
3 The restaurant was full, so we ________ (cannot eat) there as I ________ (not book) a table.
4 He ________ (break) his foot while he ________ (skateboard).
5 I looked up and ________ (realise) I ________ (not see) him before.
6 My computer ________ (crash) and I lost all my work because I ________ (not save) it.

B **Complete the story with the correct form of the verbs in brackets. More than one answer may be possible.**

This [1]________ (happen) when we were on holiday in Australia. We [2]________ (visit) my sister, who [3]________ (live) in Sydney at the time. One day we [4]________ (decide) to go scuba-diving. My sister [5]________ (want) us to see the Great Barrier Reef, but we [6]________ (not do) much scuba-diving before, so we [7]________ (feel) a little bit nervous. However, our guide was very friendly. He [8]________ (calm) us down and [9]________ (explain) how all the equipment worked. As we [10]________ (travel) out on the boat, I [11]________ (look) out at the calm sea and [12]________ (feel) very relaxed. At the beginning of the dive I [13]________ (enjoy) looking at all the different coloured fish and coral. It was beautiful. But soon the water [14]________ (start) to get murky and before long I [15]________ (cannot) see anything at all. We [16]________ (swim) against a strong current and looking for the rest of the group, but we [17]________ (cannot) find them. We [18]________ (decide) to go back up to the surface of the water. When we got there we [19]________ (realise) the current [20]________ (take) us a long way from the boat. Luckily the team [21]________ (look for) us, and they soon found us. But I'm never going scuba-diving again!

3.2

A **Complete the conversation with the words in the box.**

have (x3) shouldn't (x2) to (x2) try had didn't must should

A: So, tell me about this survival course.
B: It was great. We lived in the woods for a week.
A: What about food? Did you [1]________ to learn to hunt your food?
B: Yes, but we [2]________ have to use guns. That was optional. Some of us went fishing instead.
A: So, do you [3]________ to be super-fit to do the course?
B: You don't have [4]________ be like an Olympic athlete, but it helps if you're in good shape. I found it difficult and realised I [5]________ have done more exercise before the course started.
A: I see.
B: You [6]________ do this course unless you're ready. There was one guy who complained the whole time. He shouldn't [7]________ been allowed on the course. He gave up after three days.
A: Seriously? They [8]________ have let him do it. Did you have [9]________ do any tests beforehand?
B: I [10]________ to have a medical check-up. That's all.
A: OK. I really [11]________ try something like this. I've been saying for years I want to do a survival course.
B: You should [12]________ it.

B **Rewrite the sentences using the words in brackets. Use three words, including the word in brackets.**

1 It's a bad idea to work with that company. (shouldn't)
You ________ that company.
2 We can attend the ceremony if we want to, but it's not compulsory. (don't)
We ________ attend the ceremony.
3 You can keep the books for a week. After that, you need to return them. (must)
You ________ books after one week.
4 I didn't study for my exam. I regret it. (should)
I ________ for my exam.
5 You bought me a present! That wasn't necessary! (have)
You ________ buy me a present!
6 Why did we sell the house? It was a mistake! (shouldn't)
We ________ the house!

3.3

A **Underline the correct alternatives to complete the conversation.**

A: Can I talk to you [1]*for/about* something?
B: Yes.
A: It's [2]*about/from* your apple tree. The branches have grown too big. This is [3]*making/doing* it impossible to see through the upstairs window. Would you be [4]*possible/able* to cut them?
B: I'm ninety years old. I can't climb trees any more.
A: [5]*Why/What* about getting someone to do it for you? Perhaps you [6]*could/do* hire someone?
B: Good idea. Do you need a job?
A: Yes, I do, actually.
B: OK. What [7]*but/if* I employed you to cut my branches?
A: Maybe. The [8]*one/thing* is, I've never done that kind of work before. I'm a computer programmer.
B: Well, here's your chance to start a new career!

GRAMMAR

4.1 zero, first and second conditionals

	conditional clause	result clause
zero conditional	*if* + present simple	present simple
first conditional	*if* + present simple	*will* + infinitive without *to*
second conditional	*if* + past simple	*would* + infinitive without *to*

zero conditional

Form the zero conditional using *if/when* + present simple + present simple.

Use the zero conditional to talk about a general situation which is always true.

*If you **heat** water to 100 degrees, it **boils**.*

*When you **mix** red and blue, you **get** purple.*

first conditional

Form the first conditional using *if* + present simple + *will/won't* (or a modal verb).

Use the first conditional to talk about something that is likely to happen in the future as a result of an action or situation.

*If you **work** hard, you**'ll pass** your exam.*

*She **might become** a professional if she **keeps** improving.*

second conditional

Form the second conditional using *if* + past simple + *would/wouldn't*.

Use the second conditional to talk about hypothetical (imaginary) situations.

*If I **won** the lottery, I**'d never work** again.*

*She**'d sleep** all day if she **had** the chance.*

unless

Unless + positive verb means *if … not*.

***Unless** you have a better idea, we'll do it my way.*

*He wouldn't do that **unless** someone forced him.*

as soon as

Use *as soon as* instead of *if* to show that something happens immediately.

***As soon as** I hear from her, I'll call you.*

*If there was an emergency, we'd come **as soon as** possible.*

4.2 passive reporting structures

Use the following passive reporting structures in formal writing to report opinions and beliefs.

***it* + passive reporting verb + *that* clause**

***It is said that** he lived alone and rarely spoke to anyone.*

***It was thought that** the company would go bankrupt if he left.*

***It has been suggested/estimated/claimed that** increasing the price of unhealthy products would result in a drop in their use.*

subject + passive reporting verb + infinitive clause

***It is thought/reported/estimated to be** one of the world's biggest killers, accounting for 15 million deaths in 2017.*

***He was claimed to be** the world's greatest athlete.*

4.3 hedging

hedging
I guess/I suppose … presumably may/might/could perhaps maybe possibly (not) particularly (not) really
vague language
kind of/sort of just … or something

PRACTICE

4.1

A Circle the correct answer, a), b) or c), to complete the sentences.

1 If you ____ to me, I'll write back.
a) were written b) wrote c) write

2 As ____ as I know my schedule, I'll tell you.
a) if b) soon c) when

3 I'll be there at 6a.m. ____ my flight is delayed.
a) if not b) will c) unless

4 If she ____ nuts, she gets sick.
a) eats b) ate c) will eat

5 I'd help you if I ____.
a) can b) possible c) could

6 Where ____ you go if you could go anywhere?
a) would b) do c) were

7 If you ____ attend, you don't get paid.
a) aren't b) don't c) wouldn't

8 If we don't leave early, we ____ get there in time.
a) haven't b) wouldn't c) might not

B Underline the correct alternative to complete the text.

If I had to recommend one book about science for the non-scientist, it [1]*would/can* be Bill Bryson's *A Short History of Nearly Everything*. As [2]*soon/once* as you read the first page, you realise this isn't a book for experts, but for members of the public. Bryson educates us by telling stories.

So how useful is this book? If you wanted to learn about atoms, what [3]*do/would* you do? Maybe go online? But [4]*as soon/unless* you already know the basics, you won't understand much. What about scientific journals and papers? If I try to read journals, I always [5]*get/got* bored. The concepts and the writing are too dense. With Bryson it's the opposite: he makes complicated ideas seem simple.

If you want a well-written guide to science, I [6]*recommended/recommend* this fantastic book.

4.2

A Rewrite the sentences using the correct form of the verbs in brackets.

1 People think that the government will lose the election. (think)
It is ____________________.

2 People say that taxes are going to increase. (say)
It ____________________.

3 Research indicates that a sugar-heavy diet causes an increased risk of heart disease. (report)
A sugar-heavy diet is ____________________.

4 Scientists have said that eating dark chocolate improves brain function. (suggest)
It ____________________.

5 Research shows that staying physically and mentally active is a good way to prevent memory loss as you get older. (claim)
Staying physically and mentally active
____________________.

6 Studies have proven that mindfulness meditation reduces stress. (show)
Mindfulness meditation has ____________________.

B Find and correct the mistakes in the sentences. One sentence is correct.

1 Going for a five-minute walk is thought be a good way to increase your energy in the afternoon.
2 Taking short breaks when you work is claim to increase your productivity.
3 Studies shown that being around positive people helps you to feel more energised.
4 It is thought that using relaxation techniques helps to reduce stress.
5 Studies suggests that extreme physical exertion or emotional upset may trigger heart attacks.
6 Coffee drinkers are said that live longer.

4.3

A Put the words in the correct order to make sentences.

1 visit / the / we / later / might / museum ____________________
2 knows / where / us / presumably / find / to / he ____________________
3 that / I / be / good / would / a / idea / guess ____________________
4 on / I'm / hamburgers / keen / not / particularly ____________________
5 a / kind / it's / of / pastry ____________________
6 I / get / guess / could / or / take-away / something / we / a ____________________

GRAMMAR

5.1 quantifiers

uncountable	countable	countable and uncountable
a bit of a little (too) much (a large) amount of a great deal of	(too) many one or two several a couple of a few each a large number of	enough a lot of/lots of loads of plenty of some all

Some quantifiers are used with uncountable nouns only.
We had ***too much luggage****.* (*Luggage* is uncountable. We can't say *one luggage, two luggages*, etc.)
He drank ***a little water****.*
The ***amount of effort*** *it took was incredible.*

Other quantifiers are used with countable nouns only.
Several people *came to our house.* (We can count people: *one person, two people, three people*, etc.)
I saw him ***a few times****.* *We spent* ***a couple of days*** *there.*

Some quantifiers can be used with both countable and uncountable nouns.
We have ***plenty of time****.* (*Time* is uncountable.)
I brought ***plenty of friends****.* (*Friend* is countable.)

Common errors with quantifiers

little **and** ***a little*** **(uncountable)**
Little means *almost none*. It is used in a negative way.
A *little* means *more than none*. It is used in a positive way.
I have ***little time*** *for that kind of behaviour.*
We have ***a little bread*** *left. Would you like some?*

few **and** ***a few*** **(countable)**
Few means *almost none*. It is used in a negative way.
A few means *more than none*. It is used in a positive way.
Unfortunately, I have ***few friends*** *I can trust.* (*not many* – a bad thing)
I have ***a few books*** *you might like.* (*some* – a good thing)

too
Too means more than necessary. It is used in a negative way.
I hate this club. The music is ***too loud****, there are* ***too many people****, and the drinks cost* ***too much money****.*
We don't usually use *too* in a positive sense.
~~*This party is too wonderful!*~~

of
Some quantifiers are always followed by *of*.
I have ***a couple of*** *close friends.*
He's in ***a great deal of*** *trouble.*
We did ***a bit of*** *research.*
I eat ***plenty of*** *vegetables.*
We know ***a lot of*** *people here.*
Other quantifiers sometimes use *of* and sometimes don't. If the quantifier is followed by the noun only, it doesn't use *of*. If the quantifier is followed by adjectives, articles or pronouns, it uses *of*.
A few people *came.*
A few of us *came.*
A few of my *friends came.*
I knocked ***several times****.*
Several of the *players were injured.*
The report affected ***several of the*** *committee members.*

5.2 *-ing* form and infinitive

Certain words in English are usually followed by the *-ing* form or the *to*-infinitive.

use the *-ing* form	examples
after certain verbs (*like, love, hate, enjoy, fancy, mind, miss, imagine, can't stand*, etc.)	Do you **fancy going** out for a pizza? I **miss** not **going** to the beach every day.
after prepositions (e.g. after phrasal verbs: *look forward to, give up*; after fixed phrases ending in prepositions: *be keen on*)	I'm really **looking forward to seeing** them. He's just **given up smoking**.
as a subject or object (noun)	**Walking** is a great way to keep fit. Have you ever tried whitewater **rafting**?
use the *to*-infinitive	**examples**
after certain verbs (*seem, want, tend, promise, agree, manage, decide, refuse*)	I don't **want to be** difficult, but … We **decided to change** our plans.
to express purpose	He went to the library **to do** some research.

5.3 express your opinion

Well, if you ask me, … Personally, I'm (not) convinced … As I see it, … / The way I see it, …	It seems to me that … I'm absolutely convinced that … I have the feeling that … / I feel that …	You can take it from me that … I (don't) think that … In my opinion, …

PRACTICE

5.1

A Complete the texts with the words in the boxes.

plenty many few deal of enough

I spend a great [1]________ of time packing before my adventure trips. You hear lots [2]________ stories of people who die because they weren't prepared. I carry all the essentials – tent, waterproofs, [3]________ of dried food, etc. Also, I pack [4]________ water for an extra day. There have been a [5]________ occasions where I was trapped overnight and needed it. I think too [6]________ people underestimate the dangers of the wild.

of loads number bit much several

My friends say I always pack too [7]________ stuff. It's true: I bring [8]________ of equipment. But on [9]________ occasions my stuff has saved our lives. Once we were attacked by a large [10]________ of mosquitoes. Fortunately, I had a couple [11]________ cans of repellent, so we were OK. It's a [12]________ of a pain carrying extra equipment, but it can be the difference between life and death.

B Do these sentences need *of*? Add *of* to the underlined parts where necessary.

1 Several my friends went to the Amazon rainforest last year.
2 That route takes too much time.
3 There are a large number venomous snakes in Australia.
4 We had enough water to last us the whole trip.
5 There were a few people at the site.
6 I spend an enormous amount time in airports.

5.2

A Complete the sentences with the correct form of the verbs in brackets.

1 Do you fancy ________ (go) to a party later?
2 I'm not very keen on ________ (listen) to loud music.
3 Do you mind ________ (turn) down the volume a little, please?
4 He refused ________ (answer) his phone.
5 ________ (eat) healthily is important to me.
6 They tend ________ (get up) late in the morning.
7 I can't stand ________ (live) in this country any longer.
8 She's decided ________ (study) economics at university.

B Underline the correct alternatives to complete the conversations.

1 A: Do you like living here?
B: Yes, I can't imagine *be/to be/being* anywhere else.
2 A: Where's Julian?
B: I'm not sure. He promised *meet/to meet/meeting* us here.
3 A: Where are they going on holiday?
B: To Madeira *visit/to visit/visiting* relatives.
4 A: Where are you off to?
B: I'm going out. I can't stand *listen/to listen/listening* to everyone argue.
5 A: Have you tried talking to her about it?
B: Yes, but it doesn't seem *make/to make/making* any difference.
6 A: What does it feel like when you go paragliding?
B: It's the closest you can get to the feeling of *fly/to fly/flying* like a bird.

5.3

A The conversation has some missing words. Find the correct place to include each of the words in the box.

I'm ask seems way take think have opinion

A: You can it from me that Beijing is one of the best places in the world to live.
B: Personally, not convinced. I mean it's got serious problems with pollution. The I see it, a perfect city needs to have clean air and green spaces, and you don't get much of either of those in Beijing.
A: That's true, but Beijing is a good city for professionals though. It to me that if you're looking for a good job, Beijing has lots to offer. Salaries might not be as high as in some Western countries, but in my the cost of living is lower too. I that you can live a pretty good life in the city.
B: Well, if you me, it's a really stressful city. With more than 21 million people, it's one of the most heavily populated cities in the world. I feel this too many people for one place. It's just too busy! I'm convinced that there are much better places to live.
A: I the feeling I'm not going to be able to convince you about this one.
B: You're right about that. I can't imagine I'd change my mind about it.

GRAMMAR

6.1 modals of deduction

really certain	will	He always arrives at nine. He**'ll be** here any minute. It's nearly 8 o'clock already. There **won't be** enough time to eat before we leave.
	must, can't	That road is closed. There **must be** a better route to the airport. There **can't be** only one way to access the account.
very likely	shall	The train has just left, so I **shall be** there in about twenty minutes. I'm going out for lunch but I **shan't be** long.
	should	I filled up with petrol, so there **should be** enough to get us to Glasgow. It **shouldn't be** too difficult to change the tickets.
possible	might, may, could	Adriano is moving to Canada, so this **might be** the last time we see each other. There are two appointments left for this afternoon, so we **may be** able to fit you in. Bring that book. It **could be** useful.

6.2 third and mixed conditionals

third conditional

conditional clause	result clause
if + past perfect	*would* + *have* + past participle

Use the third conditional to talk about imaginary or hypothetical situations in the past. These are unreal or impossible situations.

*If I **had been** alive in the sixteenth century, I **would have hated** it.* (It's impossible that the speaker was alive in the sixteenth century.)

*We **would have helped** you **if we'd known** about your problem.* (We didn't know about it.)

spoken grammar

It is common to hear people using a *would* clause twice in a third conditional sentence.

~~*If I would have seen you, I would have spoken to you.*~~

At present, this is considered incorrect grammar, but this might change in the future.

mixed conditional

conditional clause	result clause
if + past perfect	*would* + infinitive without *to*

Use the mixed conditional to talk about imaginary or hypothetical situations in the past with results in the present. The *if* clause refers to the past. The *would* clause refers to a hypothetical present.

*If I **hadn't broken** my leg, **I'd be** a professional athlete now.*

*We**'d be** in Turkey now if our plane **hadn't been delayed**.*

We can also use the mixed conditional to talk about a present or future condition with a past result. The *if* clause refers to the present. The *would* clause refers to a hypothetical past.

*If you **were** French, you **would have understood** what the man said yesterday.*

*I **would have been** a model if I **were** taller.*

It is also common to use *would* + *be* + *-ing* form in the result clause.

*If the TV **hadn't broken down, I'd be watching** the film!*

*We**'d be sleeping** now if the baby **hadn't woken** us up.*

6.3 ask for and express agreement/disagreement

asking for agreement (using a question tag)	That's definitely one of the keys, **isn't it?** Getting eight hours of sleep is important, **right?**	It's so important, **isn't it?** You like listening to music, **don't you?**
agreeing	Yes, definitely. Absolutely. I (totally) agree. That's right./You're so right. Totally!	Tell me about it! (slang) No doubt about it. That's so true./That's probably true. It really does!
disagreeing	Really? I don't think so. No way! (strong)	Not necessarily. I'd say the opposite.

PRACTICE

6.1

A Underline the correct alternatives to complete the sentences.

1 I'm sure he'll find a job soon. = It *could/won't/should* be long before he finds a job.
2 Perhaps you're right. = You *might/will/can't* be right.
3 I'm sure you're joking. = You *shall/must/may* be joking.
4 That's definitely not a good sign. = That *must/may/can't* be a good sign.
5 I'm going out but I'm sure I will be home soon. = I *might/won't/can't* be long.
6 You have taken some medicine, so you will probably feel better soon. = You *shouldn't/should/must* feel better soon.
7 There are no more rooms available. I'm sure the hotel is full. = The hotel *may/can't/must* be fully booked.
8 They have done nothing all morning. I'm sure they're bored. = They *shall/can't/must* be really bored.

B Rewrite the second sentence using modal verbs. Start with the words in brackets. More than one answer may be possible.

1 All the lights are out. I'm sure they haven't got here already. (they)
They can't be here already.
2 These figures don't add up. It's possible that you're making a mistake. (you)
3 Their plane landed two hours ago. I'm sure they'll be here any minute now. (they)
4 You're going to jump out of an aeroplane? I'm sure you're crazy! (you)
5 We'll arrive ten minutes before the start of the show. I'm fairly sure there will be enough time to collect the tickets. (there)
6 Charities are sending money and food. I don't believe that is the best way to help them. (that)
7 I'm going to the shopping mall. The website says it's open until nine. (the shopping mall)

6.2

A Write one third conditional sentence for each pair of sentences. Start with the idea in the second sentence.

1 I didn't go to the dinner. I didn't have time.
If I'd had time, I would have gone to the dinner.
2 Amanda missed the plane. She got stuck in a traffic jam.
3 It was expensive. You didn't buy tickets online.
4 I didn't finish the race. I felt sick after one mile.
5 He didn't become famous. He died young.
6 They failed the test. They didn't study.
7 She didn't escape. The police found her.
8 I didn't buy the books I wanted. I didn't have enough money.

B Underline the correct alternatives to complete the sentences.

1 If we *notice/had noticed* his gambling problem earlier, he wouldn't be in prison now.
2 I'd be relaxing in my beach villa if you *haven't/hadn't* lost that lottery ticket!
3 If *I'd seen/I'd been seeing* the car coming, I wouldn't be in hospital now!
4 We'd know the answers if we *would have/had* paid attention in class.
5 He wouldn't be working here if he *hadn't finished/didn't finish* his degree.
6 You'd understand the situation if *you'd heard/you would hear* the discussion last night.
7 I'd *written/write* to her every day if I hadn't lost her email address.
8 If I *hadn't lost/wasn't losing* the key, I'd be at home now.

6.3

A Complete the conversations with the words/phrases in the boxes.

necessarily think so right really

A: If you want to be happy, I think you need to do a job which you feel passionate about, [1]________?
B: Not [2]________.
A: What do you mean?
B: Well, I think doing nothing might be the answer.
A: [3]________? I don't [4]________.

no doubt way that's probably isn't it

A: I think *Loud* is Rihanna's best album, [5]________?
B: Absolutely! [6]________ about it.
A: I also like *Rated R* though.
B: No [7]________. I don't like that one. It's too depressing.
A: Yes, [8]________ true.

definitely isn't it it really does tell me don't you

A: You really enjoy discussing politics, [9]________?
B: Yes, [10]________. It's so important, [11]________? It actually makes a difference to people's lives.
A: [12]________! It's how we change the world, right?
B: [13]________ about it!

7 LANGUAGE BANK

GRAMMAR

7.1 making comparisons, *so* and *such*

as + adjective + as

Use *as* + adjective (or adverb) + *as* to say something is equal to or the same as another thing. We can use *nearly* or *almost* to say the two things are not exactly the same.

*She's **as tall as** her sister.*

*This car **is nearly as old as** mine.*

Use *not as* + adjective (or adverb) + *as* to say something is less than another thing.

*Our house **isn't as big as** yours.*

*He doe**sn't sing as beautifully as** you.*

so and such

So and *such* have similar meanings.

Use *so* + adjective/adverb to show emphasis or strong feelings about something. Without *so*, the sentence would still be complete.

*That was **so kind** of you!*

*She paints **so brilliantly**!*

Also use *so* + adjective/adverb + *that* clause to describe something that leads to a result. In this use, without *so*, the sentence would not be complete.

*It was **so cold** that we needed coats.*

*The sofa was **so big** that it couldn't fit through the door.*

Use *such* + article (+ adjective) + noun to show emphasis or strong feelings about something. An adjective often comes before the noun. Without *such*, the sentence would still be complete.

*She's **such a great player**!*

*We had **such a nice day** at the beach!*

*He's **such a fool**!*

We also use *such* + adjective + noun + *that* clause to describe something that leads to a result. In this use, without *such*, the sentence would not be complete.

*It was **such a sad film that I cried**.*

*They had **such a good time that they returned the next day**.*

spoken grammar

We sometimes omit *that* from *so/such* sentences with a clause.

I was so tired (that) I fell asleep.

It was such a good deal (that) we bought two of them!

7.2 *be/get used to* vs *used to*

present habits

Use *be used to* + *noun/-ing* to talk about something you are accustomed to doing; it's usual for you to do this.

*I'm a postman, so I'**m used to getting up** early.*

*The weather is very hot but we live in Spain, so we'**re used to it**.*

Use *get used to* + *noun/-ing* to talk about something you become accustomed to; it is no longer unusual or strange.

*At first I didn't like the food but I soon **got used to it**.*

*I don't think I'll ever **get used to their accent**. It's difficult to understand.*

past habits

Use *used to* + infinitive (without *to*) to talk about a habit or state in the past, which is usually something you don't do now or is no longer the case. In negatives and questions, change *used to* to *use to*.

*We **used to live** on the edge of a forest. We don't live there anymore.*

*I **didn't use to enjoy** rap music but now I quite like it.*

7.3 responding to suggestions

questions	Is it really? Are you serious?
a *so* or *such* sentence	That's such a nice thing to do. That's such a good idea. You're so clever!
that sounds/that's* + adjective/*that's a …	That sounds interesting/terrible/great/amazing. That's good/wonderful/unfair! That's a good idea.
***how* + adjective**	How awful! How interesting!
one-word comment	Brilliant! Congratulations! Excellent! Great!

PRACTICE

7.1 **A** Add *so* or *such* to the sentences for emphasis.

1 He's a liar!
He's such a liar!
2 The exam was difficult that no one passed.
3 That's not a great idea, Tom.
4 I'm hungry I could eat a horse!
5 We watched a boring film I fell asleep halfway through.
6 He runs fast that I can't keep up.
7 It was a terrible waste of time.
8 You're good at maths!

B Rewrite the sentences using the words in brackets.

1 The music was too loud for us to chat. (so, couldn't)
The music was ____________________.
2 The book was brilliant. I read it twice. (such, that)
It was ____________________.
3 Carlos plays well. Sara plays better. (doesn't, as)
Carlos ____________________.
4 He had a bad headache. He went to the hospital. (such, that)
He ____________________.
5 I was angry. I turned red! (so)
I ____________________.
6 The new building is tall. It's the same height as the old building. (as)
The new building ____________________.

7.2 **A** Find and correct the mistakes in the sentences. Two sentences are correct.

1 When we lived in Italy, we used to eating a lot of pasta.
2 After living in such a big house, it's hard to get used to live in a small apartment.
3 Didn't your grandparents got used to live in that village?
4 The government has warned that we may need to be used to increased taxation.
5 We've lived in Manilla for a long time, so we're used to the hot weather.
6 Kate and I used to work together in marketing.
7 I don't think I would ever getting used to living in such a dangerous place.
8 I'm really not get used to this new work schedule.

B Complete the conversations with *used to*, *be used to* or *get used to*.

1 A: How are you finding life in Bangkok?
B: It's great, thanks, but it's very different to what ________.
2 A: Were you shy as a child?
B: Yes, I found it really hard to talk to people. I ________ feel too embarrassed.
3 A: Did you enjoy student life at university?
B: Yes, although I never ________ living together with so many people. It was always too noisy and too messy for me.
4 A: What did you find difficult when you first came to the UK?
B: I found it hard to ________ the weather. It's always raining!
5 A: I haven't lived here for very long.
B: Really? Where did you ________ live?
6 A: Be careful! Remember to drive on the left.
B: I know but I just can't ________ it.

7.3 **A** Complete the responses with the words in the box.

serious	awful	excellent	sounds	such	that's	so	it

1 A: Why don't we go to that new restaurant?
B: ________ a good idea.
2 A: My plan is to host a surprise ninetieth birthday party and invite all his old friends.
B: That ________ amazing! And it's very kind of you.
3 A: He told us to bring six water bottles each!
B: That's ________ ridiculous! No one needs that much water!
4 A: My suggestion is that you fix the roof yourself.
B: Are you ________? I know nothing about roofs!
5 A: I've decided to go to college for three years, then try to start a business.
B: That is ________ a great plan!
6 A: It's a good idea to get there two hours before it starts.
B: Is ________ really? Isn't that far too early?
7 A: The plan was to retire there, but then the house burned down.
B: Oh no! How ________!
8 A: We're hoping to expand the office to Asia.
B: ________! That could make a big difference.

GRAMMAR

8.1 relative clauses

defining relative clauses

Defining relative clauses give essential information about a person, place, thing, etc.

- Use relative pronouns to join the main clause and the relative clause.

subject	relative pronoun	example
person	*who* or *that*	She's the woman who I spoke to.
thing	*which* or *that*	This is the pen which he used.
place	*where*	This is the city where she grew up.
time	*when*	That was the day when everything changed.
possession	*whose*	That's the man whose house burned down.

- It is possible to leave out the relative pronouns *who*, *which* and *that* when this word is not the subject of the relative clause.
  That's the man (who) I spoke to today. (The subject is *I*, not *who*, so we can leave out *who*.)
  That's the man who works with me. (The subject is *the man*, so we cannot leave out *who*.)

non-defining relative clauses

- Non-defining relative clauses give non-essential, extra information about a person, place, thing, etc. The sentence is grammatically correct without the non-defining relative clause.
  Richard, who I've known for ten years, is my best friend.
  Richard is my best friend.
- Use commas before and after the relative clause.
  Istanbul, where I was born, is a beautiful city. NOT
  ~~*Istanbul where I was born is a beautiful city.*~~
- In non-defining relative clauses, we cannot leave out the relative pronoun.
  The film, which starred Brad Pitt, was great. NOT
  ~~*The film, starred Brad Pitt, was great.*~~
- In non-defining relative clauses, we cannot use *that* instead of *which* or *who*.
  The teacher, who I met when I was six, became a good friend. NOT
  ~~*The teacher, that I met when I was six, became a good friend.*~~

8.2 future forms

***be going to* + infinitive**

Use *be going to* + infinitive for a prediction based on evidence.
*Watch out! You**'re going to crash**!*

will/won't

Use *will/won't to* make general predictions about the future.
*Mobile banking **will** help people in poor countries.*
*You **won't** need to carry cash in the future.*

probably *will/won't*

You can make a prediction less certain by adding *probably.*
*Mobile banking **will probably help** people in poor countries.* (We think this is likely but we're not certain.)
*You **probably won't need** to carry cash in the future.* (It's not likely.)

may/might

Use *may/might* to make predictions which are less certain.
*You **might need to** bring an umbrella.* (We can't be sure if it will rain, but it's possible.)
*It **may be** the last time we see each other for a while.* (We're not sure when we'll next meet, but it probably won't be soon.)

NOTE: *Might not* can be contracted to *mightn't* but *may not* cannot be contracted to *mayn't.*
*His idea **mightn't/may not** work.* NOT ~~*His idea mayn't work.*~~

be due to

Use *be due to* for something that is expected to happen/is planned.
***I am due to** finish work in November.*

be about to

Use *be about to* for something that is going to happen very soon.
*She's not working at the moment because she**'s about to** have a baby.*

be likely to

Use *be likely to* for a prediction that is probable.
*We**'re not likely to** leave in the next thirty minutes.*

be bound to

Use *be bound to* for a prediction that is very likely.
*Don't worry. You**'re bound to** find a job sooner or later.*

8.3 guessing and estimating

guessing	
Perhaps … I'd imagine … Is it something to do with …? it might be …	It could be … It can't be … There's no way it's …

estimating numbers
approximately more or less I'm not sure, but I'd estimate … At a rough guess, I'd say …

PRACTICE

8.1

A Underline the correct alternatives to complete the story.

Intruder cleans up

Last Thursday, Mike Bazantkis returned from Croatia, [1]*which/where* he'd been on holiday, to discover that his front door was unlocked and the windows open. Bazantkis, [2]*whose/who* lives alone, immediately searched the house for objects [3]*what/that* might be missing. To his surprise, he found none. A painting [4]*which/who* was worth over 5,000 pounds was untouched, and the intruder had also left televisions and computers [5]*where/that* were worth thousands. In fact, the intruder, [6]*whose/who* identity remains unknown, hadn't stolen anything and had cleaned the house. Bazantkis said, 'I panicked. It was one of those moments [7]*which/when* you think your world has ended. But then I saw that the 'burglar' hadn't taken anything, had tidied up, and left me some food in the fridge. It was almost as if my mother had broken in!' Bazantkis reported the break-in to the police, [8]*who/which* said they were 'completely baffled' by the incident.

B Join the sentences using relative clauses. Use the words in the box. Add punctuation and omit words where necessary.

which (x2) when where who whose

1 Can you see that hospital? You were born there.
That's the hospital ________________.

2 Do you know that woman? Her daughter is a famous dancer.
That's the woman ________________.

3 The dress is black. It arrived today.
The dress, ________________ black.

4 A girl talked to me. She was from Ethiopia.
The girl ________________ Ethiopia.

5 It was 2a.m. At that moment, the phone rang.
It was 2a.m. ________________.

6 I worked as a waiter. I hated it.
I worked as a waiter, ________________.

8.2

A Find and cross out one extra word in each sentence.

1 I can't believe I'm will about to start my new job.
2 You're not to very likely to meet them while you're staying.
3 We'll probably to travel across the Alps towards Italy.
4 I have to get this work finished tonight, as I'm might due to hand it in tomorrow.
5 Enjoy the concert. We might will probably see you there.
6 Have you seen Tamara yet? She is due to will arrive any minute.
7 They're flying direct so they're bound about to get there before us.
8 I've just got the tickets. We're going will to San Francisco for our holidays!

B Circle the correct answer, a), b) or c), to complete the text.

My wife and I [1]____ start a new business called Mini-me Baby, selling baby clothes online. We're really excited about it because we've never had a business of our own before. Karolina is very creative, with good ideas about design, so she [2]____ in charge of choosing the collection and dealing with orders, whilst I [3]____ look after sales and marketing. Most of our customers [4]____ women working in offices, who don't have much time for shopping. We [5]____ also attract customers who live outside the city so they do their shopping online. It [6]____ really hard work, and we [7]____ make a lot of money to start with, but if we have a good strategy then we [8]____ start making money within a couple of years. The website [9]____ launch later this month. Look out for us!

	a)	b)	c)
1	a) are about to	b) is going to	c) am about to
2	a) will probably	b) 's going to be	c) might to be
3	a) will to	b) due to	c) will
4	a) are due	b) is likely to be	c) are likely to be
5	a) might	b) may be	c) about to
6	a) are bound	b) 's bound to be	c) will probably
7	a) probably may	b) don't due to	c) probably won't
8	a) 'll probably	b) probably will to	c) might to
9	a) is due	b) is due to	c) is likely

8.3

A Complete the conversations with the words in the box.

rough do approximately less could estimate

1 A: What's the world's population?
B: More or ________ seven and a half billion.

2 A: What is philology?
B: I think it's something to ________ with the study of language in texts.

3 A: How many countries are there in the world?
B: I'm not sure, but I'd ________ about 200.

4 A: How many people live in Madrid?
B: At a ________ guess, I'd say 3 million.

5 A: Is *The Lord of the Rings* the most popular novel of all time?
B: It ________ be. I'm not sure.

6 A: How long can a person survive without eating?
B: I don't know. My guess is ________ thirty days, but it depends on the person.

Lesson 1.1 MULTI-WORD VERBS

A

B

C

D

E

1 A Match captions 1–5 with pictures A–E.

1 She seemed perfect for the job, so we **took** her **on**. But she got bored and **took up** parachuting.
2 You have to **hand in** your valuables at the front desk. They **hand them back** when you leave.
3 We've **put together** a plan to raise money to rebuild the house. We can't **put it off** any longer.
4 You can't spend your whole life **looking back** at your mistakes. You should always **look ahead**.
5 While he was sleeping, my husband **kept on** talking about monsters! Then today he told me to **keep to** the main road!

B Match the multi-word verbs in bold in Exercise 1A with definitions 1–10. Put the multi-word verbs in the infinitive.

1 stay on a particular path or course of action
2 delay something
3 think about something that happened in the past
4 return something
5 employ someone
6 start a new hobby/activity
7 prepare something by collecting ideas and information
8 continue doing something
9 think about/plan for the future
10 give something to someone in authority

Lesson 1.3 EVERYDAY OBJECTS

1 A Match words 1–10 with photos A–J.

1 plug
2 button
3 envelope
4 cushion
5 adapter
6 lighter
7 shoelaces
8 belt
9 flash drive
10 stool

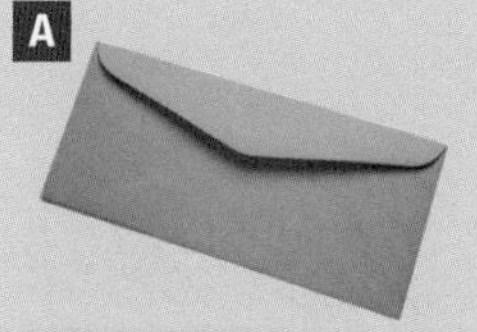
A

B

C

D

E

F

G

H

I

J

B Complete the sentences with words from Exercise 1A.

1 This chair is very uncomfortable. Could you pass me that ________, please?
2 I want to light this candle but I need a ________.
3 Before you go for your run, make sure you tie your ________ tightly.
4 He was sitting on a ________ at the hotel bar.
5 I've got my laptop, but I need an ________.
6 You should save your presentation on a ________.
7 She put the letter in a pink ________.
8 Oh no! The ________ just fell off my jacket.
9 These trousers are too big for me to wear without a ________.
10 I think it will work if you try pushing the ________ into the socket.

Lesson 2.2 PARTS OF A BUILDING

1 A **Work in pairs. How many of the words in the box do you know? Write them in the correct places in pictures A–C.**

ceiling hallway basement attic balcony gutter solar panel chimney roof veranda

B **Work in pairs. Answer the questions about the words in Exercise 1A. More than one answer may be possible.**

1 Which of these is good for the environment?
2 Which might be used more in winter? Why?
3 Which is good for storing things?
4 Which might get blocked sometimes?
5 Which might you sit on when there's beautiful weather?

Lesson 2.2 SUFFIXES

1 **Complete the words in the sentences with the suffixes in the box.**

-ment -able -ful -ion -ness -ous -ish

1 The new policy could have disastr____ effects on the economy.
2 It's been a dread____ hurricane which has caused so much damage.
3 I'm not sure that this dress is really suit____ for the occasion.
4 It was a fabul____ party. We had a lot of fun.
5 I'm sure she'll handle the job well. She's perfectly cap____ .
6 I've got my final exam today, so I'm feeling a bit nerv____.
7 Unfortunately, we lost a lot of money. It was not a wise invest____.
8 We've had a wonderful time here. We really appreciate your kind____.
9 I have a lot of admirat____ for the way he deals with people. He's a very good boss.
10 It would be fool____ of us to refuse the invitation.
11 They looked up at the shooting stars in amaze____.
12 He only ever thinks of himself. He's completely self____.

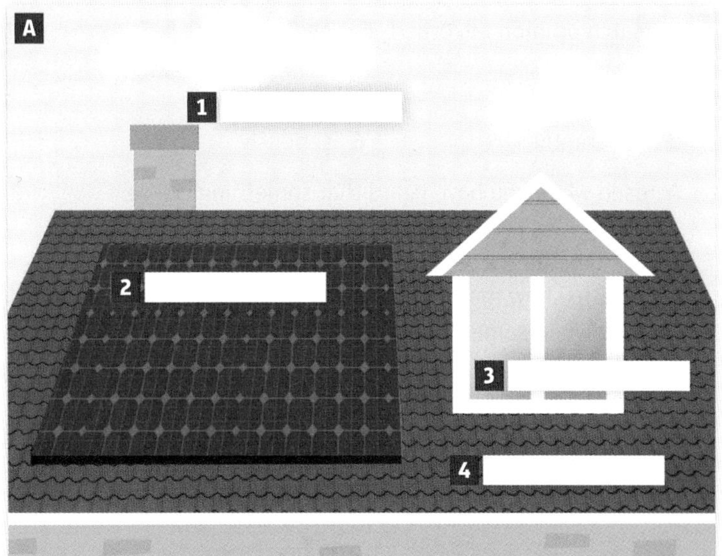

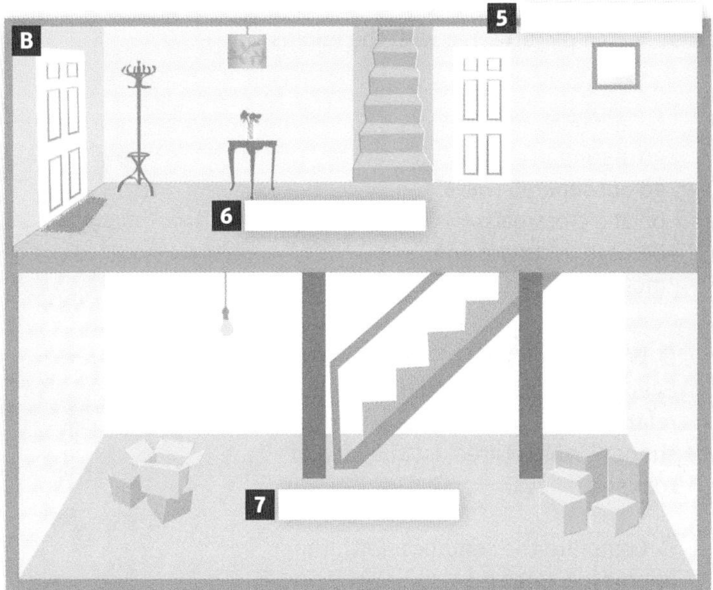

Lesson 3.1 OPINION ADVERBS

1 A Match opinion adverbs 1–6 with definitions A–F.

1 obviously
2 honestly
3 apparently
4 definitely/certainly
5 personally
6 seriously

A used when you have heard that something is true but you are not completely sure about it
B used to emphasise you are giving your own opinion
C used to show that what you're saying is not a joke
D used when something is easy to notice or understand
E used to emphasise that what you are saying is true (even if it is surprising)
F used to mean 'without any doubt'

B Underline the correct alternatives to complete the sentences.

1 The forecast is good. It's going to be hot at the weekend, *apparently/seriously*.
2 I'm *apparently/seriously* worried about Eve. She hasn't been to work all week.
3 He hasn't even started his report! He *obviously/personally* has more important things to worry about.
4 There is no doubt in my mind. I *definitely/apparently* think you should take the job.
5 *Personally/Definitely*, I don't think much of that idea. I feel we should look for an alternative.
6 I *apparently/certainly* never expected to become famous. It came as a complete surprise.

Lesson 3.2 IDIOMS

1 A Match pictures 1–6 with the idioms in the box.

be at a dead end go around in circles go our separate ways be at a crossroads be back to square one move in the same circles

B Work in pairs. All of the idioms in Exercise 1A can be used to talk about relationships. Which three include shapes? Which three use the idea of roads/journeys?

C Complete the sentences with the idioms in Exercise 1A.

1 We split up because our relationship was *at a dead end*.
2 We're not getting anywhere in this discussion. We're just __________.
3 I never met your friend. He's a singer and I'm a banker. We don't __________.
4 After a year of arguing, my boyfriend and I decided to __________. We're happier without each other!
5 They're __________. They could either split up or get married!
6 Our business plan was rejected by the bank manager, so we're __________.

1

2

3

4

5

6

Lesson 4.1 SCIENCE

1 A Work in pairs. Read the text. What do the words in bold mean?

Three big issues in science today

Genetically modified food has the potential to reduce starvation as it allows us to produce large quantities of food that is **immune** from insects and disease. However, we still don't know if it has long-term effects on health or the environment.

Another issue is **fossil fuels**: petrol, coal and natural gas. Fossil fuels take millions of years to form and we are using them up too quickly. Also, the way we use them contributes to **global warming**. There is currently a movement to use **renewable energy** instead of fossil fuels.

A third issue is **cloning**. We have the technology to reproduce life forms from their **DNA**, and this may prevent the **extinction** of some animals. However, cloning is unnatural and not part of **evolution** and many believe it is **unethical**. The answer may lie in **nanotechnology** – a method for manipulating extremely small quantities of **matter** such as atoms. Nanotechnology can allow us to regenerate injured body parts by growing them.

B Which of the words in bold in Exercise 1A can you use to describe pictures 1–8?

1

2

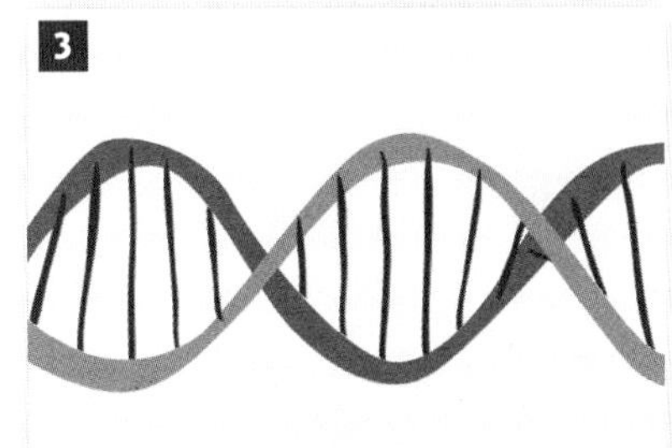
3

4

5

6

7

8

Lesson 4.2 COMMONLY CONFUSED WORDS

1 A Work in pairs. What is the difference between each pair of words in the box?

remember, remind
dessert, desert
journey, travel
fun, funny
receipt, recipe
nervous, irritable
sympathetic, nice (to describe someone)

B Complete the sentences with words from Exercise 1A.

1 I've got a terrible memory. Please can you ________ me to call my wife later?
2 He gets very ________ when he's driving, and shouts at other drivers.
3 It was wonderful to meet Katie after all this time. She was so ________ and welcoming.
4 I hope your ________ here was OK and there weren't too many delays.
5 You had a party? Oh that sounds ________.
6 A: That'll be twenty-five euros.
B: Thank you. Can I get a ________, please?
7 I hope you enjoyed your meal. Would you like to see the ________ menu?

Lesson 5.1 NATURE

1 A Match pictures 1–6 with the words in the box.

predator ecosystem endangered species prey reptile mammal food chain

1

2

3

4

5

6

B Work in pairs. Answer the questions. Then turn to page 133 and check your answers.

1 Which predator kills most frequently?
2 Which wild animal is usually said to be at the top of the food chain?
3 What is the world's largest mammal?
4 What is the largest type of reptile in history?
5 Which of these is NOT an endangered species: cheetah, red wolf, rhinoceros, giraffe, polar bear?
6 What two words were combined to create the word *ecosystem*?

Lesson 5.2 DESCRIBING PEOPLE

1 A Match the words in the box with definitions 1–10.

ambitious bad-tempered big-headed anxious charming bossy dependable impulsive upbeat sociable

someone who:
1 gets angry a lot
2 is pleasant and attractive
3 worries a lot
4 can be trusted and is reliable
5 likes telling other people what to do
6 is cheerful, optimistic and full of energy
7 thinks they are very important/the best
8 has big ideas and wants to do well in life
9 likes spending time with people
10 likes to act quickly on an idea (without thinking about it carefully)

B Underline the correct alternatives to complete the sentences.

1 It was good that I failed. It stopped me from getting too *big-headed/charming*.
2 I love the way he's always so *anxious/upbeat*. It really cheers me up.
3 I worry about her decisions. She can be a little *impulsive/sociable*.
4 She was *charming/bossy* and easy to work with.
5 Turgay has been such a help – really *dependable/impulsive* and trustworthy.
6 She is incredibly *anxious/ambitious* and wants to be prime minister one day.
7 I don't really get on with my older brother. He's too *charming/bossy*.
8 He's very *sociable/big-headed*, always going to parties or inviting people to the house.

Lesson 6.2 MONEY

1 A Find words in each sentence that match definitions a) and b).

1 Our accountant says the company will go bankrupt next month! We need money!
   a) without enough money to pay debts and continue as normal: *bankrupt*
   b) a person whose job is to write or check financial records: ____________

2 She's an investor. She bought shares in a company that was later sold for $100,000,000.
   a) equal parts into which the value of a company is divided: ____________
   b) someone who gives money to a company in order to make a profit: ____________

3 There are no jobs because the economy has collapsed and the country is in a recession.
   a) a time when there is very little trade and business: ____________
   b) the wealth and resources of a country, especially how its money and goods are produced/used: ____________

4 We pay a lot of tax in my country and we also have a problem with high inflation, so many people have difficulties buying food for their families.
   a) money you pay the government for public services: ____________
   b) when the price of things keeps increasing: ____________

B Work in pairs. Choose two questions to ask your partner.

1 Do you think taxes are too high in your country? Why/Why not?
2 If you were an investor, what companies would you buy shares in?
3 Do you remember the last time your country was in a recession or had high inflation?
4 What are the qualities of a good accountant? Would you be good at this job? Why/Why not?

Lesson 6.3 HAPPINESS

1 A Put the letters in brackets in the correct order to complete the expressions for describing happiness. Then match the expressions with pictures A–H.

1 I'm over the ____________ (omno).
2 He's walking on ____________ (rai).
3 He's on top of the ____________ (drolw).
4 I'm on ____________ nine. (duloc).
5 I'm in seventh ____________ (veehan).
6 I've never been ____________ (retetb).
7 They're in good ____________ (tipsris).
8 She's in a good ____________ (domo).

B One word in each sentence in italics is wrong or missing. Correct the wrong words or add the missing words.

1 We're so pleased about your results. *We're absolutely on the moon.*
2 I wouldn't disturb him at the moment. *He's not with a very good mood.*
3 Everyone was having a wonderful time. *They were all good spirits.*
4 I feel great. *In fact, I've never be better.*
5 I absolutely love my new job. *I'm in seven heaven.*

Lesson 7.1 VISUAL ARTS

1 A Complete definitions 1–8 with the words in the box.

filmed	Greek	dreams	body	looks	past	patterns	technical

abstract art: shapes and ________ that don't look like real things or people

figurative art: art that includes images of the human ________

conceptual art: art in which the ideas and concepts are more important than ________ skill

video art: art that uses ________ moving images

modernism: a style of art that rejected the ________ and focused on experimentation

classical art: art using traditional forms based on Ancient ________ and Roman styles

realism: a style which tries to show nature or life accurately, exactly as it really ________

surrealism: art that mixes strange, unrelated images from ________ or the unconscious mind

B Work in pairs. Which of the types of art in Exercise 1A do you like? Which don't you like? Can you name any artists who use these styles?

Lesson 7.1 MULTI-WORD VERBS 2

1 Some multi-word verbs have more than one meaning. Read the pairs of sentences. Underline the multi-word verb in each sentence and match it with its meaning, a) or b).

1 We made up a story using the pictures.
2 I missed two days of work when I was sick but I'll make up the time next week.
  a) work when you don't usually work because you haven't done enough
  b) invent

3 My car broke down yesterday.
4 We need to break down the instructions into simpler stages.
  a) stop working (e.g. a machine) because something has gone wrong
  b) separate into smaller parts to make something easier to understand

5 Elizabeth gave up smoking.
6 He spent hours looking for the keys but eventually he gave up.
  a) stop trying because something is too difficult to achieve
  b) stop doing something, especially something you do regularly

7 Can you turn down the music?
8 The job didn't offer enough money, so I turned it down.
  a) turn a switch on a machine so it produces less heat, sound, etc.
  b) refuse an offer, request or invitation

9 By playing so badly, we let down our fans.
10 Can you let down the rope so I can climb to the top?
  a) disappoint a group of people
  b) move something into a lower position

11 He works out every day in the gym.
12 We need to work out a solution to this issue.
  a) decide or plan something in order to solve a problem
  b) do exercises that make you stronger

Lesson 8.1 LEXICAL CHUNKS WITH *MAKE, DO, TAKE*

1 A Match the comments in each set with their explanations, a), b) or c).

Expressions with *make*

1 'Sorry! My dog ate my essay!'
2 'Everyone except John has to go to the gym.'
3 'I tried my hardest.'

a) She made an exception (for him).
b) She made an excuse.
c) She made an effort.

Expressions with *do*

4 'Our dog never hurt anyone or broke anything.'
5 'I washed the plates and forks.'
6 'I did the job for her, for free.'

a) He did the dishes.
b) He did her a favour.
c) He didn't do any harm.

Expressions with *take*

7 'I did all the work on my own! It was all me!'
8 'I believe you.'
9 'Tell me more about this.'

a) She took an interest in the subject.
b) She took the credit.
c) She took his word for it.

B Complete the sentences to make them true for you.

1 I take an interest in …
2 I hate it when people take the credit for …
3 I might take someone's word for it if …
4 The last time I made an excuse was …
5 I always make an effort when I'm …
6 The last time I did the dishes was …
7 I'm always doing favours for …
8 It never does any harm to …

Lesson 8.3 IDIOMS

1 A Work in pairs. What do idioms A–J mean? Discuss. Then check your answers in a dictionary.

laugh your head off

feel under the weather

sit on the fence

add fuel to the fire

have a face like thunder

keep a straight face

make ends meet

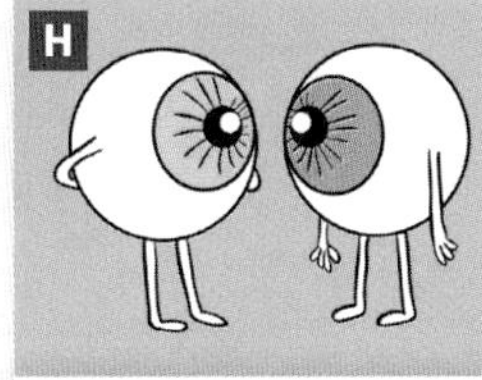

see eye to eye

get the sack

take something with a pinch of salt

B Match idioms A–J in Exercise 1A with definitions 1–10.

1 delay making a decision/be unable to commit to a decision
2 make a situation worse
3 have enough money to buy what you need to live
4 laugh a lot/laugh loudly
5 not completely believe something you are told because you think it may be untrue
6 be dismissed suddenly from a job
7 manage to stop yourself from smiling or laughing
8 be or feel ill
9 agree with someone
10 look extremely angry

C Complete the sentences with idioms from Exercise 1A.

1 Sophie is off work. She's feeling a bit ________.
2 They're both working really hard just to ________.
3 It was so funny. I really struggled just to ________.
4 I wouldn't ask the boss right now. She's got a ________.
5 You'll have to make a decision. You can't just ________.
6 Have you heard about George? Apparently, he ________ for stealing stationery.
7 I wouldn't believe that. You need to take what they say ________.
8 He's furious already. If you tell him about the car being stolen, it will only add ________.
9 We never really got on very well. We didn't see ________.
10 It was one of the funniest sights I've ever seen. I laughed ________.

D Choose two or three of the idioms in Exercise 1A to make sentences about your life. Then work in pairs and share your sentences.

My sister and I rarely see eye to eye about things.

Lesson 2.1

5 B Student A: follow these steps.

1. Read the information about your invention.
2. Prepare to answer the questions in Exercise 5A about your invention. Make some notes.
3. Work with Student B. Ask and answer questions about your inventions. Do not tell Student B what your invention is. Can you guess his/hers?

Science > Inventions

Microwave

Inventor: Percy Spencer
Year: 1964

This object was designed by mistake. At the end of World War II, an engineer was looking for another use for a magnetron, a device which generated microwaves used in radar systems. One day he was standing next to the machine when he noticed the bar of chocolate in his pocket had melted. He started to experiment and soon discovered that the machine worked well on popcorn, too!

Lesson 3.3

9 A Student A: read your roles and think about what you are going to say.

Situation 1

You bought a phone that was described as 'unbreakable'. You dropped it and it broke. You want a refund.

Situation 2

You are a manager. Your employee posted negative comments about the company on social media. Ask him/her not to do it again because it makes the company look bad. This is a formal warning.

Situation 3

You live with three others in a flat. One flatmate often leaves a mess in the kitchen. You (and the two others) think he/she should clean the kitchen after using it.

Lesson 4.4

6 A Student A: read about your scientist and make notes in the table on page 53.

Antonie van Leeuwenhoek was born in Delft, Dutch republic on 24 October 1631. He is best known for his work on the development of the microscope. Leewenhoek did not come from a family of scientists – his father was a basket maker – and he had no fortune or higher education. However, while working as a cloth merchant in Amsterdam, he saw his first microscope. He bought one of these simple microscopes for his own use, and over the years he started to develop the glass lenses to improve the magnitude of the microscope. He used his new, more powerful microscope to observe small insects, like bees. He is often known as 'the Father of Microbiology', having made some of the most important early discoveries regarding single-celled animals and plants, bacteria and red blood cells.

Lesson 6.1

2 B Student A: read the second part of the article and answer the questions.

1. What benefits does doing good have?
2. What was the experiment involving money hidden inside books trying to achieve?
3. What did Chris Topping do with the money he found? Why?

The science behind being GOOD

According to scientific studies, selfless behaviour is good for your health, mood and longevity. So in what ways can being nice actually be good for you?

Firstly, there is the feeling of pleasure you get from doing good – the 'helpers' high' – caused by the production of certain chemicals in the brain. Secondly, it seems that people who help others suffer fewer health problems themselves.

So, how can we encourage more people to be kind? Can one good deed lead to another? In one experiment, people buying books in the UK were astonished to find £5 notes inside them, with a note saying: 'Hi, if you are finding this money, then the universe is smiling at you today. Enjoy a cuppa* on me or pass it along to give another smile to someone else! Have a great day!'

Chris Topping, from Liverpool, decided to do something meaningful with the money he found. 'We bought some sandwiches and drinks for a few homeless people on the way home,' he said. 'I see them in the same spot every day, so I thought I'd buy enough for everyone.'

*Enjoy a cuppa on me. = Let me buy you a cup of tea. (UK)

Lesson 8.5

5 B Read the answers to the quiz questions.

1 Library of Congress, Washington D.C., USA
2 from the word *googol*, which is a term for a huge number (1 plus a hundred zeros)
3 generally thought to be Canada; about half of Canadian adults have been to university

Lesson 2.2

3 A Student B: read the text and answer the questions in the table on page 24.

Cave Digger

Sandstone rocks in Abiquiu, New Mexico

Ra Paulette has been creating artistic caves out of sandstone since 1987. Based in New Mexico, USA, Paulette digs into the earth to make the caves. Then he sculpts rooms and walls, columns and roofs, with beautiful designs and shapes. The result is a series of incredible underground interiors.

So far, Paulette has completed more than a dozen of these caves. They look as if they have been built by a team of engineers, architects and artists, but they haven't. Paulette has constructed them alone, with just his dog for company, and using only hand-held tools. He does it for the love of the process. 'When you're doing something you love, you want to do it all the time,' he says. 'I see this as an environmental project. I'm trying to open up people's feelings.'

Paulette has no qualifications as either an architect or a builder. He dropped out of college, hitchhiked across America and did odd jobs for years: postal worker, security guard, farm worker. In the summer of 1985 he got a job digging wells. This gave him the idea that he wanted to work with his hands. When he built his first cave, local people saw his amazing talents and began commissioning him to make more.

In recent years, his work has gone on the market. The caves' owners are able to sell the caves for around a million dollars, but Paulette hasn't made much money. He charges just $12 an hour for his services as a sculptor/builder.

In 2014 Paulette suddenly became famous when a documentary about him, called Cave Digger, was nominated for an Academy Award. Fame hasn't changed him at all.
He has just continued digging, sculpting and making places of rare beauty.

Lesson 4.5

1 b)	3 f)	5 a)
2 d)	4 c)	6 e)

Lesson 5.3

9 Student A: read about a policy for teaching maths in Shanghai. Prepare to tell your group about the policy and try to persuade them to include it. Then read about the criticism of one of the other policies. Be prepared to ask the speaker about it.

Shanghai: A model for teaching maths

In Shanghai, schools use a system for maths called the 'mastery approach'. Students in the class are not taught according to their individual ability; rather, the highly-trained, specialist teachers move through the programme slowly until every student understands. The system has resulted in students that are better at maths than anywhere else in the world.

Criticism for the Poverty in Peru project

Rural poverty in Peru remains high, and more investment in health and education is needed. Corruption is also a problem, particularly as the country's economy slows.

Lesson 7.3

7 A Student A: read about your hacks. Plan what you will say to your group.

Exercise hacks – keeping fit

- New to exercise? Run for just one minute a day. Add an extra minute every day.
- Listen to music while exercising. Fast rhythms means faster exercise.
- Listen to an audio book (in English!) while exercising.
- Add frozen fruit to your water bottle. It keeps water cold/adds flavour.
- Planning an early morning workout? Sleep in your exercise clothes.

Lesson 2.1

5 B Student B: follow these steps.

1. Read the information about your invention.
2. Prepare to answer the questions in Exercise 5A about your invention. Make some notes.
3. Work with Student A. Ask and answer questions about your inventions. Do not tell Student A what your invention is. Can you guess his/hers?

Science > Inventions

Chewing gum

Inventor: Thomas Adams

Year: 1870

Thomas Adams was experimenting with a substance called 'chicle', the sap from a South American tree. He was trying to use it as a substitute for rubber. However, his experiments kept failing and the inventor was feeling frustrated. Without thinking very much about it, he put a piece of the 'chicle' in his mouth and discovered he really enjoyed chewing it. This substance now comes in brightly-coloured packets you can buy in the supermarket. The bright colours help to make more sales.

Lesson 3.3

9 A Student B: read your roles. Think about what you are going to say.

Situation 1

You work at a phone shop. A customer bought an 'unbreakable' phone, but he/she broke it. The customer wants a refund. You are not allowed to give refunds. You can only replace the phone.

Situation 2

On private social media, you commented about bad things happening at work. Your comments were fair and accurate, but your manager is unhappy with you. You believe that what you say and do in private is not your company's business.

Situation 3

You live with three others in a flat. You are the only person who cleans the floors and the windows and tidies the living room. You do not clean the kitchen because you think they should do some housework.

Lesson 4.4

6 A Student B: read about your scientist and make notes in the table on page 53.

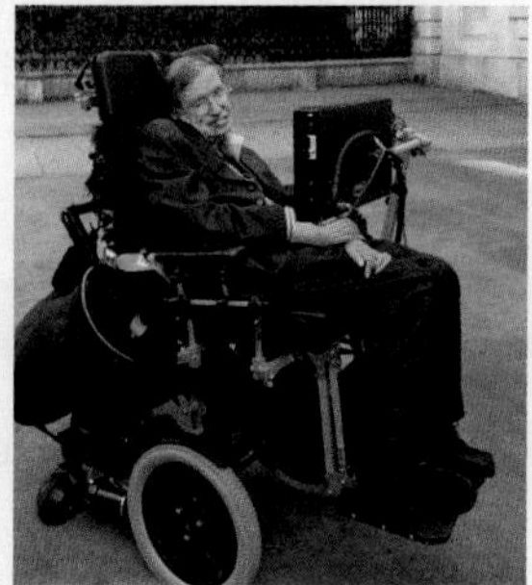

Stephen Hawking was born on 8 January 1942 in Oxford, England. He wanted to study Mathematics at university, but the college where he was accepted did not offer this course, so he studied Physics instead. He later went to Cambridge to study Cosmology. Hawking worked to understand the basic laws which govern the universe, using Einstein's theory of relativity to try and understand how the world began and what is the exact nature of a black hole. Aged twenty-one, he was diagnosed with ALS, a motor neurone disease, which meant that for much of his life he was confined to a wheelchair and had to use a computerised voice system. However, he continued his research into theoretical physics and also wrote many books and gave public lectures. He died on 14 March 2018.

Lesson 7.1

9 A Check your quiz results.

- If you chose mainly a), you are very creative. You probably like to make things in your free time.
- If you chose mainly b), you have an average level of creativity.
- If you chose mainly c), you aren't very creative, but you are probably very logical and sensible.

Lesson 7.3

7 A Student B: read about your hacks. Plan what you will say to your group.

Travel hacks **for happier holidays**

- Before leaving, scan your passport. Email the scan to yourself in case of theft or loss.
- Write *FRAGILE* on your luggage. Baggage handlers will treat it better.
- Freeze your water. You can't take bottled water through security. You can take ice.
- Use airport ATMs to get foreign currency and avoid changing money (bad rates and fees).
- Buy water/snacks in a supermarket. Hotel food is twice the price.

Lesson 8.3

8 Student A: read about your idioms. Then explain to Student B where these idioms came from.

1. ***Spill the beans:*** to vote, Greeks placed beans in a jar. A white bean was a yes. A brown bean was a no. The beans were counted in secret. If the container was knocked over, the beans were spilled and the secret was out.

2. ***Get side-tracked:*** if you get side-tracked, it means you get diverted from your objective. Early railroads only had one track. Sometimes trains would approach in the opposite direction, which caused a problem. So they built side tracks – short tracks next to the main track so that trains could park temporarily. Side tracks didn't go anywhere.

Lesson 2.2

3 A Student C: read the text and answer the questions in the table on page 24.

Lesson 5.3

9 Student B: read about a policy to get people to stop smoking in Australia. Prepare to tell your group about the policy and try to persuade them to include it. Then read about the criticism of one of the other policies. Be prepared to ask the speaker about it.

Australia: a solution to stop smoking?

Smoking is the leading cause of preventable death, leading to around 6 million deaths per year. In Australia people are giving up smoking at much higher rates than anywhere else. Why? They have some of the world's toughest anti-smoking laws. You're not allowed to smoke in public places, including playgrounds, train platforms and taxi ranks. Also they have some of the world's highest cigarette prices, strict laws about plain packaging and a huge media campaign. The government also introduced a digital app to help people give up.

Criticism for the model for teaching maths in Shanghai

Shanghai: The high pressure schooling system is often criticised because success is often linked to many hours of homework and extra tuition.

Shelter helper

Since 2015, California resident Elvis Summers has been building homes for the homeless. The first home he built was for sixty-year-old Irene McGee. She was living on the street, without even a cardboard box to sleep in. Summers saw her every day and decided to help her. He bought some materials and asked for donations of wood, and then he built the shelter, adding wheels to make it mobile. The home is roughly the size of a shed – one room, large enough for a person to lie down and store a few possessions.

Summers had himself videoed building the house in order to publicise what he was doing. The clip also showed the beautiful moment when Summers handed over the keys to Irene McGee. The video went viral and raised awareness of homelessness in Los Angeles. Since building that first home, Summers has launched a fundraising campaign which has raised over $100,000 in donations. A local church has also helped, offering 10,000 square feet of space in which wooden homes can be placed. Although his plans have received some opposition from the city, which has removed some of the homes because they were on public property, Summers says he'll keep on building.

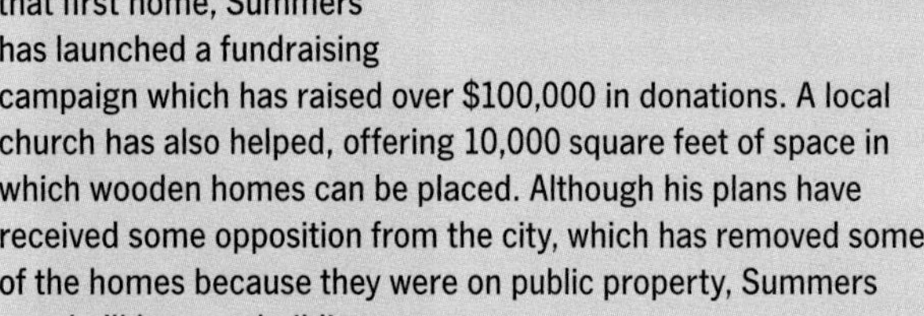

He and friends have now constructed over forty of the wooden shelters, allowing the homeless of Los Angeles to have some security, privacy and dignity. He has also been working on developing a mobile shower unit. In his own words, 'How we treat and care for those who are suffering and less fortunate determines what kind of society we are and how our future generations will act.'

Lesson 8.2

10 A Student A: Ask Student B questions to get the information you need to complete statistics 1–6. Then give Student B they information they ask for to complete statistics 7–12.

Crazy statistics

1. ________ % of humanity lives on less than $10 a day.
2. The average American will spend ________ months of their life talking on the phone.
3. If everyone on Earth properly washed their hands, nearly ________ lives would be saved every year.
4. Human life expectancy has increased more in the past 50 years that in the last ________ years.
5. You will probably spend about ________ months of your life on the toilet!
6. The average person will walk ________ km in their life. That's more than 3 times around the world!
7. Your probability of living to more than 110 years old is 1 in 7,000,000.
8. Your chance of eating a spider while you are asleep is actually close to 0%.
9. The average person will yawn about 250,000 times during their life.
10. Men in the United States have a 43.31% chance of getting cancer during their lifetime.
11. 0.3% of solar energy from the Sahara is enough to power the whole of Europe.
12. The human eye blinks about 4,200,000 times a year.

Lesson 4.4

6 A Student C: Read about your scientist and make notes in the table on page 53.

Ernest Rutherford
was born in New Zealand on 30 August 1871. He was a physicist who became known as the father of nuclear physics. In his early work he focussed on radioactivity. He developed a new form of radio receiver and also differentiated between alpha and beta radiation. He was awarded the Nobel Prize in Chemistry for his work into the chemistry of radioactive substances. In 1907 he moved to the University of Manchester, where he started work on splitting the atom in a nuclear reaction. During the first world war he worked on a top secret project to help submarines avoid detection.

Lesson 5.3

9 Student C: Read about a policy to reduce poverty in Peru. Prepare to tell your group about the policy and try to persuade them to include it. Then read about the criticism of one of the other policies. Be prepared to ask the speaker about it.

Peru: cutting poverty

Peru has cut its poverty rate in half in just ten years. After decades of economic growth, an inclusive economic policy has helped many of the poorest in the country. The government introduced schemes to provide basic services such as piped water, sanitation and electricity to slum areas, and supported social programmes for children, families and the over sixty-fives. This has helped to lift 7 million people out of poverty in the last five years. Communities played a role in the success of the programme, putting pressure on governments through direct action such as protests and roadblocks.

Criticism for the Australian anti-smoking policy

Some people have criticised the plans saying that governments shouldn't try to control our behaviour and that the policies lead smokers to feel excluded from society. Recent attempts to ban smoking in prisons led to some of the worst riots in recent history.

Lesson 6.1

2 B Student B: read the third part of the article and answer the questions.

1. How can fear of negative judgement from others affect our behaviour?
2. What kinds of people tend not to worry about being judged?
3. According to the article, what are the possible benefits of thinking only about yourself and not concerning yourself with others' opinions?

How being selfish can lead to success

Fear of doing something that results in negative judgement from others is very common. However, this fear can stop us from doing things like giving a presentation or complaining about poor service.

People who worry a lot about what other people think of them can be more easily manipulated by others. Self-centred or antisocial people don't worry about being judged and tend to be more successful.

It could be argued that once you start living for yourself and nobody else, you get a lot more done. This is a trait of many high achievers. It may not be 'good' to be 'bad' and not care about other people, but it clearly pays well.

Lesson 7.3

7 A Student C: read about your hacks. Plan what you will say to your group.

Tech hacks – make the most of your machines

- Need to charge your phone quickly? Put it into aeroplane mode. It charges twice as fast.
- Overheating laptop? Put two forks under it.
- Want to talk to a human when calling customer service? Keep pressing 0.
- Writing an essay? Paste it into Google Translate and listen. You'll hear mistakes.
- Emailing? Forgot to send an attachment or pressed 'Send' too soon? Enable Gmail's 'Unsend' button.

Lesson 8.3

8 Student B: read about your idioms. Then explain to Student A where these idioms came from.

1 ***Turn a blind eye:*** it means 'pretend not to see something'. In 1801 British naval officer Lord Nelson was told his commander had put up flags ordering a retreat. Nelson was blind in one eye. He looked through the telescope using his blind eye and pretended not to see the commander's order. Instead, he attacked and won the battle.

2 ***Miss a deadline:*** a deadline is a time limit. But the expression comes from the US civil war. Prisoners had to stay within a boundary, often just a line scratched in the ground. The guards told them, 'If you cross this line, you're dead.' Soon they began calling it a deadline.

Vocabulary bank, Lesson 5.1

1 B Read the answers to the questions.

1 human beings
2 the lion
3 the blue whale
4 the dinosaur
5 giraffe
6 *ecology* and *system*

Lesson 4.4

6 A Student D: Read about your scientist and make notes in the table on page 53.

Albert Einstein was born in Germany on 14 March 1879. When his family moved to Italy for work, Einstein stayed in Germany to finish his studies. He later moved to Switzerland where he took the exams for the Swiss Polytechnic. Despite his obvious capabilities in science and maths, his other grades were often poor and Einstein had a tendency to rebel against authority. Einstein's main area of research was related to gravity and in 1915 Einstein announced his general theory of relativity, for which he is most famous. In 1921 he won the Nobel Prize for Physics and is considered to be one of the most influential physicists of the twentieth century. .

Lesson 8.2

10 A Student B: Give Student A the information they ask for to complete statistics 1–6. Then ask him/her questions to get the information you need to complete statistics 7–12.

Crazy statistics

1 80% of humanity lives on less than $10 a day.
2 The average American will spend 6 months of their life talking on the phone.
3 If everyone on earth properly washed their hands, nearly 1,000,000 lives would be saved every year.
4 Human life expectancy has increased more in the past 50 years than in the last 200,000 years.
5 You will probably spend about 3 months of your life on the toilet!
6 The average person will walk 120,000 km in their lifetime. That's more than 3 times around the world!
7 Your probability of living to more than 110 years old is 1 in ________.
8 Your chance of eating a spider while you are asleep is actually close to ________%.
9 The average person will yawn about ________ times during their life.
10 Men in the United States have a ________% chance of getting cancer during their lifetime.
11 ________% of solar energy from the Sahara is enough to power the whole of Europe.
12 The human eye blinks about ________ times a year.

AUDIO SCRIPTS

Unit 1 Recording 3

M1 = Man 1 W1 = Woman 1 P = Presenter
M2 = Man 2 W2 = Woman 2 W3 = Woman 3

M1: When I was young, when we came back from holiday, what did we do? We'd roll up our sleeves, we'd hold forearms together to compare how brown we were, to show how good the holiday was. If you think about what the post-holiday ritual is now, we come back and we look at our phones with mock horror. And we say, 'Pff ... I had nearly a thousand emails when I came back from holiday. And then the person next to you says, 'Pff ... I had two thousand.'

W1: Busy-ness is a competition. By saying the number of hours you've worked, by saying the number of emails you've done, by saying the amount of things that you do – that's your badge of honour.

P: Hello, how are you today? Actually, don't say it. I know what's coming. The pre-programmed response to that question used to be, 'Oh, I'm fine.' Now it's much more likely to be, 'Oh, you know, busy.' I say it all the time and it's the truth. But if I'm honest, I also want you to think I'm busy. I mean, what kind of loser has nowhere he needs to be?

M1: Busy has become a brand. Somehow it speaks to our self-importance, it speaks to how essential we are to our world, if you like.

P: Tony Crabbe is a psychologist and the author of a book about busy-ness.

M1: And when we tell people we're busy, we persuade them with great detail about quite how busy we are because there's a need we feel for other people to validate our busy-ness.

P: And when everyone around you is constantly proclaiming their busy-ness, it's like it's contagious. David Drever is a manager at the internet payment company WorldPay, and busy-ness has been on his mind ever since he grabbed a copy of Tony's book while racing to catch a plane.

M2: I began to realise, albeit subconsciously, that whether you're in the lift, whether you're in the canteen, whether you're at home, whether it's my wife, every time you ask somebody, 'How are you?' 'Yeah, busy,' and it's really hard not to say it.

W2: If you're not busy, you're seen as not somebody that's delivering or potentially somebody that's lazy, so you're pre-conditioned to actually say that you're busy to showcase the fact that you're there for a reason almost.

P: That's Yasmin, who works with David. This need we seem to feel to demonstrate our busy-ness is so common these days you can lose sight of how strange it is. When did never having a spare moment become something to boast about?

M1: So, in the past, status was about bigger car, bigger house, bigger castle – depending on how far you go back – and these were the things that gave us status. Now, I don't think we've left those behind, but where does status really come from today? Status comes from our reputation – the stuff that we can share on Facebook – so actually, it's our experiences, it's the things that we can show people that we're doing.

P: Stephanie Brown is a psychologist who works in Silicon Valley in the US. And as the economy's become more and more competitive there, she's watched people become ever more obsessed with demonstrating their busy-ness.

W3: People began comparing their ninety-hour weeks and 'busy' was equated with progress and success. And we are always after success and how best to exhibit that.

Unit 1 Recording 6

1 I'm trying to get up at five a.m.
2 I'm really busy at the moment.
3 I try not to work in the evenings.
4 Before I know it, two hours has disappeared.
5 He's always looking at his phone.

Unit 1 Recording 7

A: So, my first item is my passport. I think it would be top of the list, definitely. That's indispensable. I mean, you need it to prove who you are.

B: Yeah, absolutely. I've got that, too.

A: And then I've got my laptop and hard drive. You know, most of my important documents and photos are on there, so that's essential, too.

B: Definitely. I agree. I've got my mobile phone. That's got everything on it – all my contacts and photos, and you can use it to get online.

A: Right. So ... phone. Yeah, that's vital.

B: What have you got next?

A: Umm, next I've got a blanket.

B: A blanket? Why have you chosen that? I mean, it's quite big to carry.

A: Well, yeah, but it's really special. It's made of really soft wool; my sister gave it to me. And I always wrap it round me when I'm feeling sad or anything, so I think that would be useful. And it would keep you warm. You can wear it.

B: OK, that's quite practical. A blanket. Anything else?

A: My coffee pot.

B: You're kidding!

A: No, I love this coffee pot. You know, it's one of those Italian ones. I bought it when I was travelling there. It makes really strong coffee.

B: That's not really essential though, is it? I don't think that would be my first choice.

A: Hmm, I take your point. I guess not.

B: In fact, I don't even drink coffee.

A: Ah, well, that would explain that. OK, how about a penknife? That's more useful. You can use it to cut up food, make some dinner. I'd say a penknife is pretty important.

B: Hmm ... I was thinking the same thing. And a cooking pot.

A: Cooking pot? Ooh I'm not sure about that.

B: No, I've got this great cooking pot. It's a bit heavy but you can cook anything in it. I always take it when we go camping, so you can always have a meal.

A: OK, I guess that sounds useful.

B: And my guitar. I'd have to bring my guitar.

A: Oh yeah, definitely. I've got music on my phone, but yes, a guitar. That should be on the list. And also, my ring.

B: Your ring? Tell me about it.

A: Well, it's a silver ring I was given on my sixteenth birthday, so it's pretty special.

B: OK. Yeah, I've got my dad's watch, too. It's no good for telling the time, but it has sentimental value.

A: Great!

Unit 1 Recording 9

I spent eight years working as a lawyer in New York. My clients were Wall Street corporations. I was dancing with the devil every day. The money was amazing and I loved the fast pace of life. But after eight years I got burned out, so I moved to a small town on the coast of Ecuador and started living the quiet life. My new house cost less than my bicycle in New York.

I was definitely healthier when I was living in Ecuador. I ate better food, did more exercise and found time to relax. I loved experiencing nature and the ocean, going for walks, looking at the stars.

Overall, it's hard to say which kind of lifestyle I prefer. I stayed in Ecuador for two years, but I came back because I missed the buzz of my work. I also felt a bit isolated at times, with my family and friends so far away.

In an ideal world, you'd do both: spend part of the year in big cities and part of the year putting your feet up by the sea or in the countryside, but I know that's not possible for most people.

Unit 2 Recording 1

P Presenter D = Danny

P: Hi, and welcome back to *Genius Designs*, where we're talking to Danny Schwartz about some of the latest designs to come out of the design show. So, Danny ...

D: Hi.

P: Hi, Danny. So, first of all, can I ask you what you know about some of these designs?

D: Sure. Let's look at this first one. It's called Birdy and it's a flight simulator. Basically, you climb onto the machine and it simulates the flight of a red kite flying over New York City.

P: Wow! The view of the city from above must be stunning.

D: Yeah, it's pretty cool. But what's amazing about it is that the flight of the machine is actually controlled by your body.

P: Really? So as you move, you control the flight of the bird?

D: Yeah, exactly.

P: So who developed the idea?

D: It was developed by scientists at the Zurich University of the Arts.

P: Amazing! But does it have any kind of functional use? Or is it just for fun?

D: I'm not sure. I think it's just a fun gadget – you know, perhaps something that tourists might like to try out.

P: Yeah, I'd have a go on that. It looks fun.

D: Yeah, looking down over New York City as if you were a bird.

P: OK, so I'm looking at these strange sort of

spoons now. Can you tell me if these are really edible?
D: Yes, they are. Anatolly Omelchenko spent six years developing these special edible spoons.
P: Six years? And what was the idea behind them? Why would you want to eat your spoon?
D: Well, basically, he was looking for a way to reduce the amount of plastic that's being used for takeaway foods.
P: OK.
D: So, he developed a spoon that's durable enough to use to eat your meal, but it's made out of dough, so when you've finished eating, instead of just throwing it away, you eat the spoon as well.
P: And do you know what it tastes like? Is it tasty?
D: Well, the dough can be flavoured however you like, so you can match the flavour of the spoon to the meal you're having.
P: I like that – it's very flexible. It's actually quite a groundbreaking idea. They're much better than plastic spoons, definitely – even biodegradable ones. But Danny, I have to say the design I'm most looking forward to hearing about is this one: horse sneakers. Now, this has to be a joke!
D: No, it's serious. This is a really novel product – I've never seen anything like it. These are the first ever running trainers designed specifically for horses.
P: Trainers for horses? I'm sorry, don't you think that's a bit ridiculous? I mean, horses have steel horse shoes, right? How useful is it really for them to wear these trainers?
D: Well, traditional horse shoes can be quite slippery on roads. These trainers are made of plastic, so they're lighter and they move with the horse's hooves, so it's more comfortable for both the horse and the rider. And also, they're clip-on, so you can put them on and take them off really easily.
P: Hmm … I'm not convinced, I'm afraid. I mean, who do you think would actually buy trainers for a horse?
D: You'd be surprised. People *are* buying them.
P: You're absolutely right, I *am* surprised. Now, what have we got here? Some very expensive water by the look of it.
D: Yes, well, this water was invented by coffee enthusiasts. …

Unit 2 Recording 7

1
A: I looked up this grant and it's for anything up to ten thousand pounds. It could solve our financing problems. I mean, at least the equipment and personnel. What do you think?
B: What's the name of the organisation?
A: Grey Fox Arts.
B: Grey Fox?
A: Yeah. I think it has potential.
B: What's the deadline?
A: A couple of weeks. It's a few forms to fill in. We have to include a description of the project with things like budget, personnel, equipment – that kind of thing.
B: OK, that sounds great. Let's take a look together.

2
A: So, the schedule.
B: I'm thinking we start filming mid-afternoon on Friday, around three. How does that sound?
A: Friday? Can't we begin on Thursday?
B: The weather forecast says it's going to rain on Thursday, so that's a non-starter.
A: Oh OK. We can't film in the rain.
B: No way. So around three on Friday?
A: I'm not sure that'll work because of the light. Can we start earlier, before it gets dark?
B: One-ish?
A: Yeah, that would be better.

3
B: Hey, great news! Mark James has agreed to be in the film.
A: Woah! Fantastic! He was amazing in that crime drama!
B: And he'll do it for nothing.
A: Amazing! How on earth did you manage that?
B: I know his wife, Sandra. I told you ages ago, remember?
A: Oh yeah.
B: So, I spoke to her and then she had a word with him and he agreed.

4
B: Well, we need to film in a shelter, and it has to be somewhere quiet. So, I was thinking, there's an old public shelter by the river.
A: OK. That's a possibility.
B: Down the far end …
A: You mean in the park?
B: Yeah.
A: That might work.
B: There's a shaded area with lots of trees. The shelter's there. It's quiet and I think it'll look fantastic.
A: Excellent! I like the sound of that.

Unit 2 Recording 9

That's amazing!
It's fantastic!
That's excellent!
How wonderful!
It's marvellous!
That was brilliant!
She's awesome!

Unit 3 Recording 3

1 You don't have to stay.
2 You shouldn't have stayed.
3 We should have told him.
4 We had to tell him.
5 I didn't have to do it.
6 I shouldn't have done it.

Unit 3 Recording 4

1
A: Since as long as I can remember, I've had problems making friends. It's not that I *wanted* to fit in. I just didn't like the kind of things that other kids liked.
B: You mean music, hobbies, clothes …
A: Yeah. All that stuff just seemed meaningless to me. I didn't want to hang out with the cool kids. I'm just not a cool kid and I don't want to be.
B: And do you think it's connected to your family background?
A: Oh, definitely. My parents are really quiet and although there's four kids, we live in a quiet household. We read, we eat together, we're very respectful of each other's space, and we're just not into partying.
B: So do you see this as a problem at school – like when you're trying to make friends?
A: Um, a little bit. It's not so much a problem – more a feeling that I'm just very different. Like when other teenagers are starting to go out and have boyfriends and stuff like that, I'm happier staying in and studying. It's more a question of looking for similar people, wanting friends who have the same interests. Friends like you, actually!
B: Have you ever been teased or bullied about being quiet and studious?
A: Never bullied, no. But I suppose there's some low-level teasing. Like, 'Why are you always reading? Why don't you come out with us?' But I think the important thing is to feel comfortable in your own skin and not try to pretend to be someone you're not.
B: Yeah, cos that won't work.
A: People see through that. You have to be yourself.

2
A: I'm going to finish my studies soon and I'll need to get a job – and that's going to be a big challenge.
B: Definitely.
A: I remember my dad saying the toughest time of his life was when the economy collapsed around 2008 and he lost his job. It became very hard to make ends meet, but he said it wasn't just the money. You also want to do something useful for society and contribute – you know, not just sit at home. But there was nothing available, so he did a lot of temporary work, which he hated. He just couldn't deal with it.
B: Manual labour – that kind of thing?
A: Yeah. There's nothing wrong with manual labour, but he was on day-to-day contracts, so he never knew whether he'd have work tomorrow. So, for me, that's one of the things I know will be challenging after I finish university. What's next? What am I going to do with the rest of my life? Will there be a job for me? So the thing I dread the most is the uncertainty.
B: Yeah. I think when you're at school or university, everything is kind of organised for you, but then you have to take a leap into the unknown and it can be kind of scary.

3
A: I think the most difficult challenges are usually transitional moments, and becoming old is one of them. You become invisible. I think it happens when you reach a certain age. People just don't take any notice of you or value your opinion.
B: Do you think it's something to do with the way society is set up? Society is all about being young, isn't it? Fashion, TV, film, music – all those things are really aimed at young people.

A: To a certain extent. And what I've noticed is that sometimes I'll walk down the street and I'll catch someone's eye, and in my head I'm a young person with ideas and energy, but to the other person I'm just old and grey; I'm a grandma and I have nothing to offer.
B: And older people have so much to offer.
A: I know. We have experience and wisdom. And the thing is, I love being with young people. I love new technology and ideas. I'm not constantly saying how much better it was in the old days, but it's still difficult to have your opinions valued.

Unit 3 Recording 6

E = Eric D = Daniela

E: Hi, how are you?
D: Fine, thanks.
E: Look, there's something I need to talk to you about.
D: Oh yeah?
E: I have an exam coming up and I'm studying, and … well, the problem is there's a lot of noise coming from your flat at night.
D: Oh, you mean last weekend?
E: Yeah, well, kind of every night. I mean last weekend but also during weekdays.
D: Really? We had a party on Saturday.
E: Yeah, the thing is, I can't study because of the noise.
D: Oh, sorry.
E: That's OK.
D: I didn't realise, to be honest.
E: It's OK. So I'm thinking perhaps you could lower the music?
D: I can turn the music down.
E: Yeah, or would you be able to wear headphones?
D: Sorry?
E: What about wearing headphones?
D: It's not just me who listens though. We kind of listen to music together.
E: Oh, OK. Um … I wonder if you could just keep it down.
D: When's your exam?
E: It's coming up next week.
D: Right. Well, you know what? We can just play music quietly for a week or two. That's not going to kill us. And then maybe when your exams are finished, we can have a massive party for you! Because I think we all go to the same university and we're all taking exams. What do you reckon?
E: That sounds like a great idea! Thanks a lot. What's your name?
D: Daniela. And yours?
E: I'm Eric.
D: Well, great to meet you properly, Eric, and sorry about the noise. I've seen you around. What do you study?
E: Um, music.

Unit 3 Recording 9

One of the biggest problems in Hong Kong is overcrowding, so in many parts of the city you find people living in these terribly cramped conditions, whole families living in one very small room or apartments which have been divided up into small sections for people to live in. It's literally like living in a shoe box, with no room to move, no room to keep your possessions, no window. The issue is that real estate is very expensive in Hong Kong, so landlords make the rent really high, which means that people who need to live in the city for work but are only earning a low wage can't afford anywhere better to live. It's a real problem. Sometimes the government pulls down the old buildings, like they did with the slum that was Kowloon Walled City, where the houses were built so closely together that it was always dark. It was extremely overcrowded and living conditions were terrible. They turned the area into a huge green park, which is great for tourists, and now it's a lovely space to sit and eat your lunch or to go for a walk. But the housing problem still remains. One solution would be to put a limit on how much the landlords can charge for rent. Or perhaps introduce a system for increasing the wages for lower-paid jobs so that families can afford somewhere better to live. I think those two things would certainly help.

Unit 4 Recording 1

AW = Anthony Walker JN = Janice Neil

AW: I'm Anthony Walker. Citizen science is one of the biggest trends in the scientific world. It's allowing normal people like you and me the chance to contribute to scientific projects that can help save the planet. I talked to research scientist Janice Neil about its impact.
What do citizen scientists study?
JN: Citizen scientists study all kinds of things, including the weather, plants, animals, rivers and forests. There are no limits. If it's in the natural world, they study it.
AW: How important are the contributions of citizen scientists?
JN: If we didn't have citizen scientists working on these research projects, we wouldn't be able to do them. It's as simple as that. There's just too much work. Let me give you an example. Every year, we name nineteen thousand species of animal. Of that nineteen thousand, citizen scientists are responsible for sixty percent. Amateurs discover and name nearly twelve thousand species a year.
AW: Who are these scientists and what exactly do they do?
JN: There's a lot of variety. As I said, if it's in nature, it can be studied. There are schoolchildren in the States who observe the sky each morning and send their observations to NASA. There's a group of retired people who search for fossils in dry river beds. If they find something, they record it by adding it to a database. There's a project in the Congo in Africa. The people there use smartphones to collect data about the natural habitat. So there's a lot of variety.
AW: How is technology a part of this?
JN: Technology plays a big part. If you don't have the tools, you can't do the work, particularly when that work involves so much data. One big area at the moment is using data to simulate the real world, to make models. So, for example, if you can make a model of how a disease like malaria might spread, you'll have a chance to stop it. Well, making models is something we can only do with the right technology.
AW: Can citizen science make the world a better place?
JN: Citizen science is about understanding the environments we live in. Unless we find out what's happening to the natural world, we can't protect it. So yes, ultimately, the idea of citizen science is to make the world a better place.

Unit 4 Recordings 4–6

1
A: OK, so, um … let me see … I guess I would start with the obvious sites – things like Facebook, Instagram, Twitter …
B: Snapchat?
A: Yeah, Snapchat. So I'd delete my profile from those sites. Presumably, you can do that, right?
B: Yes, I think so. Though some of those sites, like Facebook, I think you can, you know, deactivate the account; but I'm not sure you can actually delete it.
A: Right. So that might be a problem – you know, ones you can't delete. But I guess you can delete most of them.
B: Yeah, like YouTube.
A: Oh, hold on, I didn't think about YouTube. I've got a YouTube channel. In fact, when I start to think about it, I've got loads of different accounts, so getting to them all wouldn't be easy.
B: Yeah, I know. Me too.
A: So maybe a website like this one would be useful after all. You just tell them about your accounts and they go through them all for you.
B: Yes, perhaps it would …
2
A: Right, so why would you do it?
B: Well, I guess one reason might be that you've experienced some kind of bullying – I mean cyberbullying or something.
A: Yes, I suppose that's possible.
B: Or maybe you posted something really stupid, like an article or something, and now you regret it.
A: Personally, I don't really understand it, you know, the idea that you can just disappear from the internet. It's like dropping out of society because you don't like how society behaves. I don't really think the way to change it is to drop out. And it's kind of the same on the internet.
B: But what about if you've had a really bad experience?
A: Hmm … I don't know. I think maybe you just have to learn to deal with it. Or ignore the problem or something.
B: I suppose so. But, I mean, sometimes online bullying can lead to people being afraid in real life. People who are afraid to leave their homes, for example, because of threats they've received online.
A: OK. So, obviously, that's terrible but I don't think you solve it by disappearing offline. I

think you have to learn to ignore it or fight back.

3

A: Not really. I don't need to. You see, for me it's quite simple. I just avoid social media in the first place.

B: Really? You don't use it at all?

A: Nope.

B: And don't you feel like you're missing out?

A: Not really. I mean, I guess it's partly my age, but I really don't see the need for it. The thing is, if I want to talk to someone, I arrange to meet up, go for a drink or a meal or I call them up for a chat. I honestly think that is a much more valuable type of social interaction. You know, talking to someone face-to-face.

B: Well, yes, obviously, but a lot of the time, when people meet up, they can chat about things that they've been sharing on social media. So, when I meet someone, they know that I've just come back from holiday because they've seen the photos, so we can talk about that.

A: Hmm … but you see, I just don't think it's particularly interesting. You know, I don't really need to see what you had for breakfast this morning. I'd rather talk about something else.

B: Exactly. And a lot of the time someone has posted an interesting article or something, so you can talk about that.

A: Really? I'm not sure. It seems to me that people just post all kinds of rubbish on social media to try and make themselves popular.

Unit 4 Recording 8

1 What sports do you enjoy?
2 Which is your favourite restaurant?
3 What will you be doing in five years' time?
4 When will you next see your best friend?
5 What did you do last weekend?
6 Where are you going on your next holiday?

Unit 5 Recording 2

1 My utopia? There's no doubt about it: I love reading, so I fancy spending time on Book Lovers' Island, where everywhere you look there would be shelves of books – new books, old books, books in different languages, cookery books, art books. On Book Lovers' Island people would spend their days lying around in hammocks reading books. There'd be no television, except maybe for the showing the occasional film of a book. In the evenings people would get together for poetry readings or discussion groups, where you can talk about the book you're reading. You might have themed evenings, so, for example, if you're talking about a book which is set in India, then you might eat some Indian food. Every month or so there'd be a literary festival where authors of books would be invited to give talks, so you could look forward to meeting the author and talking to him or her about the book. Anything that's not allowed? Yes, kindles, e-readers. All the books on the island would need to be real books – nothing on a screen. So no e-books. In fact, no computers or computer games. Kids on this island would spend their time playing on the beach, swimming or reading books.

2 My island would be a gadget island, so everyone would be a super techie, gadget-lover like me. People would spend all their free time playing around with new gadgets, finding out how they work, experimenting. So you would always have the latest phone and computer, all the latest computer games. There would be super-fast mobile and wi-fi signal everywhere, so you'd never have to plug anything in or recharge it. And all the houses would have all the latest technology – they'd be smart houses, where you only have to think about what you want to do, and it happens for you – I don't know, robots cooking and serving the food … Everyone would work in these amazing fun offices – you know, a bit like the Google offices. And none of the technology would ever break down – you know, everything would always work, and if there was ever a tech problem or you didn't know how to do something, there would always be someone right there, on hand, to help you. So none of those telephone call centres to deal with tech problems.

3 OK, so my island would be like a teenage utopia, where only teenagers can hang out, no adults. And we are not expected to do anything, so we could spend our time doing whatever we want, like just playing on computer games or on our phones, and no one would hassle us. We could get up late – like, maybe in the afternoon – eat whatever we want to eat, whenever we want – like, just go to the fridge and eat whatever you can find, and not need to sit at the table or anything like that. There'd be loads of music and cool places to hang out together, doing not very much. We would refuse to go to school. There would be no teachers or exams or anything like that. People would just learn to do things by themselves or teach each other. People would just spend time chilling out with their mates or you could practise surfing or doing beach sports. Yeah, that would be great.

4 Right, well, my island would be an island dedicated to the one thing which is essential in every person's life and about which I feel so passionate. I tend to spend a lot of time cooking, so my utopia would be a foodie-utopia, where every meal is an explosion of exotic tastes and flavours. There would be fruits of every shape and size, fresh vegetables and amazing cuisine from all around the world, so you could visit different areas of the island that would specialise in certain types of food, like Thai or Chinese or Korean food in one place, and Portuguese or French cuisine somewhere else. So you could try all the different types of food. And everything would be prepared freshly from scratch. Nobody would be allowed to eat fast food, or pre-prepared food on the island, so bread would be freshly baked in the morning – no sliced bread – and everyone would be expected to get involved in growing the food, and would help to prepare the food as well as enjoy eating it. I'm getting hungry just thinking about it!

Unit 5 Recording 4

A: OK, so this is the first idea, and well, if you ask me, it's a really good idea. In Bermuda they have no natural water resources, right?

B/C: Yeah.

A: So the only water that people have access to is rainwater. So what they did is build these special roofs on the houses, Bermuda white roofs with steps, and they are designed specially to collect, purify and store rainwater, so each family is responsible for their own water supply.

B: OK.

A: And obviously, this means that people are really careful about how much water they use.

B: Right.

A: So, the way I see it, this is the kind of idea that could easily be adapted to other countries where access to water is a problem.

B: Hmm … Personally, I'm not convinced. Don't you think it would be better if the government was responsible for making sure that everyone has access to clean water and sanitation? I mean, for health and everything.

C: Yeah, and what about if you're in a country where it doesn't rain much?

A: Well, yes, I guess that's a good point, but I feel that the idea of personal responsibility is a good one.

B: Yes, that may be true. But I still feel that ultimately, it's the government's responsibility.

A: Which is why the government requires all new buildings to have these special roofs.

B: OK, fair point. What about this one? Japan has managed to virtually eradicate gun crime.

A: Really?

C: Wow! How have they done that?

B: Well, they teach their policemen to use martial arts instead of relying on their weapons when dealing with violent criminals.

A: That sounds good. But how does it work? I mean, as I see it, karate isn't much good to you when someone's pointing a gun in your face, surely?

B: Well, what happens is that when the police are faced with a violent criminal, rather than use their gun, they use these big futons, you know, mattresses, and they actually wrap the criminal inside these mattresses, like a big burrito, and carry them back to the station to calm down.

C: Excellent. That's quite funny.

B: Well, funny, yes, but I'm absolutely convinced that kind of approach can really work. You know, not reacting to violence with more violence, but trying to calm down the situation.

C: Nice one.

A: I'm not sure about that. I think it might work some of the time.

B: Well, it seems to be working in Japan.

A: Yeah, but there might be other reasons too. I'm not sure if it would work in America, for example.

C: Well, it might be worth a try. They seem to have quite a problem there. Anyway, here's my idea. This one is from Estonia. So, Estonia, when it separated from Russia, it decided to try and become a pioneer in digital services. The government pioneered a digital revolution, and it's been an amazing success story.

B: Sounds interesting.

C: Yeah, well, in my opinion, the country is one of the best examples of how a country can run online. It has one of the fastest broadband speeds in the world and it was the first to allow online voting in a general election.

A: OK.

B: Really?

C: All the classrooms are online, all the medical records are online, you pay for your car parking online. Apparently, the entrepreneur who developed Skype comes from Estonia and there are more start-ups per person than Silicon Valley in California.

A: Wow, that sounds good!

B: Hmm … I don't know. I think there are more important things the government could spend its money on in Estonia.

C: It seems to me that this one is working pretty well. So which policies should we include in our perfect country?

B: Well, I'm absolutely convinced that …

Unit 5 Recording 7

When people talk about Detroit, the first thing they say is it's a place where they make cars. The city is famous for it. Or it was in the past. It was a big old industrial town which got beaten up by the economy and by cheaper cars from Japan and Europe. They say Detroit has collapsed. It's a broken town. The buildings are empty, there's no jobs, there's crime, it's a Third World city in the middle of America. Well, some of that is true but there's a side people don't know about. This is a music town. Always has been. Jazz, gospel, rock 'n' roll, rap, hip-hop, techno. Detroit produced some of the biggest names in music, particularly African American singers. You may never have heard of them but they probably influenced every musician you ever did hear of. Without Diana Ross, there's no Beyoncé. Without Stevie Wonder, there's no Michael Jackson. And the music scene is still alive here. There's all kinds of tunes coming out even today, when people can barely put food on the table. That's the hidden side of Detroit.

Unit 6 Recording 4

A: And we finish with a heartwarming story from Brazil. João, a twenty-year-old, living in poverty in the northeast of Brazil, worked as a garbage sorter. Every day he would dig through mountains of rubbish to find recyclable objects. One day recently, he found something rather more valuable: a package containing one thousand four hundred dollars in cash. It had been put in the rubbish by mistake, of course, and the owner, a man named Bruno, was desperately looking for it.

B: Bruno had taken out the money for a trip to Europe. He'd hidden it in a roll of paper in his car. But his seven-year-old nephew found it and thought it was rubbish. So he threw it out.

A: Bruno then spent an evening in the recycling centre looking for his money, but he couldn't find it.

B: The next morning, João, the garbage sorter, went to work and found the money. He'd heard that another man was looking for it, so what did he do? He returned it immediately – every last cent.

A: This garbage sorter lived in a tiny wooden shelter with his family, but he was so honest that he says he didn't even think of keeping the money.

B: This is a tale with not one but two happy endings. The story hit the news in Brazil and was noticed by a famous rap singer called Gabriel.

A: Gabriel was so moved by the story that he wanted to give João a reward. So he asked his friends for donations. In the end, they collected a kitty worth ten thousand reais, or three thousand dollars. Gabriel gave the money to João, saying, 'This is a present from the heart.'

B: The second happy ending was this: Bruno, the man who'd lost his money and got it back, owns a construction company. As a way to say thank you, he offered João a job, with double the salary that João had made as a garbage sorter.

A: It shows us: honesty pays.

B: Certainly does.

Unit 6 Recording 5

1. would
would have
would have been
I would have been late.
2. would
wouldn't
wouldn't have
wouldn't have seen
I wouldn't have seen her.
3. would
would you
would you have
Would you have come?

Unit 6 Recording 6

A: I have something that I would consider to be one of the top five things that would mean a happy life.

B: OK.

A: Number one for me is being outside in nature.

B: Yes, definitely.

A: Absolutely. Do you like doing that?

B: Absolutely!

A: So last year I went to Wales for the first time and … uh, I didn't know the beaches were so good in Wales, and on the coastal path, there's a national coastal path, and …

B: Oh that scenery must be just breathtaking!

A: Oh it's incredible!

B: That's definitely one of the keys, isn't it?

A: And there was no one there, and I remember thinking, 'Where is everyone?' It was kind of a holiday time …

B: Oh gorgeous!

A: And I felt this real stillness when I was there. It was incredible. I'd never experienced it, living in a city all my life …

B: It does make you happy.

A: It … Absolutely. (It really does.)

B: And I think music is one of my keys to happiness (*A: OK*) for sure, because it can change your mood completely. (*A: Yeah.*) If you're down, you can listen to something and it will cheer you up. (*A: Yeah.*) Or if you're uptight, you can relax with some calming music. (*A: Yeah, yeah.*) I think that's amazing and I also think … increasingly, we are focused on the future and I will be happy when this happens or when that happens, (*A: Yeah.*) and I think it's all about the now, the present. (*A: Yeah.*) Past is done. (*A: Yeah, yeah.*) Future hasn't happened yet. It's all about living in the moment.

A: That's hard to do, I think – sometimes.

B: That's number three, I think.

A: Yeah, focusing on the moment, I agree. Yeah, that's definitely on my list.

B: What else?

A: Uh … um, this one's a bit boring, but getting eight hours of sleep at night.

B: No, it's not at all – that's a luxury.

A: Getting eight hours of sleep, right?

B: Yes! How wonderful!

A: It's so true. I never do. I never do.

B: No, I think very few people do. But it is so important, isn't it?

A: I have one of those sleep apps on my phone, where it actually measures how much I sleep and somehow it can measure the quality of my sleep, and I'm amazed that it's always less than six hours a night.

B: Oh, well, yeah, it's so important.

A: So, like, I have to change what time, I have to change something about my lifestyle, about what I do in the evening, how early I get into bed …

B: Ah … Oh, another one: cooking and good food. But I mean …

A: Really?

B: Yeah, incredibly important!

A: I never do that. I never cook for myself.

B: Well, you see, you are what you eat. (*A: Wow!*) You stop at (*A: Gosh!*) you know, fast food restaurants (*A: Yeah.*) and wonder why you don't feel good because …

A: Well, that's probably true.

B: … It is so important, I think. To be happy, you've got to put good food (*A: Yeah.*) into your system. (*A: Yeah.*) Really healthy stuff.

A: OK, here's another thing, which is kind of partly to do with focusing on the moment, is focusing on the simple things. The simple things. And for me, one of those things is not eating on the run, even though I'm not cooking my own food.

B: Now there you go.
A: But not eating on the run, walking up to get public transport, and have something in my hand, which I'm eating breakfast that way. Sitting down, taking a moment, a coffee or some tea, and just, for five minutes, kind of settle the mind before the day gets going.
B: Bliss. Let's do it now.

Unit 6 Recording 7

1
A: Are you coming out later?
B: Yes, definitely!
2
A: I love it when it rains.
B: Really?!
3
A: Eating good food is so important.
B: I don't think so.
4
A: I think laughing at your problems really helps you to stay happy.
B: It really does!
5
A: I need eight hours sleep.
B: Absolutely.
6
A: Exercise is essential.
B: I totally agree.
7
A: It's important to do a job that you love.
B: That's right.
8
A: Life is too short to be angry all the time.
B: You're so right.
9
A: I only eat raw food.
B: No way!
10
A: You need to be in love to be happy.
B: Not necessarily.
11
A: Sundays are so relaxing. It's my favourite day of the week.
B: No doubt about it.
12
A: Good friends are really important.
B: Totally!
13
A: One thing that stresses me is when I have too much to do.
B: Tell me about it!
14
A: The only way to be happy is to be rich.
B: I'd say the opposite.
15
A: It's best to keep things simple.
B: That's so true.
16
A: The best advice is just not to worry. Things will be fine.
B: That's probably true.

Unit 6 Recording 8

1 War is one of the biggest problems of our times.
2 It's essential that people have access to free healthcare.
3 Staying at home and watching TV is a great way to be happy.
4 People today worry too much about everything.
5 Money is the most important thing, isn't it?
6 If you work hard at a job you love, you will be happy.

Unit 7 Recording 1

1 as good as – He's as good as me.
2 better than – She's better than me.

Unit 7 Recording 2

big as
as big as
He's as big as a bear.

strong as
as strong as
She's as strong as me.

intelligent as
as intelligent as
I'm not as intelligent as you.

smaller than
I'm smaller than you.

quieter than
They're quieter than us.

dangerous than
more dangerous than
It's more dangerous than you think.

Unit 7 Recording 4

I've always been a massive fan of music. Um, my mum used to have so many CDs, um, and tapes and records and I used to listen to all sorts of things. I used to do a lot of my listening in the car on the way to school, um, and we'd listen to a tape or whatever that we'd chosen from the supermarket at the weekend.
Um, she had such an eclectic taste in music – from, er, classical music like Beethoven, Mozart, to seventies bands such like Shakatak, um, it's just amazing.
Um, and I've always, always listened to electronic music and dance music. Um, it started when I was about thirteen years old, um, I used to go to, um, like, raves for young people when I was at school and I've just always been into it and I've never ever grown out of it.
One thing that I can't get into is country and western. My boyfriend is a massive, massive fan and I just cannot get used to it. Um, I really have tried. I think as far as I will go is listening to the odd Dolly Parton track, but it's the sort of music that makes my toes curl. Um, just can't, yeah, I just cannot get used to it.
But if I look on my iPod now, a lot of the music that I listen to now, I probably listened to back when I was four or five years old, er, with the exception of some of the dance tracks which came in when I was a teenager. So yeah, I'd like to say that I listen to a wide spectrum of music, um, and, yeah, I've got my mum to thank for that.

Unit 7 Recordings 5 and 6

A: OK, I have a few suggestions for making life easier. Firstly, travel.
B: Go on.
A: Packing. You know when you fold your clothes and put them in the suitcase and you finally arrive and the clothes are all wrinkled?
B: Yeah.
A: Instead of folding them, roll them.
B: Roll them? Oh, I see. Like wrapping paper or posters. And they don't get wrinkled?
A: Nope.
B: Does it actually work?
A: Apparently. And on the same subject, if you're travelling and you have dirty laundry, keep it in a separate plastic bag, but put a bar of scented soap in the bag as well.
B: To stop the clothes from smelling bad?
A: Yep.
B: That's a good idea.
A: Next one. You're on holiday and you get bitten by mosquitoes.
B: OK.
A: Lick your finger and dip it in salt. Then rub the mixture of salt and saliva on the bite. It heals after a few minutes.
B: Oh wow – that sounds so easy! I'll try it.
A: I know that one cos mosquitoes love me.
B: Me too.
A: And talking of mosquitoes, if you're at home and there are mosquitoes in the house buzzing around, you …
B: Not likely where I live.
A: You switch on a fan and sit in the breeze. Mosquitoes are very light and can't fly in the wind.
B: Oh that's good.
A: I've got a couple more.
B: Go on then.
A: You're on the beach and you want to go for a swim but you're scared someone will steal your stuff.
B: Yep.
A: Well, before you go to the beach, make a container out of an old sun lotion bottle. One of the rectangular ones.
B: OK.
A: First, you clean it out. Then you cut the top off so you can fit your phone, keys and money in it. Then you fit the top back on. If it looks old and nasty, people are much less likely to steal it.
B: I get it. That's such a good idea.
A: I think so too. OK, last one. You get caught in the rain with no umbrella, but you have to get somewhere on foot.

B: Take a taxi?
A: No, you're walking.
B: Put a plastic bag over your head?
A: No, you'll suffocate, silly! No, you stop at a café or bar and ask for an umbrella.
B: Eh? I don't get it.
A: Cafés and bars have lots of umbrellas that people leave there by mistake.
B: Oh, right.
A: The café owners don't know what to do with them, so if you ask for one, they'll give it to you.
B: Oh that's true. Very good. Nice life hacks.
A: Thank you. Thought you'd like them.

Unit 7 Recording 8

1
A: I drink coffee every morning.
B: Me too.
2
A: I don't write in a notebook.
B: Me neither.
3
A: I sometimes wash the dishes.
B: Me too.
4
A: I don't like mustard.
B: Me neither.
5
A: I work long hours.
B: Me too.
6
A: I don't listen to classical music.
B: Me neither.
7
A: I like DIY.
B: I don't.
8
A: I don't have a sedentary lifestyle.
B: I do.
9
A: I water the plants at home.
B: I don't.
10
A: I don't own an umbrella.
B: I do.

Unit 7 Recording 9

It's no secret that I *love* street art. Whenever I travel to a new city, it's one of my favourite things to see. I love the vibrant colours and the exciting atmosphere that street art creates. I'm always on the lookout for good art or graffiti as I wander around a city with my camera. So, when I travelled to Lima, I was so excited when a friend told me about the Barranco district. The Barranco district is the cliff area of Lima. In the 1920s it was where the rich and famous Peruvians built their summer houses, but later in the century many of its buildings fell into decline. Now, however, the area is inhabited by artists, photographers and musicians. Many of the brightly-coloured buildings have been restored and taken over by artists' collectives. The result is that the walls of the houses, both inside and out, are covered with the most amazingly imaginative and colourful murals. I went on a walking art tour of the area with my guide Cecilia, from Lima Art Tours. She knew a lot of the artists personally, so as we walked around, she was able to explain the meaning of many of the murals to me. Some of the artworks have been painted by a collaboration of artists from Colombia, Argentina and Chile. They were so beautiful, and it was really fascinating to hear about their history. Also, she took me down back streets to find murals that, undoubtedly, I would not have discovered without her. We also went into some of the more formal art galleries to see the art on exhibition there. And to top it all, we had a wonderful lunch looking out across the ocean and eating local food. The best thing about the tour? I learned so much about street art in Lima, I learned a lot about the city and its history, and I made a new friend too!

Unit 8 Recording 1

1 We made a deal.
2 We'll make alterations.
3 They made a pact.
4 Did you make some money?
5 It did some damage.
6 Did I do something wrong?
7 She did the deed.
8 Do your utmost.
9 Don't take him seriously.
10 Take advantage of it.
11 We took control of it.
12 Don't take it for granted.

Unit 8 Recording 2

I = Interviewer E = Expert

I: 'Big data' is set to become one of the greatest sources of power in the twenty-first century. So how is big data going to change things for us in the future?
E: Well, the amount of data we produce is enormous. And it's already being used for all kind of things, many of which I'm sure you know about, but a few that maybe you don't. First of all, let's look at healthcare. Big data is being used to help predict epidemics, like flu epidemics, by looking at what people search for on the internet – for example, people searching for 'flu symptoms' on Google – and looking at who is absent from work. Then by looking at travel data, about where people are likely to travel to, experts try to work out where the disease is going to spread to. In the future big data will be used to cure diseases like cancer by very carefully matching the patient to the exact type of treatment that will help them, by monitoring people more closely so that we can detect cancer in its very early stages. So, with the devices people wear on their arms which monitor levels of activity, nutrition, sleep patterns, blood pressure. All of this information can go towards helping to prevent illness before it happens. You know, the work that was done to decode the human genome – it took more than ten years to complete. With big data that same work can be done in just twenty-six hours. So it's really speeding things up in the area of scientific research.
I: That's amazing! So data in healthcare enables us to predict when there might be a problem, and find cures for diseases?
E: Hopefully. That's right.
I: And in what other areas is big data having an impact?
E: Another interesting area is crime prevention. Police forces in California are using big data to help reduce crime rates. They use the data to help predict where crime is likely to occur, and then send officers to the scene before the crime actually happens. When the police officers arrive at the scene where the crime is about to happen, it reduces the chances of the crime happening. And it really works. In some areas they have managed to reduce the crime rate by thirty-three percent.
I: So big data is actually making us safer?
E: You could say that, yes.
I: What about love? Big data is being used by online dating websites. Is that right?
E: Yes, online dating is another area where it's important to make accurate predictions. Information gathered from people's social networks allows companies to make much more accurate predictions of whether two people will get on well with each other. Do they like doing the same kinds of things, for example? It's incredibly easy to predict a person's personality and behaviour based on their Facebook data. Companies are able to accurately predict your intelligence, personality traits, age, gender and even religious views, based on the information you share on Facebook.
I: I see. And that information can then be used to help find a love match.
E: Exactly. Sport is another one. Video analytics can track a player's performance, so every player in a football match or a baseball game is tracked to see how well they are performing. The coach then uses the information to decide who is going play in the next match. Many sports teams even track their athletes outside the sporting environment too, using smart technology to track their nutrition and sleep, but also to monitor social media conversations allowing them to observe the emotional well-being of the players.
I: Hmm … I'm not sure about that. It seems a bit intrusive to me. I mean, the players ought to be able to have a private social life without being spied on, surely?
E: Yes, maybe.
I: And what about smart cities? What are the plans there?
E: Yes, data analytics are being used in cities to help control traffic. So in the future you'll probably never get stuck in a traffic jam because the analytics will find the best route for you to travel. In fact, by redirecting the

traffic, the system will try to ensure there are no traffic jams. And the chances are you won't be driving your own car either; it'll be driving itself.

I: That sounds a bit scary. There are bound to be problems if machines are in charge of everything, don't you think?

E: Yes, I think a lot of people do find it scary, but believe me, big data is due to change the world. And I think it will be for the better.

Unit 8 Recording 4

A: Where do you think the expression *get the sack* comes from?

B: I have no idea. Perhaps it's something like Father Christmas carrying a sack of presents. No. I don't know.

A: OK, before the industrial revolution, workers used to carry their tools in a sack. When the job was finished, the boss returned their sack. It meant the end of their employment.

B: I see.

A: What about *brand new*?

B: I'd imagine it's connected to the word *brand*, as in *supermarket brand* or *brand of food* – the company that makes it.

A: OK. Well, a brand was a fire in a furnace. It was used to make things out of metal. If you say something is brand new, it means it's freshly made from the fire.

B: I was more or less right, then.

A: Kind of. What about *giving someone the cold shoulder*?

B: Well, if you turn your shoulder to someone, it's like you're turning your back on them. Same thing, right?

A: Nope. This idiom is from the Middle Ages. The cold shoulder was food. It was the worst part of the lamb that you're eating, and you'd give it to people you didn't like. This meant they would go away and not bother you anymore.

B: Oh. I'd never have guessed that.

A: What about the expression *don't have a clue*?

B: Is it from Sherlock Holmes? You're trying to solve a mystery but you don't have any clues?

A: No, a clue was a ball of string in old English. Traditionally, if you entered a cave or a maze, you'd roll out the string so that if you got lost, you'd follow the string back to the entrance.

B: Oh, I get it.

A: If you don't have a clue, it means you don't have the ball of string, so you can't get out.

B: Oh, OK.

A: Here's another one: *beside the point*. Where does that come from?

B: No idea.

A: It comes from archery – you know, bows and arrows. If your shot is beside the point, it means that you aimed at the target and missed.

B: I see. So instead of hitting the target, your arrow went to the side of the target – beside the point.

A: Yes. OK, last one: why do we say *left-wing* and *right-wing* for political views?

B: Is it something to do with where people sat in parliament?

A: Very good! In France, two hundred years ago, King Louis the sixteenth called a large group of politicians together. The conservatives sat on his right and the liberals sat on his left. From then on, conservatives have been described as being right-wing and liberals as being left-wing.

B: I thought it was something like that. Oh well, I got one right!

A: Yes, you did. Very good! And it was …

Unit 8 Recording 5

1 There are approximately ten of them. There are more or less ten of them.
2 The keys might be in the car. The keys could be in the car.
3 I'm not sure, but I'd estimate one thousand euros. At a rough guess, I'd say one thousand euros.
4 There's no way it's more than that. It can't be more than that.

Pearson Education Limited
KAO Two
KAO Park
Harlow
Essex CM17 9NA
England
and Associated Companies throughout the world.

www.english.com/portal

First published 2018
ISBN: 978-1-2922-4153-1
Set in Aptifer sans LT Pro 10/12 pt
Printed and bound by L.E.G.O. S.p.A. Lavis (TN) – Italy

Acknowledgements
The publishers and authors would like to thank the following people and institutions for their contribution to the development of the material:
Hungary: Tom Boyle; **Italy:** John Waddington; **Poland:** Konrad Dejko; **Spain:** Victoria O'Dea; Pilar Álvarez Polvorinos/Maria Del Pilar Álvarez Polvorinos; **UK:** David Byrne, Sally Fryer

We are grateful to the following for permission to reproduce copyright material:

Illustration acknowledgements: Richard Duckett 95; Fred Blunt 13, 61, 68, 120, 121, 122, 123, 124, 125, 126, 127; Ben Hasler 47, 59, 71, 94; Harry Malt 11.

Photo acknowledgements
The publisher would like to thank the following for their kind permission to reproduce their photographs:

(Key: b-bottom; c-centre; l-left; r-right; t-top)

123RF.com: 23bl, 72t, 74tc (right), 120b (G), 120b (I), 120b (J), 23bl, 72t, 74tc (right), 120b (G), 120b (I), 120b (J), 23bl, 72t, 74tc (right), 120b (G), 120b (I), 120b (J), ginasanders 35tr, Nataliia Kelsheva 55bl, michaeljung 72bl, mihtiander 23cr, photobac 31t, Pierangelo Roberto 82t (C), siraphol 15 (K), sumikophoto 129t, temis 23tr, yevhenholovash 14 (E); **Alamy Stock Photo:** Theo Alers 82t (A), Art Directors & TRIP 14 (A), Atzen 93, Radim Beznoska 82b (J), Blend Images 67t, blickwinkel 31bc (left), 35tl, Kevin Britland 79t, Ivan Chiosea 82t (E), John Davidson Photos 79bl, Foto Arena LTDA 34, Fotograferen.net 83b, John Gaffen 2 55bc (right), 62tl, Gl0ck 120b (H), Granger Historical Picture Archive 81, 91bl, Robert Grubba 19t, Peter Horree 92br, 128tr, Image Source 38tr, imageBROKER 31br, 40-41, Johner Images 7t, Andriy Kravchenko 44tc (right), LiliGraphie 7bc (right), 14 (F), Buddy Mays 56tc (left), MBI 10tl, 74tc (left), Ronnie McMillan 38tl, NG Images 130r, Panther Media GmbH 67bc (left), 98 (B), Pablo Paul 98 (G), Photoco 14 (C), photonic 10 120t (B), Pictorial Press Ltd 92tr, 132, 133, Morley Read 56tr, robertharding 55br, 64-65, Sport In Pictures 33, Charles Stirling 129b, Björn Wylezich 14 (B), Xinhua 62tr, YAY Media AS 14 (I), Feng Yu 120t (A), Zoonar GmbH 38bl; **BBC Worldwide Learning:** 16 (inset), 28-29t (Headshots), 40 (inset), 52-53t (Headshots), 76-77t (Headshots), 100-101t (Headshots); **Courtesy of Procter & Gamble UK:** 21bc; **Courtesy of the Estate of Gill Conquest/ Extreme Citizen Science group, UCL ; ; :** 44tr; **Thomas Dambo, www.thomasdambo.com :** 107; **Getty Images:** AFP 31bl, 32tl, Giuseppe Cacace 91bc (left), 96, DragonImages 10tc, Bobby Longoria 24tl, Lucas Oleniuk 24tc, SolStock 74tl, Eszter Tokar / EyeEm 73, Westend61 10tr, Sam Yeh 79br, 88-89; **Monkey Business:** 20tr, 22c; **Nucleo/twinpixelvideo.com:** 20cr, 22b; **Pearson Education Ltd:** Mark Bassett 50, Coleman Yuen. Pearson Education Asia Ltd 86t (D), Coleman Yuen 120t (E); **Psalt Design:** Psalt Design 20bl (above); **Scottish Viewpoint:** Peter Scott 7br, 16-17; **Shutterstock.com:** 86t (B), 111, 86t (B), 111, Natasa Adzic 67bl, Africa Studio 15 (O), 19br, 28-29, 86b (I), Natig Aghayev 95 (buildings), AkeSak 43bc (left), Alter-ego 98 (A), Carlos Amarillo 97, ANCH 14 (J), Andresr 67bc (right), Galyna Andrushko 55t, Aquiem / Solent News / REX 20br, 22t, Aquiem / Solent News / REX 20br, 22t, arek_malang 74tr, artjazz 86b (G), Mile Atanasov 15 (L), Atstock Productions 31bc (right), Baloncici 120t (C), bikeriderlondon 44bc, Maksym Bondarchuk 82b (G), Grisha Bruev 95 (black car), DBtale 19bc (left), Tommaso Delpiano 9, Ditty_about_summer 75b, djile 79bc (left), Pichugin Dmitry 55bc (left), 61, Dean Drobot 25t, Edible Spoon Maker / Solent News / REX 20cl, Daniel M Ernst 14tr, Everett - Art 80 (B), 80 (C), Everett Historical 92tl, 92bl, Flik47 92b, Fotos593 67br, 76-77, Francescomoufotografo 44tl, 44tc (left), Francescomoufotografo 44tl, 44tc (left), GaudiLab 51, Matt Gibson 23br, Gil C 82t (B), Peter Gudella 99 (H), guruXOX 26, Ruslan Guzov 37, David Hartley / REX 58, HQuality 43t, Image Point Fr 14cr (below), John_T 95 (tree lined street), Muellek Josef 82b (I), Kiwisoul 82b (L), Leszek Kobusinski 15 (N), Yuganov Konstantin 91br, 100-101, D. Kucharski K. Kucharska. 56tc (right), Denis Kuvaev 82b (K), Ennio Leanza / Epa / REX 20c, Lexan 95 (white car), lightwavemedia 15t, Jacob Lund 7bc (left), mantinov 38br, mayakova 86 (A), Megasus / Bournemouth News / REX 19bl, 20tl, Megasus / Bournemouth News / REX 19bl, 20tl, Mimagephotography 95 (woman and luggage), 95 (woman on phone), MrGarry 128bl, My Good Images 86t (E), NAAN 117, Vitaliy Netiaga 7cr, Suwit Ngaokaew 43br, 52-53, NodPod / REX 21br, Odua Images 14 (H), OlegDoroshin 130l, Pakhnyushchy 95 (sky), pathdoc 91t, pelfophoto 86b (H), Pepsco Studio 43bc (right), Dusan Petkovic 95 (man), Photodonato 95 (billboard), Photofollies 120b (F), Photon photo 79bc (right), Dario Lo Presti 19bc (right), Ragma Images 91bc (right), 98 (F), Rawpixel.com 63b, Dr. Morley Read 56tl, Bella Reji 95 (lamppost), Rob Hainer 36, rozdesign 15 (M), Runrun2 82b (H), Dennis M. Sabangan / EPA / REX 62tc, sagir 120t (D), Saltwater Brewery / Solent News / REX 20tc, Scanrail1 95 (tablets/phones), SeDmi 98 (E), Roman Sigaev 86b (F), simongee 14 (G), Sipa Press / REX 32, sirtravelalot 98 (C), Dmitrij Skorobogatov 86b (J), Syda Productions 83tr, Tatiana Popova 14 (D), Toasteroid / Solent News / REX 20bl (below), Tuzemka 95 (woman's head), Twinsterphoto 72br, Kiselev Andrey Valerevich 83tl, Serge Vero 82t (D), VILevi 23tl, Alexandr Vlassyuk 86t (C), wavebreakmedia 35tc, Zentilia 95 (traffic lights), zhangyang13576997233 98 (D), Andrii Zhezhera 80 (A), Zurijeta 82t (F); **Elvis Summers, www.mythpla.org:** 131l, 131r.

All other images © Pearson Education

We are grateful to the following for permission to reproduce copyright material:

Text
Extract on page 11 from content taken from BBC Radio 4 programme 'In Four' episode 'Busy-ness is NOT a competition', and obtained upon permission from the BBC; Extract on page 13 adapted from *The Upside of Downtime: Why Boredom is Good*, Robinson (Mann, Sandi) Little, Brown Book Group; Extract on page 47 adapted from 'Is Technology Changing Our Brains?', *BBC Focus Magazine*, Issue 300 (J, Carlowe 2016) © Focus / Immediate Media; Book cover on page 1 from *The Lost City of the Monkey God*, 1.ed, Head of Zeus (Douglas Preston); Extract on page 62 adapted from content taken from BBC World Service programme 'The Compass' episode 'My Perfect Country' (use of concept), and obtained upon permission from the BBC Extract on page 68 adapted from Good vs Evil, *BBC Focus Magazine*, Issue 297 (2016) © BBC Focus Magazine / Immediate Media; Extract on page 74 adapted from The Happiest People On The Planet?, *BBC Focus Magazine*, Issue 303 (2017) ©) BBC Focus Magazine / Immediate Media; Extract on page 85 adapted from Understand the Power of Music, *BBC Focus Magazine*, Issue 297 (Powell, John 2016) © BBC Focus Magazine / Immediate Media

Video produced by Silversun Media Group for Pearson Education